ROMAN IMAGES

Selected Papers from the English Institute
New Series

Roman Images

 Selected Papers from the English Institute, 1982

New Series, no. 8

Edited, with an Introduction,
by Annabel Patterson

The Johns Hopkins University Press
Baltimore and London

© 1984 by the English Institute
All rights reserved
Printed in the United States of America

The Johns Hopkins University Press, Baltimore, Maryland 21218
The Johns Hopkins Press Ltd., London

Library of Congress Cataloging in Publication Data
Main entry under title:

Roman images.

   (Selected papers from the English Institute; 1982,
new ser., no. 8)
   1. English literature—Roman influences—Addresses,
essays, lectures. 2. American literature—Roman
influences—Addresses, essays, lectures. 3. Rome
(Italy) in literature—Addresses, essays, lectures.
4. Virgil—Influence—Addresses, essays, lectures.
5. Classicism—Addresses, essays, lectures.
6. Literature, Modern—Roman influences—Addresses,
essays, lectures. I. Patterson, Annabel M. II. Series:
Selected papers from the English Institute; new ser.,
no. 8.
PR127.R65 1984   820'.9'3245632   83-17560
ISBN 0-8018-3127-X

Contents

Introduction

The seed of this volume of *English Institute Essays* was sown at the 1981 meeting, when Ronald Paulson gave the paper "The Representation of Revolution (1789–1815)," with a provocative focus on the Roman paintings of David. At the 1982 meeting, it germinated in a panel on Rome in the European imagination. The principle of this panel was that anything could be discussed *except* the officially "neoclassical" in art and literature. The object was to show how continuously potent was the idea of Rome in Western cultural history; and, by implication, to call into question the special status of eighteenth-century neo-classicism, as merely a better-publicized phase of an unbroken intellectual process.

We must assume that the point was made, well enough at least to indicate the richness of the topic, and to persuade the Executive Committee to commit to Rome the entire 1982 volume. Of the eight essays collected here, three, those by Margaret Ferguson, Jerome McGann, and myself, were part of the original panel. The other five, by Elizabeth Block, Patricia Craddock, Ralph Johnson, Robert Miola, and William Vance, were requested especially for this volume. I want to take this opportunity to thank all of the contributors for their efficiency, courtesy, and enthusiasm for the project; both those who produced new essays to rather stringent specifications, and those who revised, expanded, or contracted. Nobody stood on his or her dignity. Nobody missed the deadline. We worked together, as collaborators. I am grateful for the experience.

What should now be apparent is not merely the richness of the topic but its inexhaustibility. William Vance's superb essay on the Colosseum in the American imagination still mourns its deleted examples from European painting. Just one of his American exemplars, Henry James—hardly a minor figure—receives in Elizabeth Block's essay the more intense and minute focus that James would have approved. Ralph Johnson's subtle polemic encapsulates the Roman view of Rome from Cato to Vergil; it could easily be the preface to a new major project. The same could be assumed of Jerome McGann's powerful survey of Romantics in and about Rome, from Goethe to Stendahl. Robert Miola's essay on *Cymbeline,* tantalizing by its status as summation and counterexample to the Roman plays, actually *is* an excerpt from his new book, *Shakespeare's Rome,* forthcoming from Cambridge University Press. Margaret Ferguson's daring leap from Du Bellay to Wallace Stevens alerts us both to her larger study of Du Bellay (in *Trials of Desire: Renaissance Defences of Poetry* [New Haven, 1983]) and to Thomas Greene on "Du Bellay and the Disinterment of Rome" in *The Light in Troy* [New Haven, 1983].

If the eighteenth century is now well represented by Patricia Craddock's elegant essay on Gibbon, French neoclassicism still gets very short shrift in this volume. Another of its roaring silences is on the Middle Ages: the *Roman d'Enéas;* the *Faits des Romains,* one of the great "publishing" successes of the early thirteenth century. Chaucer's Monk cites Lucan and Suetonius as his sources for the three Roman "lives" in his lugubrious tale, reminding us that Roman historiography was always a force in European culture, even when it was imperfectly known. Also, our comparatively light emphasis on the Renaissance should be seen in the light of another recent collection of essays, *Rome in the Renaissance: The City and the Myth* (1982), the papers of the Thirteenth Conference of the Center for Mediaeval and Early Renaissance Studies at Binghamton.

If one of the things to notice about this volume is, then, the salient omissions that provoke more work, more thought, another must surely be the community of tone and method between the eight authors. It is not just that Vergil, Spenser, Gibbon, Montesquieu, and James, appear in more than one essay, nor that in pursuit of our great subject we have crossed our normal chronological and disciplinary boundaries, classicists engaging in literary criticism, "English" specialists in art history, everyone in comparativism of a sort. It is, rather, that these essays could not have been written without a regard for historicity. They take different positions, perhaps, on the wide scale of what that can mean, from the pleasing vagueness of James's "impressions" of history in the Eternal City to the crucial significance of dates in Stendahl's experience of Rome; but no one (not even Stevens) can write ahistorically about Rome. The very fact that the English Institute has chosen to express itself on this topic in 1982 gives credence to the belief that a new historicism is abroad in the profession, built, with respect, on the ruins of the old. On the other hand, it is wise not to make large claims. The strata of which cultural history is built up are paper-thin these days. We all face runaway obsolescence. By the time this volume actually appears, the Institute will have moved on to other concerns; and Rome, the place of memory, will be back in her place.

ROMAN IMAGES

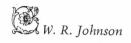 W. R. Johnson

Vergil's Bees:
The Ancient Romans'
View of Rome

Th' abuse of greatness is when it disjoins
Remorse from power.
Julius Caesar 2.1.18–19

I

Patient, unimaginative, superstitious, loyal, brutal, humorous, mildly tolerant, tenaciously practical, ferociously disciplined. We get our word *rational* from them, but for them *ratio* meant, essentially, "counting"; we get our word *reality* from them, but by *res* they meant, mostly and finally, "money" and "real estate." They worshiped, as most human beings do (but they were disarmingly honest about it), food and sex, property and luck, health and the gene pool, sickness, death, and the unquiet dead. Fathers were really gods; mothers, who never ceased to be their fathers' daughters, whatever their married state, whatever sons they bore, were revered and necessary goddesses (revered because necessary), lucky sharers in the glory; momentary for this man, everlasting for his clan, of the father, the farmer, the warrior, the judge, the priest, and the king whose priestess she became on that fateful day when she passed over his threshhold, yesterday a child, today a woman. We see them, not least through the eyes of Cecil B. De Mille and his fellow artisans, in their familiar costumes, now streaming, now trudging, out from their overgrown country town, that stolid, limitless energy radiating out over the world, both civilized and uncivilized, until the picture (it is the map in our high school history book) is complete. *Mare nostrum.* Our sea. Our world.

Wherever they came, whether to forest or desert, to Spanish hamlet or Greek metropolis, their marvelous highways came with them, and their aqueducts and arches; their forums, law books, amphitheaters; taxmen, ledgers, jails, firemen; census and sanitation; streets geometrized and clean; schools, banks, baths. In their wake, after a decent interval, would follow the Greeks, with Homer and *Tischmusik,* with tragedy and comedy, with Great Books and professors to teach them, or to explain the ruins to those who did not care to read. Bread and circuses; brandy and guns. But after a while there was, or so it seemed, no need for guns, for the world had been pacified. *Culture* is their word; *civilization* is a word derived from their words. *Cultura* is unwearying labor; clearing away the wilderness; planting, pruning, manuring, guarding; extending slowly, sometimes imperceptibly, what one has received to pass it on, improved, to heirs one will never see; the god-given plants entrusted to one's care, not for oneself, but for the future. Cicero's Cato says it all in *De senectute,* and says it beautifully.

There is nothing in any of this to sneer at, certainly. But is it true? Yes and no. And did they themselves believe it, does Cicero's garrulous old gentleman speak for them? Yes and no. Cato the Elder, both Cicero's portrait of him and the obscure yet vivid figure we patch together from Plutarch and Livy and from fragments of his own writings, was at home in his skin; was at home in the glorious, not yet magnificent, city whose streets he walked and whose destiny and myth, he as much as any single man, shaped in his life and, especially, in his art. Cato believed what he said. Cicero wanted to believe in Cato's city, its past, the living history of its hills and buildings, its divine mission, its unique fate; and, at the time he was composing *De senectute,* wanted to believe it with a special intensity. After him, the doubts of some of his fellow countrymen would proliferate, just at the time when Cato's dream was crystallized by the genius of Augustus, and the glorious, humble brick found the magnificence of its marble veneer, and the first Rome, paradigm of all later Romes, became eternal.

II

But before we examine these doubts, those of Cicero and his heirs, let us look more at the dream of Cato. In 196 B.C., having successfully intervened in the muddle of Greek politics, the Romans, through the agency of the *imperator* of the Roman forces in Greece, Titus Quinctius Flamininus, magnanimously proclaimed the freedom of all Greece at the Isthmian games. Livy, writing during the Augustan principate some hundred and fifty years after the event, re-creates with his usual verve and poise the rapturous response of the audience to that proclamation (33.32), then analyzes the thoughts and feelings that underlie this dramatic moment in a passage that, if it does not perhaps exactly imagine what the Greeks felt on that occasion, suggests what he himself and many of his contemporaries wanted to think about what their city had stood for, and what it might, after the chaos of the recent civil wars, come to stand for again. In other words, he provides, in a skillfully novelistic frame, a lapidary statement of the traditional Roman view of Rome, its character and its destiny. In 33.33, after sketching the perilous affections of the Greek throngs as they seek to honor and thank Flamininus, Livy goes on to remark that this effusion of delight and gratitude did not cease once the spectacle of freedom was over and the audience had left the theatre. For days afterwards people went about expressing to one another their amazement and delight, saying such things as these:

> There exists one nation on the face of the earth which, at its own expense, with its own exertions, heedless of hazard, wages war on behalf of the freedom of other people [*pro libertate aliorum*]. This nation is not concerned merely for the liberty of their neighbors, of peoples in their immediate vicinity or whose lands border theirs; no, they are prepared even to cross the sea to make sure that there can be no unjust empire anywhere on earth [*ne quod toto orbe terrarum iniustum imperium sit*], and that justice, its divine sanction, and the rule of law [*ius, fas, lex*] shall be everywhere triumphant. [*ubique potentissima sint*]. (33.33. 5–7)[1]

Never mind that just at this period this passion for human liberty, this willingness to undertake any toil or danger anywhere to guard freedom and justice, are being subtly undermined from without and from within. Livy and his contemporaries, like their immediate predecessors, if they are unwilling or perhaps unable to entertain the

notion that power tends to corrupt, never tire of repeating that
money does corrupt.[2] The *locus classicus* for this chastening wisdom,
accepted rather late in the game, was Cato, into whose mouth Livy
puts an elegantly worded version of this sober fact, which had been
endlessly elaborated by the great censor during his long public service.

A year after Greece was granted its freedom and was beginning to
see that freedom meant peace and quiet combined with taxation
without representation and political impotence, Cato the Elder felt
himself called upon to speak against a motion to repeal the Oppian
Law, an emergency measure passed during the worst days of the
Second Punic War, which forbade women to own more than half an
ounce of gold, to wear gowns trimmed with purple, or, except on
religious occasions, to ride in a carriage within the city. The women
of Rome, having become bored with the law and perhaps with what
it stood for, began to demonstrate against masculine vanity and for
the law's repeal; it was perhaps both the obvious justice of their
demands, the likelihood of their success, and their surprising show of
political savvy and political power that elicited from Cato the polished, wicked, unfair, and hilarious oration that Livy gives him.[3] One
imagines that Cato knew that his cause was doomed and that, having
other, bigger fish to fry, he hardly cared; it was a splendid chance to
reassert his place as supreme macho, to castigate feminine wiles and
feminine deficiencies, to upbraid unseemly un-Roman uxoriousness,
and to point out, again, yet again, the real threat to Rome, to her
greatness and her power:

> You have often heard me complaining of the extravagance not only of
> women, but also of men; not merely of private citizens but even of our pub-
> lic officials; have often heard me warning you that our city is beset by two
> quite opposite vices, avarice and luxury [*diversisque duobus vitiis, avaritia et
> luxuria*], which are diseases that have brought to utter ruin all great empires.
> And the better and happier the luck of our republic is from day to day, the
> more our empire grows—we have already crossed over into Greece and Asia
> Minor, places chock full of all the seductions to depravity, and we are even
> pawing now over the treasuries of kings—the greater our empire becomes,

the more frightened I get that this wealth will take hold of us rather than our taking hold of it. (34.4.1–3)

Like many great statesmen, Cato was something of a showman; that is to say, he knew that the process of governing needs some razzle-dazzle, not only to avert our gaze from what will not bear looking at, but also to assuage the mere tedium, the killing boredom of grimy chores. And it also needs to be dramatized. From Livy's re-creation, it looks as though Cato has cast himself in his favorite role, that of farmer-warrior-citizen, *Ur-pater-familias*, struggling gallantly but futilely with the demon of modernity and the specter of decadence, a dual role which Lucius Valerius, who speaks for tolerance and women's rights and common sense and for the repeal of outmoded, old-fashioned law, foolishly and eagerly embraces—thereby winning a cheap, quick victory, while Cato emerges with what he wanted: a stunning but honorable defeat, which will enhance the authenticity of his image as protector of *Romanitas*.

Cato means what he says, of course; he really believes, in fact he knows, that wealth will undermine discipline, and he sees, or nearly sees, the essential dilemma, that a republican empire is something of a contradiction in terms. Cato does not anywhere suggest that it is wrong to go into Greece and Asia Minor and take whatever is to be found there, that picking through the regal treasuries is unethical.[4] Booty, as Montesquieu saw, is the outward sign of the inner glory, which is the heart of *Romanitas* and its destiny.[5] The problem is how to shape an adequate attitude toward the wealth that inevitably accompanies power and influence. That Rome had a right and a duty to dictate war and peace to those with whom it came in contact, Cato never doubted for a moment. But the speed and the confusion that were beginning to attend on the unfolding of Rome's mission and destiny bothered him. Indeed, as Livy has him put it, it frightened him. He was as quintessentially Roman as he claimed to be, his character no persona but an accurate if heightened mimesis of Roman values. The Roman way was prudence, caution, patience; waiting for the opportunity, careful pacing, slow change, methodical trial and error. If, after the victory over Carthage, Romans began to act like Greeklings, the game was over.

The dream of Cato, then, the essential Roman dream, is a rather peculiar one. As Montesquieu saw very clearly, the Romans loved making war, as had the Greeks, almost for war's own sake.[6] In equal measure, almost, they loved freedom—that is, not being told what to do by others—again, like the Greeks. But unlike the Greeks, the Romans combined their love of war and freedom (for themselves) with an instinct for passionate cooperation and teamwork, in which the individual almost automatically sacrificed himself for the common good. This nexus of characteristics proved to be unbeatable, and also proved finally to be, as Cato feared, unable to withstand the complexities of sheer size. As the boundaries of empire widened, the ferocious passions dwindled, faded into the welter of responsibilities and conflicting claims and new styles of life.[7] Freedom, cooperation, and the fun and glory of winning came to be taken for granted, and so got lost in the shuffle. Cato lost (as doubtless he knew he would). This is Montesquieu's view of the matter; clear-eyed it is, cynical it is not; and it seems to me essentially the correct view.

Montesquieu's Rome is astounding, awesome—he did not deny it, in the title of his exquisite essay on Rome, its claim to grandeur—but it is not pretty, and it is not, as it stands, very elevating. Passion for everyone's freedom, passion for everyone's welfare, passion for peace, always and everywhere. The words and the music of the proclamation of Greek freedom and the Isthmian games receive their last and perfect re-creation in the ancient world some four hundred years after Livy wrote, just as the last vestiges of Roman Rome merge into the first lineaments of European Rome; just as Namatianus, with a poignance that verges on the noble, bids farewell to the Eternal City to return to Gaul: *Exaudi, Regina tui pulcherrima mundi. . . . Exaudi, Genetrix hominum Genetrixque deorum. . . . Crebra relinquendis infigimus oscula portis* [Hear me, o loveliest of the queens of your world. . . . Hear me, o mother of men, o mother of the gods. . . . I kiss again and again the gates I must abandon] (*De reditu suo* 1.47, 49.43). To ridicule the feelings that shape this haunting farewell would be no less unwise than to assume that Namatianus speaks

here with historical objectivity, that he provides us with a holistic
Roman view of Rome:

> fecistic patriam diversis gentibus unam:
>   profuit iniustis te dominante capi.
> dumque offers victis proprii consortia iuris,
>   urbem fecisti quod prius orbis erat.
> auctores generia Venerem Martemque fatemur,
>   Aeneadum matrem Romidulumque patrem:
> mitigat armatas victrix clementia vires,
>   convenit in mores nomen utrumque tuos:
> hinc tibi certandi bona parcendique voluptas;
>   quos timuit superat, quos superavit amat.
>   (*De reditu suo* 1.63-72)

[From and for nations widely sundered you have made a single nation; to be
taken over has been, under your dominion, advantageous even for the unre-
generate. And when you made the conquered partners in the Law that is
yours alone, what was only a world you transformed into a City. We boast
Venus and Mars as the shapers of our nation, she, the mother of the sons of
Aeneas, he, father of the sons of Romulus. Triumphant mercy softens weap-
oned force, hence both names are suited to your nature and your manners,
hence that good and double joy, in fighting and in forgiving—whom she
feared, she overcomes; whom she overcame, she loves.]

If the reader, then and now, does not think of Livy's Isthmian
proclamation or of Augustus's own words, the *Res Gestae* carved in
gold, he may very well have at the back of his mind *Aeneid* 6.583
(*parcere subiectis et debellare superbos*) as he listens to Namatianus's
grieving, heartfelt praise. Montesquieu's *certandi voluptas* is here, but
it is a *voluptas* that has been carefully qualified—it is not the crimson
joy of battle only; it is *bona,* because it is also *parcendi voluptas.* So,
amat first blends with *superat,* then obscures it. One world, one city,
a city of Law and of Love. It is the Stoic dream now, fashioned from
Cato's dream. It is, though Namatianus was hardly a Christian, the
beginning of a Christian dream of Rome. Cato's soldiering farmer,
jealous of his liberty, quick to see the main chance, frugal, moderately
sensual, good at team sports, now marches, in Namatianus's imagination, under a standard that would have appalled him:

iustis bellorum causis nec pace superba
    nobilis ad summas gloria venit opes.
              (*De reditu suo* 1.89–90)

[Through a series of wars fought for just causes, through peace treaties imposed without arrogance, your noble glory has come to the summit of wealth.][8]

Cato's farmer-soldier would have liked this couplet; but the emphasis on clemency, compassion, the brotherhood of nations would doubtless have struck him as so much hypocrisy.

That Namatianus should have felt these things, when the Visigoths were loose both in Italy and Gaul, is understandable. But even Namatianus might have been slightly puzzled had he anticipated how the myth would eventually develop. As Charles Norris Cochrane articulated it in 1944:

> Under the aegis of Eternal Rome, Greek and Latin, African, Gaul, and Spaniard remained free to lead their own lives and achieve their own destiny; as late as the end of the fourth century it was still possible for Augustine to speak (in his own words) "as an African to Africans." But, while local and racial differences continued to exist, citizens of the empire discovered a bond of community with one another on the plane of natural reason. It was on this account that the Roman order claimed a universality and a finality to which alternative systems of life could not pretend.[9]

"On the plane of natural reason"? The ignorant, cunning, indefatigable farmer whom Cato discovered and invented had come a long way in a thousand years. From the stubborn acres of Latium and its border skirmishes to the splendors of Roma Aeterna, which the Visigoths had failed to destroy (because *Romanitas,* partly through their agency, merged solidly with *Christianitas* to resist them) Cato's farmer has somehow been transformed by Geistesgeschichte into a philosophical paradigm of total unity and rational order. Propertius, looking at the phenomenon of Roman history in a different light from a different angle of vision, seems to have seen something less grand, less marmoreal:

Moving naked over Acheron
    Upon the one raft, victor and conquered together,

Marius and Jugurtha together,
                        one tangle of shadows.[10]

III

As long as the empire of the Roman People maintained itself by acts of service, not of oppression [*beneficiis tenebatur, non iniuriis*], wars were waged
in the interest of our allies or to safeguard our supremacy [*de imperio gere-
bantur*]; the end of our wars was marked by acts of clemency or by only a
necessary degree of severity; the senate was a haven or refuge for kings, tribes,
and nations; and the highest ambition of our magistrates and generals was to
defend our provinces and allies with justice and honor [*aequitate et fide*].
And so our government could be called more accurately a protectorate of the
world than a dominion [*patrocinium orbis terrae verius quam imperium*]. (*De
officiis* 2.8.26–27)[11]

In this section of his great, final work, *On Responsibilities,* Cicero is
engaged in a discussion of how men may best go about the business
of winning friendship and securing influence honestly and effectively.
The book is addressed to his son, and Cicero wants to offer him (and
other readers) certain practical suggestions on how to go about con-
ducting one's public and private lives. He is very aware of the difficulty of ethical and political choice, not only because it is difficult
to be honest with one's self about one's motives and desires but also
because there are in fact or in appearance genuine conflicts between
the good and the expedient. That he does not succeed in resolving
this conflict need not surprise us. Discerning readers through twenty
centuries have been grateful for his efforts, and we might do well to
follow their example. *De officiis* is Cicero's sanest, most heartfelt
book, and it is packed with the shrewd, slightly naive, wavering com-
monsense that is uniquely his. Traces of silliness and pomposity are
not absent, but here they are less obtrusive, less insistent, than usual.
As he writes this book he is also writing the final Philippics. He
knows that he and his world are doomed; he does not whine; and he
more than rises to the terrible occasion. Surrendering to his destiny,
he comes upon something like the nobility he had searched for
through five frantic decades.

In the passage I have quoted, it is true, there is a faint smell of sour grapes, and the evil Julius, to whom he is about to allude, is here as elsewhere in *De officiis* much on his mind. But here both his own foibles and fumblings, and the wicked luck and genius of his prime antagonist are peripheral. He is trying to probe deeper sorrows; and he is about to make a startling admission. When he suavely terms the republic's empire a *patrocinium* rather than an *imperium* he is indulging in conventional, sentimental, rationalization. What might seem to the uninitiate expediency or opportunism or even greed and powerlust is in fact virtue. The dream of Cato is, then, satisfied, and Livy's Isthmian spectacle intact. But having elegantly reformulated the old myth of innocent and benevolent empire, the mind and the mood waver:

> This policy and practice [i.e., *patrocinium*] we had begun gradually [*sensim*] to modify even before Sulla's time; but since his victory we have departed from it altogether. For the time had gone by when any oppression of the allies could appear wrong, seeing that atrocities so outrageous were committed against Roman citizens. (27)

The emphasis here is on Sulla's behavior during and after his civil war, on the aftermath of that behavior, chiefly as it prepared the way for the demon Julius. But the delicate "gradually" hides more than it illumines, beautifies Cato's dream rather than exposes it. *Patrocinium* had been a lie from the beginning; only as one moved away from its origins did it come to take on, in the shining distances, the shape and candor of truth. There are two possible readings of this passage: either, we have come to treat each other as badly as we have always treated our allies, that is to say, our alien victims; or, we have fallen into the habit of mistreating our allies openly, unashamedly, now that we, corrupted by money and power, persistently, mechanically, mistreat each other. The first is the bitter truth; the second, a sentimental evasion. Julius had caused a model of the city of Marseilles, one of Rome's great "allies," to be carried in his triumphal procession, as if it were in fact a defeated enemy. "I might mention," adds Cicero, "other outrages against our allies, if the sun had ever beheld anything more infamous than this particular one" (28) [*Si hoc uno quicquam sol vidisset indignius*]. The hyperbolic indignation appears because he has come, unawares, to the heart of the matter. "Justly, therefore, we are being punished [*iure igitur plectimur*]. For if we had not allowed the crimes of many to go unpunished, so great a license would never have centered on one individual" (28).

> And so in Rome only the walls of her houses remain standing—and even they wait not in fear of the most unspeakable crimes—but our republic we have lost forever. . . . It is because we have preferred to be the object of fear rather than of love and affection that these misfortunes have fallen upon us. And if such retribution could overtake the Roman People for the injustice [*iniuste imperanti*], what ought private individuals to expect? (29)

This is a moment of genuine poetry. The houses are empty (the great, good citizens are mostly dead in civil war), the empty houses are terrified. And the republic is gone, lost, irretrievably. Our empire is gone, our republic is gone, our freedom is gone. Rome is Rome no more. But what exactly is the punishment for? "If we had not allowed the crimes of so many to go unpunished . . . " [*nisi enim multorum impunita scelera tulissemus . . .*] Cicero cannot quite bring himself to say it, or even to think it.

It was left for the magisterial, irritable, sublime Samuel Johnson to say it for him. In 1755 Dr. Thomas Blackwell had the bad luck to publish the second volume of his *Memoirs of the Court of Augustus,* attacking Augustus and defending the cause of the ardent republicans, Brutus and Cassius. Dr. Johnson was not impressed:

> He is come too late into the world with his fury for freedom, with his Brutus and Cassius. We have all on this side of the Tweed long since settled our opinions: his zeal for Roman liberty and declamations against the violators of the republican constitution, only stand now in the reader's way, who wishes to proceed in the narrative without the interruption of epithets and exclamations. It is not easy to forbear laughter at a man so bold in fighting shadows, so busy in a dispute two thousand years past, and so zealous for the honour of a people who while they were poor robbed mankind, and as soon as they became rich, robbed one another. Of these robberies our author seems to have no very quick sense, except when they are committed by Caesar's party, for every act is sanctified by the name of a patriot. [12]

"While they were poor robbed mankind." The republic, and with it its freedom and empire, had not been lost through greed, as Cato had feared. It had been lost through injustice. The republic and its empire were corrupt from the beginning. Cicero glimpses this: *iure igitur plectimur; nisi enim multorum impunita scelera tulissemus.* But his mind, naturally, whirls to the loss of freedom, to the person who destroyed it, not what that person embodied. Others would also grieve for the loss of freedom, of the republic, for different reasons, in different ways, at different times: Asinius Pollio and the other opponents of Augustus;[13] Lucretius and Catullus; Horace, Propertius and Ovid;[14] Lucan[15] and Tacitus. But deeper than their various perspectives was a bad conscience that knew why the freedom had been lost.

We are told that Scipio Aemilianus wept at the destruction of Carthage.[16] Weeping, he murmured Hector's words, "The day will come when holy Ilium will perish, and with it Priam and the people of Priam, he of the good ash spear" (*Iliad* 6.448–49). Was Scipio grieving for Carthage, for *lacrimae rerum,* all humankind, for Rome and its mortality, for dim intuitions of hybris, of overreaching? This is the stuff of history; a beguiling anecdote, susceptible of various embroideries. We don't know exactly what Polybius, its eyewitness and source, said about this scene. Maybe he misunderstood what he saw and heard, maybe he misremembered it. Maybe smoke got into Scipio's eyes and he made a little joke about it?

This is much too cynical, as the interpretation of Mommsen is much too Romantic. Mommsen saw the tears as symbols of guilt, presentiments of the retribution (*Vergeltung*) that must someday surely overtake Rome for its sins.[17] Not impossible, not likely. But for all its sentimentality, its imprecision as historical re-creation, the intuition of Mommsen has much to recommend it. The story of the tears of Scipio (whether or not there were tears, whatever they meant) is not a metaphor (tears = guilt) for something the Romans came more and more to feel about themselves, their empire, and their city. It is rather a symbol, now luminous, now opaque, that suggests, evokes, but does not define, a complex cluster of feelings and notions Roman literature and Roman monuments sometimes faintly suggest but most often disguise—in the grandeur that was Rome. National pride, the swagger of luck, a sense of achievement earned through loyalties and discipline; delight in power and wealth, complacency and boredom; the anxiety of success; fear, shame; guilt. *Iure igitur plectimur.*

IV

> In my sixth and seventh consulships (28, 27 B.C.), after I had extinguished
> civil wars, and at a time when with universal consent I was in complete control
> of affairs [*per consensum universorum potitus rerum omnium*], I transferred
> the republic from my power to the senate and people of Rome [*rem publi-
> cam transtuli*]. For this service of mine I was named Augustus by decree of
> the senate, and the door-posts of my house were publicly wreathed with bay
> leaves and a civic crown was fixed over my door and a golden shield was set
> in the Curia Julia, which, as attested by the inscription thereon, was given me
> by the senate and people of Rome on account of my courage, clemency, jus-
> tice and piety [*virtutis clementiaeque et iustitiae et pietatis causa*]. After this
> I excelled all in influence [*auctoritate*], although I possessed no more official
> power [*potestatis*] than others who were my colleagues in the several magis-
> tracies.[18] (*Res Gestae* 34)

Rem publicam transtuli. In this, the coda to his history of his reign, Augustus makes a claim that seems to have baffled some of his contemporaries and has continued to baffle the students of and heirs to Roman civilization through the centuries. Like the tears of Scipio, Augustus is a symbol of what Romans felt about their city. Restored the republic? Isn't that what all revolutionaries claim to be doing? Tacitus smelled, and in savage poetry exposed, what he took to be the evil hypocrisy of this claim. After that, endless variations on the two themes: defense of Augustus, defense of Tacitus.[19] Mommsen, again in the grip of his Romantic moods, but now in a soberer frame of mind, thought that Augustus meant that he had founded in Rome, invented for it, a dyarchy, a sharing of power between himself as *princeps* (first citizen) and the senate: so, essentially, the republic was restored.[20] In our own time, Hammond has modified Mommsen by interpreting the Augustan claim as meaning that he recognized "a single final authority," not himself "but the Senatus Populusque Romanus"; that he saw himself as "the servant extraordinary" of the

senate, "acting as its agent," the senate itself "acting directly for the
Roman people."[21] Tacitus and his followers would hardly accept this
sleight-of-hand. And yet it is not inconceivable that this is how Augustus saw the matter, or came to see it sometime before he wrote
his *Res Gestae,* in his "seventy-sixth year." The *Res Gestae* is a model
of its genre, the testament of a Hellenistic king. How is it that the
king, then, can talk so blandly, or so humbly, of the republic? Perhaps because he is no less the heir of Cato than he is the heir of Alex-
ander. If *res publica* is to be defined essentially in terms of the liberty
that it confers, then Augustus's claim is, for the most part, inaccurate
at the least. But is that Cato's definition? Is that what he said and
meant, is that what he dreamed? *Res publica,* the public thing, the
thing in common, the common good. But the individual surrenders
his rights, his happiness, his life, his *libertas,* for the common good
(whenever circumstances require that surrender). Is liberty, then, the
substance of the city, or is it one of its accidents? The republic, the
city, Cato's dream, does not mean liberty, it means *imperium.* Augustus had in fact restored the republic by saving its *imperium,* by
making possible its present and its future, whatever the cost to himself, to others.

Yet magnificent as it is, not least in its superb understatement,
neither the *Res Gestae* itself nor the shrewdly edited, official versions
of Augustan history that have come down to us could have created
and sustained the grandeur of Rome—the awesome beauty of its
buildings and the power, good fortune, stability and endurance that
those buildings betokened and continued to token through the centuries, even after they had been defaced and pillaged and had begun
their long ruining. After Augustus, the buildings would grow steadily
more magnificent in proportion, perhaps, as the political realities
they were designed to show forth declined. But what Namatianus
had in mind when he said his beautiful farewell to the city, what centuries of pilgrims have seen there or hoped to see there, was the
Rome of Augustus. Or rather, the Rome of Vergil, for it is Vergil's
art that makes good the deficiencies both of the *Res Gestae* and its
writer's own historians. Without Vergil, Augustus and his Rome
would still be magnificent, of course, and would have "their place

in history" much as they have it now. But the special effulgence, the
fathomless, elusive, yet blazing radiance that enfolds and guards
them—without Vergil, this they might very well lack. And this is
one of those peculiar, almost unintelligible paradoxes that history is
so lavish of. For if Vergil is the author of Jupiter's great speech to
Venus, of Anchises's revelations to his son of the course and meaning
of Roman history, of the splendors of the Shield of Aeneas, he is no
less the author, in the same poem, of another poem.

Inside the foundation epic, with triumphant Augustus at the center
of the Shield of Aeneas, is a poem about *innatus amor habendi* [the
inborn love of having] (*Georgics* 4.148); a poem about the mechanism of greed and of glory, of the injustice that informs them; a
poem in which the grandeurs and the desolations of *res Romanae* are
steadily and violently evoked, contemplated, and let go. It is a theme
he had touched on in the *Georgics,* most memorably at the close of
the second book (458ff.) where he surveys varieties of human happiness. Farmers, the poet himself (475ff.), are, could be happy, removed from the great world, pondering the world, the natural world,
as it is. Philosophers are happy; so, too, are those who follow the old
Italian religion—for both philosophers (Epicureans) and the rustic
worshipers of nature have put behind them the prime causes of humankind's fear, that fear in which all its unhappiness and wickedness
are rooted:

> Blest is he who has looked on things as they are,
> Who has trampled under him fear and pitiless fate
> And the roar of hungry hell. And happy, too,
> That man who knows the truth of rural gods,
> Of Pan and old Silvanus and the Nymphs:
> Him the people's favor cannot bend,
> Nor royal splendors fright, nor civil war,
> Nor barbarous armies massing in the North,
> Nor Rome's own force, nor kingdoms soon to fall.
> Who plucks his fruit from willing boughs, he feels
> Neither the bite of envy for the rich
> Or pity for the poor, nor gazes on
> The public archives and the iron laws,
> The forum in its madness. Others with oars

Harrass the blind surge, plunge to iron wars,
Break past rich portals into the regal hall.
To sip from jewelled beakers or to drowse
Wrapped in the lustre of Tyrian sheets, for this
They mark for doom the city and its houses. (490-506)

I have here mistranslated *res Romanae* as "Rome's own force," not merely for the sake of alliteration, but because the phrase defies translation. *Res* has here all its political connotations: property; possessions; interest (advantage, benefit); business; acts, events, history; commonweal, commonwealth—*our thing*. Something that constrains, overwhelms. The nations soon to fall of course add to the sum of *res*. The independent farmer, humble of means but not starving, secure in his kinship with his land and its ancient deities, can withstand this immense power, can disassociate himself from its history of murder, its rigid, opportune legalities, and its insane public assemblies. *Insanum forum,* a brilliant near-oxymoron, does not signify only the crazy proletariat. He will therefore not find himself sailing eagerly off to pacify the savages, spread law and order, bestow peace and commit armed robbery with leisure and impunity. The last three verses of my translation might allude to Rome and the horrors of its civil wars; they might, alternatively or simultaneously, allude to foreign adventures in military training and creative finance.[22] These verses also, no less than those devoted to the Shield of Aeneas, depict an aspect of Roman history, *res Romanae*. Remembering them, we can see Aeneas through the eyes of Dido and of Turnus. Dido and Turnus are not, of course, wholly correct in their views, do not know enough; but something they do know, and their views (as losers and victims) are not wholly wrong, either. The mission of Aeneas, though it has its glory, certainly, is not without its darker ambivalences as well. Vergil is, *par excellence,* the poet of *iure igitur plectimur.* He takes the idea of the common good, the Roman good, together with the sacrifices it requires and the injustices it promotes, turns it over in his mind and heart, and so comes upon its essential power and its central antimonies—that is to say, its tragedies and mysteries.

The bees and their beehive are a natural, an almost perfect, metaphor for *res publica,* for Rome. Vergil had come upon the essence of this metaphor, together with another of the great, central metaphors that haunts the *Aeneid,* that of the loss of Eurydice, when making his final revision of the fourth *Georgics.* There, in the rich complexities and rumbling dialectics of what purports to be a Callimachean poem on Roman agriculture, the beehive, with its bees, figures in the poem's closure as allegorical icon of the republic restored. The culture hero Aristaeus has suffered the loss of his swarm, through, as he learns from Proteus, his attempted rape of Orpheus's wife, Eurydice; bitten by a serpent, as she fled in terror from Aristaeus, she descended to death in the underworld, where, Orpheus's attempt to rescue her having failed, she now dwells forever. Her shade and that of Orpheus, dead of grief, will not be appeased—for it is their anger that killed Aristaeus's swarm—until he offers them proper atonement. This atonement duly made, his swarm is miraculously returned to him. That Aristaeus images Augustus seems fairly clear; and no less clear is the mood of thanksgiving that informs the closure of the poem, as the tale of Aristaeus and his bees is ended. Nevertheless, although it is the brighter aspects of the bee metaphor that dominate Vergil's handling of it in *Georgics* 4, the guilt of Aristaeus, if it is legally expiated and that expiation rewarded, glints steadily and ominously under the shimmering surfaces and rococo wit of Aristaeus's story— his wittily pictured visit to his mother under the sea, his encounter with Proteus, and the fortunate reversal of bad luck and destructive lust. It is the figure of Eurydice we remember, her terrible disintegration and fading when Orpheus glances back at her: the horror of loss, here as so often in the *Aeneid.*

In its first appearance in the *Aeneid,* the bee-city metaphor is positive. Aeneas and Achates, having escaped the wrath of Juno and death at sea, come to Carthage for Dido's help; before meeting her, they stand watching as the builders of Carthage energetically perform their labors. For this energy, discipline, and clear purpose, which are suffused in a kind of joy, the bees provide an apt simile:

> Just as the bees in early summer, busy
> beneath the sunlight through the flowered meadows,
> when some lead on their full-grown young and others
> press out the flowing honey, pack the cells

> with sweet nectar, or gather in the burdens
> of those returning; some, in columns drive
> the drones, a lazy herd, out of the hives;
> the work is fervent, and the fragrant honey
> is sweet with thyme. "How fortunate are those
> whose walls already rise!" Aeneas cries
> while gazing at the rooftops of the city.
> $$(611-21=430-36)^{23}$$

The lyrical charm of the simile is undercut, if at all, only by light
discord from the image of the drones. But even that possible ambivalence is overwhelmed in the brightness, speed, and sweetness of the
pictures and their sound, by these and by Aeneas's wondering delight
(envious he is not, not consciously). Nor, usually, do we feel the bitter irony, of which he is utterly unaware, in his blessing on Dido's
people. He does not know, and we seldom remember here, that this
is the city that will cause Rome such grief, that will inspire the tears
of Scipio. Vergil has not forgotten these things; but, for all that,
here the bee-city metaphor is as joyous as it is exquisitely composed.

Toward the beginning of *Aeneid* 7, near the center of the entire
epic, the bee symbol returns, not as simile but as narrative event.
King Latinus is surprised by a portent involving the sacred laurel tree
in his courtyard:

> At the laurel's crown—how strange
> to tell—a thick and sudden swarm of bees,
> borne, shrill, across the liquid air, had settled;
> they twined their feet and hung from leafy branches.
> At once the prophet cried: "In that direction
> from which the swarm has come I see a stranger
> approaching and an army nearing us. . . . "
> $$(82-88=64-70)$$

Immediately after this, the hair of Princess Lavinia bursts into flame.
Frightened by the double prodigy, Latinus hastens to the oracle of
Faunus, where he learns, dimly, something of their meaning. The
stranger is Aeneas, and it is he who will marry Lavinia. And the reader
knows that from their union, slowly, in the course of history, will

Margaret W. Ferguson

"The Afflatus of Ruin": Meditations on Rome by Du Bellay, Spenser, and Stevens

The phrase quoted in my title, from Wallace Stevens's poem "To an Old Philosopher in Rome," may sound somewhat gloomily grandiose. It points, however, to one of my major concerns in this paper: the idea of Rome as a source of poetic "afflatus," or inspiration. Rome and her famous ruins have, of course, been the subject of some great poetry as well as much that is not; it is only slightly less commonplace to observe that many poems inspired by the real or imagined sight of Rome are thematically concerned with the nature and longevity of inspiration itself. Ruins naturally conjure up fears of mortality, and for poets, ruins frequently inspire thoughts about that metaphorical death that is voicelessness. The afflatus of ruin, one might say, often produces poems about the ruin of afflatus.

The theme of ruined inspiration appears repeatedly in Du Bellay's sonnet sequences about Rome and also in his prose treatise, *La Deffense et illustration de la langue françoyse* (1549); this treatise is in part a defense against the poet's fears that he is doomed, as a late-born Frenchman, to write poetry less copiously rich than that of the ancient Greeks and Romans. Spenser too broods on the meaning of Roman ruins for his own poetic aspirations and for English civilization in general; he does so not only in the sonnets about Rome he translated directly from Du Bellay's French, but also in a little-read but fascinating minor work called *The Ruines of Time*. Stevens wrote only one poem thematically concerned with Rome. This is the "pre-elegy," as Harold Bloom aptly calls it, addressed to the old philosopher George Santayana, who chose to spend his final years tended by nuns in a Roman nursing home.[1] I shall discuss Stevens's poem in some detail at the end of this paper; for the moment, however, I would like to use it schematically to introduce my second major concern, the relation between Rome and family romance.

Freud's essay "Family Romances" (1909) describes the child's imaginative search for an improved parentage.[2] As a response to sibling rivalries, fears of being insufficiently loved, and the general ambivalence of the Oedipal situation, the child's imagination, Freud writes, "becomes engaged in getting free from the parents of whom he now has a low opinion and of replacing them by others who, as a rule, are of higher social standing" (SE 9:237–38). Stevens's "To an Old Philosopher in Rome," like the other texts I shall discuss, may be usefully regarded as a complex version of family romance—one that dramatizes some of the genre's economic and ideological implications. Although I shall argue that Stevens's portrait of Santayana as a heroic paternal figure surrounded by ministering nuns shows family romance being linked to a peculiarly American idealization of poverty, Stevens's poem also serves, more generally, to illustrate a connection between the idea of Rome as a source of inspiration or knowledge, and the idea of the city as a mythical homeland, a place where one may be reborn, as it were, in a finer tone. This connection can be traced in many meditations on Rome, including Freud's own accounts of his dream romance with "the Eternal City."[3]

In the Renaissance, Rome occupied a central place in nationalist family romance stories as well as in those of individual poets. The Tudors found the Trojan Brutus at the root of their family tree, and French monarchs also traced their lineage back to Troy, specifically, to Hector's son Francus, who supposedly settled in Celtic Gaul after his city's fall.[4] Such myths portrayed the French and English monarchies as siblings, and potential rivals, to the empire founded by another son of Troy, Aeneas. But nationalist myths also relied on a theory of history that acknowledged Rome's temporal priority while at the same time glorifying the Renaissance states. This was the old theory of *translatio imperii,* or transfer of empire, with its corollary notion of *translatio studii,* or transfer of learning.[5] According to this theory, Rome was the heir to the cultural riches both of Troy and of ancient Greece; Rome was, as well, the empire providentially chosen to unite the world and prepare it for Christianity. Providence had also decreed that the course of empire was to move from east to west, following the path of the sun.[6] The version of this theory that Catholic theologians developed to support the idea of papal authority over the Holy Roman Empire was bitterly attacked in the Reformation period; far from relinquishing the theory itself, however, Protestants transformed it into a weapon for their own nationalist and theological arguments.[7] Although the idea of *translatio imperii* might appear to adumbrate a view of history as peaceful continuity, its teleological perspective was powerful and elastic enough to accommodate catastrophes such as the fall of Rome and the break between Protestants and Catholics.

As a theory of history, as a hermeneutic tool, and as a linguistic practice, translation is at the heart of Du Bellay's and Spenser's meditations on Rome. It is, however, a complex and highly problematic topic, which has various uses for family romance. Translation may be conceived of as a peaceful means of transferring cultural riches from Roman fathers to their Renaissance heirs; but if the Roman authors look, as they often do to Du Bellay, like fathers who are refusing to die gracefully and pass on their wealth, or if they look like brothers or uncles who have taken more than their fair share of goods from the family seat of Troy, then translation may easily become a weapon in a metaphorical civil war. For Du Bellay, the issue is further complicated by the fact that the language of the ancient Romans is also the one that sixteenth-century Catholic theologians praised as a *sermo patrius* or paternal speech, while denigrating the value of the vernacular mother tongue.[8] Du Bellay's defense of French, which contains passionate arguments for vernacular translations of the Bible and equally passionate arguments against servile translations of classical texts, is a work full of contradictory theories and attitudes. In this paper I shall focus chiefly on those aspects of the text that dramatize Du Bellay's ambivalence toward ancient Rome and her famous authors.[9]

The *Deffense* may be read, from this perspective, as a text that superimposes a positive family romance story upon a negative one. In the former, the Romans are conceived of as generous guardians of a treasure of poetic inspiration. They themselves inherited this treasure

from the Greeks, and are now ready, Du Bellay hopes, to pass it on
to the French. In the second story, however, the Romans are conceived of as miserly kinsmen who keep the French in a state of
poverty and bondage. Both of these stories refract Du Bellay's biographical situation as the younger son of an impoverished branch of
a noble family. Raised, after his parents' death, by an elder brother
who seems to have treated him as shabbily as Oliver treats Orlando
in Shakespeare's *As You Like It,* Du Bellay wrote the *Deffense* in
hopes of gaining employment from his wealthy kinsman the cardinal
Jean Du Bellay, to whom the text is dedicated.[10] The cardinal had
served as a diplomatic envoy to the papal court at Rome; Du Bellay
therefore associates him with his own desires to gain real as well as
metaphorical riches from journeying to Rome in the cardinal's
retinue. Du Bellay's ambivalent attitudes toward the ancient Roman
authors and toward the city itself are inextricably linked to his complex relation to the cardinal, whom he regards both as a heroic father
figure and as a potential enemy, a man capable of frustrating a young
kinsman's desires for that wealth which should have come to him
"naturally," that is, through inheritance rather than clerkly labor.[11]

Du Bellay's positive family romance story, as I have called it,
projects onto the ancient Roman authors the qualities he hopes the
cardinal will, in the future, display toward his needy kinsman. The
Romans are presented, in this story, as benevolent masters of the art
of imitation, which they used to enrich their language as Du Bellay
hopes to enrich French. Imitation, as Du Bellay describes it in an
early chapter of the treatise, is a process that resembles agricultural
labor. The Romans illustrated this process when, "in the manner of
good farmers," they "grafted" Greek words like branches onto the
plant of the Latin language.[12] The organic metaphor Du Bellay resorts
to here pays homage to Vergil's portrait of the Romans as cultivators
in the *Georgics.* The metaphor also, I think, reveals Du Bellay's longing to assimilate his notion of imitation to a nostalgically idealized
version of feudal economy, in which land rather than commodities
was the source of wealth.

The organic metaphor of imitation, however, is ultimately an
inadequate defense against Du Bellay's awareness that neither literary

nor economic riches are likely to come to the poet who simply culti-
vates his garden. More aggressive tactics may be necessary, as Du
Bellay suggests in a later passage that compares the Roman practice
of imitation not only to an act of agricultural grafting, but also to
acts of ingestion and architectural construction:

> Imitating the best Greek authors, transforming themselves into the Greeks,
> devouring them, and after having well digested them, converting them into
> blood and nourishment, they proposed the best author as a pattern, each ac-
> cording to his natural bent and according to the argument he wished to elect;
> they diligently observed all of the rarest and most exquisite virtues of the
> model author, and treating these virtues as grafts, as I have said before, they
> grafted and applied them to their own language. By doing this (I say), the
> Romans built all those beautiful writings, that we praise and admire so
> strongly.

> [Immitant les meilleurs aucteurs Grecz, se transformant en eux, les devorant,
> & apres les avoir bien digerez, les convertissant en sang & nouriture, se propo-
> sant, chacun selon son natural & l'argument qu'il vouloit elire, le meilleur
> aucteur, dont ilz observoint diligemment toutes les plus rares & exquises
> vertuz, & icelles comme grephes, ainsi que j'ay dict devant, entoint & apli-
> quoint à leur Langue. Cela faisant (dy-je) les Romains ont baty tous ces beaux
> ecriz, que nous louons & admirons si fort.] (Pp. 42-43)

Although a contemporary critic objected to the "translation
vicieuse" in this passage's shifting metaphors,[13] the shifts in truth
seem necessary to express Du Bellay's sense that imitation involves
a violent act of appropriation which can only with difficulty be ac-
commodated within the bounds of civilized behavior. If the passage
sketches a miniature history of culture—from cannibalism to agriculture to architecture—it also testifies to Du Bellay's sense that imitation, as a means of acquiring wealth, is neither a wholly natural nor a
wholly legitimate phenomenon.

The negative version of Du Bellay's family romance acknowledges
the possibility that the ancient authors—and by implication, the
cardinal Jean du Bellay—may not wish to relinquish their wealth to
an impoverished young man. A battle for property seems an inevitable
consequence of this idea, especially since Du Bellay does not seriously
consider the possibility that the modern poet could gain the verbal

power he desires through using his own faculty of invention.[14] Indeed, Du Bellay was criticized by contemporaries for relying more heavily on imitation than on invention both in his theory and in his poetic practice;[15] his views on the necessity of imitation, more extreme than those of other sixteenth-century critics, testify to his pessimistic sense that there is a finite amount of literary wealth in the world at any given time. If the ancients presently possess it—as he insists they do when he says that "the arts and sciences are now in the hands of the Greeks and the Latins" (p. 67)—the modern poet must somehow take the treasure from them. He fears, however, that his strength to do so may be drained before he even begins the task. The modern poet, Du Bellay laments, loses so much time in acquiring rudimentary language skills that his "alacrity of spirit" and his very manhood seem to disappear before he can compete with the ancients. "Not only do we consume our youth in this vain exercise" of learning ancient languages, he laments, "but as if repenting of having left the cradle and become men, we return again to infancy, and for twenty or thirty years do nothing but attempt to speak Greek or Latin or Hebrew" (p. 66). Playing deliberately on the etymology of the Latin word *infans,* which means "speechless," Du Bellay here portrays the modern poet as a perennial child, kept by his ancient fathers in an unnatural state of arrested development.

The negative version of Du Bellay's family romance combines hostility toward the ancient authors with an idealization of Rome herself; the city is conceived as an infinitely richer mother of poets than France has ever been. Although Du Bellay refers to his native land as the "mother of arts" in sonnet 9 of *Les Regrets,* in the *Deffense* France seems to be a sadly inadequate mother—perhaps even a stepmother. She is often associated with images of sterility and disease, and is, at one point, compared to a desert.[16] For Du Bellay, it would seem, Rome is the true promised land, the once and future Eden where even common people could suck in eloquence, as he wistfully says, with their nurses' milk (p. 81).

When Du Bellay actually succeeded in journeying to Rome four years after the *Deffense* was published,[17] he found, like so many travelers before and after him, that the city he saw did not correspond with the city he had imagined; he records the experience of disappointment and bafflement in a famous sonnet:

Nouveau venu qui cherches Rome en Rome,
Et rien de Rome en Rome n'apperçois,
Ces vieux palais, ces vieux arcz que tu vois,
Et ces vieux murs, c'est ce que Rome on nomme.[18]

In the two great vernacular sonnet sequences he wrote during his stay in Rome, *Les Antiquitez de Rome* and *Les Regrets,* he repeatedly broods on the gap between Rome's name and the mysterious, contradictory realities (or unrealities) it signifies. He also repeatedly personifies the city itself as a woman, no longer the benevolent mother of genius he had imagined in the *Deffense,* but rather a mistress who both resists the French poet's courtship and lures him away from his mother country—and from the French language which he characterizes, in a witty Latin poem, as his wife.[19] Although this is only one aspect of the complex sexual drama figured in Du Bellay's Roman poetry, it is the aspect most germane for Spenser and is therefore worth discussing briefly here.

In the central section of the *Regrets,* Du Bellay compares Rome to a series of female figures who threaten the poet with literal and metaphorical impotence. Among these dangerous women are the witches Alcina and Circe; cruel Lady Fortune; painted courtesans who look like harpies or ancient sybils and who may infect the unwary traveller with syphilis; a demonic *genius loci* who can rob the poet both of his voice and his hair; and finally, Venus herself, the "Cyprian Mother" who guarded her son Aeneas but who may kill the French poet as she killed Adonis.[20] These sonnets about the erotic dangers of modern Rome stand in ironic and contrapuntal relation to the poems of the *Antiquitez* in which Du Bellay portrays the ancient city as an unattainable object of desire, an "imperial mistress" endowed, as Wayne Rebhorn has recently argued, with all the qualities Petrarch ascribes to Laura "in morte."[21] There, of course, is the rub; the speaker of the *Antiquitez* may praise Rome in phrases directly drawn from Petrarch's *Canzoniere,*[22] but he, unlike Petrarch, cannot claim ever to have seen his lady alive in all her glory. Whereas in the

Regrets, modern Rome threatens the poet with impotence and voice-lessness because of the very lavishness of her morally dubious gifts, the ancient city depicted in the *Antiquitez* threatens the poet with poverty and frustration. In the *Regrets* Du Bellay presents himself as a man pursued and captured by Rome, but in the *Antiquitez* he is the pursuer who never reaches his goal. His mistress is cold to him, not because she is virtuous (Du Bellay departs from Petrarchan convention in refusing to make that claim) but because she is dead, or only ambiguously alive beneath her ruins. The poet attempts, like Orpheus, to rescue his beloved from the underworld of death, but like Orpheus, he fails. He blames that failure not only on himself, but also on fate, which in some poems is seen as the cause of Rome's fall, and also on Rome herself, who is chastized in other poems for engendering her own ruin by her excessive pride and her penchant for civil war.

Sometime in the 1570s or 1580s, Spenser translated Du Bellay's *Antiquitez* as *Ruines of Rome;* he did not translate the *Regrets,* but that sequence about the seductive and corrupting power of papal Rome is important for understanding not only Spenser's portrait of Duessa in the *Faerie Queene* but also his ambivalence toward his own act of bringing Du Bellay's poems about ancient Rome to Protestant England. Years before he composed the *Ruines of Rome,* Spenser had translated most of Du Bellay's *Songe,* a series of fifteen apocalyptic dream visions about Rome's fall appended to the *Antiquitez;* his reasonably accurate if not altogether elegant blank verse translations were produced for Jan van der Nood's *Theatre for Worldings.* [23] Spenser later revised these poems, probably around the same time he was writing the *Ruines of Rome,* and published them, under the title *Visions of Bellay,* in his 1591 volume of *Complaints.* [24] The young Spenser was clearly impressed by Du Bellay's poignant meditations on Rome as an emblem of mutability both in *Songe* and in the *Antiquitez;* it seems fair to speculate that Spenser was also impressed by the French poet's brilliant feat of transposing the conventions of Petrarchan love poetry onto sonnet sequences about ancient Rome. But that very transposition dramatized a danger for the English imitator—the danger that in the very act of translating Du Bellay's poems, Spenser was engaging in a form of idolatry.

When he first translated the sonnets of *Songe,* which are more overtly Christian in their perspective than the *Antiquitez,* Spenser may well have felt, as van der Nood evidently did, that Du Bellay's poems were perfectly well suited to a Protestant world-view.[25] Du Bellay's characterization of Rome as the seven-headed beast of Revelation in sonnet 8 of *Songe,* for instance, is easily assimilable to the popular Protestant analogy between the Roman church and the Whore of Babylon.[26] And although Du Bellay's poems were about the ancient city rather than the Catholic church, his meditations on Rome's pride and fall appear, at first glance, no less useful for Protestant polemical purposes than Augustine's famous descriptions of Rome as the prototypical city of man, whose self-willed fate should warn us to turn our eyes to the city of God. Nonetheless, so shrewd a reader as Spenser would probably have to come to see that the sonnets of *Songe,* no less than those of the *Antiquitez,* often illustrate a form of idolatrous love on the poet's part even as they chastize Rome for her vain glory.[27] Modeled on Petrarch's canzone "Standomi un giorno solo a la fenestra" (*Rime* 323), the *Songe* poems present us with a dreamer who continues to worship Rome despite his knowledge that she was [is] "built on sand."[28]

The experience of rereading and rewriting Du Bellay's Roman sonnets over a period of years led Spenser, I think, to question the meaning of his own act of translating them. Was his admiration for them itself a form of idolatry, like Du Bellay's admiration for Rome and her pagan authors? And in giving Du Bellay's poems a new life in the English language, was Spenser endangering the spiritual health of both his readers and himself? The idol "stirreth up the desire of the ignorant: so that he coveteth the forme that hath no life, of a dead image," says the Bible (Wisdom 15:5); in reviving Du Bellay's poems as Du Bellay had sought to revive the spirits of the ancient Roman writers, was Spenser making an error similar to Redcrosse's when he seeks to revive the faint Duessa?[29] Spenser raises such questions only obliquely in the "Envoy" he attached to his translation of the *Antiquitez,* but he explores them more directly in *The Ruines of Time,* a poem which is deeply indebted to Du Bellay but also subtly critical of him.

In his "Envoy" to *Ruines of Rome,* Spenser at once compliments Du Bellay handsomely and begins, symbolically, to withdraw from his sphere of influence:

> *Bellay,* first garland of free Poësie
> That *France* brought forth, though fruitfull of brave wits,
> Well worthie thou of immortalitie,
> That long has traveld by thy learned writs,
> Olde *Rome* out of her ashes to revive,
> And give a second life to dead decayes:
> Needes must he all eternitie survive,
> That can to other give eternall dayes.
> Thy dayes therefore are endles, and thy prayse
> Excelling all, that ever went before;
> And after thee, gins *Bartas* hie to rayse
> His heavenly Muse, th' Almightie to adore.
> Live happie spirits, th'honour of your name,
> And fill the world with never dying fame.
>   (*Works* 8:154)

In the mention of Du Bartas and his heavenly Muse, Spenser implies the need for a Christian supplement to the path defined by Du Bellay and faithfully followed—up to this point—by his English translator. But the idea of a progress of poetic vision from earlier to later times and, by implication, from lower to higher sources of inspiration, works in this poem to suppress or at least defer the question of a choice between pagan and Christian modes of poetry. The problem of choice is clearly present, for Du Bartas's heavenly Muse stands in dramatic contrast to the "Divins esprites" Du Bellay had invoked, with religious awe, in the opening sonnet of the *Antiquitez.* Those spirits of ancient Rome, whose only corporeal remains are the "poudreuse cendre" ("ashie cinders") buried beneath the weight of walls, possess a dark inspirational power that the humanist poet seeks to reawaken.[30] Spenser, however, hints as Du Bellay does not at the difficulty of accommodating poetic acts of quasi-magical resurrection within a Christian framework. Spenser translates "Divins esprits" as "Ye *heavenly* spirits" [my emphasis]; he thereby adds a discordant, if not ironic, note to the pagan ceremonial resonance of Du Bellay's poem, which enacts, as Thomas Greene observes, "the quintessential humanist rite, the calling up of the ancient dead in imitation of their own gestures and their own style."[31] The poet Du Bellay imitates most closely, in this sonnet and throughout the sequence, is Vergil; Du Bellay's invocation alludes, indeed, as Greene suggests, to Vergil's own prayer to the gods of the underworld that he be allowed to "reveal [literally, throw open] truth sunk in depths of earth and gloom."[32] The Vergilian parallel dramatizes the spatial as well as the theological distance between the buried source of power and knowledge Du Bellay's opening sonnet defines and the "heavenly" source Spenser associates with Du Bartas in the "Envoy" and foreshadows in his apparently inept translation of Du Bellay's phrase "Divins esprits." Although the "Envoy" does not directly pose the question of whether a poet can serve both heaven and the ancient spirits of Rome, that question lurks in the sonnet's concern with literary immortality. The longing for fame may be, for the Christian, "that last infirmity of noble mind."

In *The Ruines of Time* Spenser grapples with his fear that he may be not only spiritually endangered but also poetically weakened by his imitative relation to Du Bellay.[33] Both aspects of his anxiety are figured in the fate of the poem's major character, Verlame. The *genius loci* of the ancient British city of Verulamium, this strange lady owes her very existence to Rome, the city which at once founded her and made her a tributary. If Rome made Verlame great, however (or at least great in a small way), Rome also caused her English daughter's fall into her present humiliating state of ruin. We are therefore not surprised to hear in Verlame's tone toward Rome a confused mixture of gratitude, envy, and resentment. Consider, for instance, a passage that looks at first like a Protestant diatribe against Rome but that then modulates into a genuine question about Rome's wealth (a pressing issue for a metaphorical child) and next into a lament for Rome and for Verlame herself:

> And where is that same great seven headded beast,
> That made all nations vassals of her pride,
> To fall before her feete at her beheast,
> And in the necke of all the world did ride?
> Where doth shee all that wondrous welth nowe hide?

With her own weight down pressed now shee lies,
And by her heaps her hugenesse testifies.

O *Rome* thy ruine I lament and rue,
And in thy fall my fatall overthrowe,
That whilom was, whilst heavens with equall vewe
Deignd to behold me, and their gifts bestowe,
The picture of thy pride in pompous shew:
And of the whole world as thou wast the Empresse,
So I of this small Northerne world was Princesse.
                          (11.71–84; *Works* 8:39)

Verlame stands in relation to Rome as Spenser stands, at this point
in his career, in relation to Du Bellay. Critics have often noted that
the opening scene of *The Ruines of Time* derives from sonnet 10 of
Songe, where the dreamer sees a nymph-like spirit of Rome bewailing
her fate on the banks of the Tiber. But they have not observed that
when Spenser translated this scene into an English equivalent, he was
commenting, with considerable irony, on translation itself, as a process that all too often makes something major into something minor.
Walking by the side of the Thames, the poet-narrator sees a woman
"sorrowfullie wailing" on the opposite bank, rending her golden
locks and, unlike Du Bellay's nymph, holding a broken rod which
she waves at the heavens (11.9–13). Paradoxically, the original detail
of Spenser's scene is precisely the one that signals his fears that he is
incapable of independent creation. The broken rod, which recalls the
oaten pipe Colin Clout despairingly breaks at the end of the January
eclogue, is a symbol of failed inspiration.[34]

Spenser had good reason to represent his own sense of poetic
impotence in Verlame, for when he looked around him for English
sources of inspiration—financial as well as literary—he saw a landscape filled with graves. The recent deaths of his patrons Leicester
and Walsingham, and above all, the death of his friend and mentor
Sir Philip Sidney, made England seem an extremely inhospitable
place for a young poet. In *The Teares of the Muses,* the poem that
immediately follows *The Ruines of Time* in the *Complaints* volume,
Spenser portrays his native country as a cultural wasteland that fos-
ters no creative labor;[35] and in the letter dedicating *The Ruines of*

Time to the Countess of Pembroke, Spenser links the sorry plight of his own "young muses" directly to Sidney's death; "togeather with him," Spenser writes, "their hope of anie further fruit was cut off" (*Works* 8:35). Verlame's unhappy relationship of dependency toward Rome seems to represent Spenser's anxiety not only about his dependence on Du Bellay, but also about his dependence on Englishmen no longer alive to help him.

Once we see the poem as an extended meditation on the problems of dependency on persons who, like parents, are perceived as alternately giving too much and too little, we can appreciate the originality of Spenser's strategy to overcome his sense of being in a state of poetic ruin. The first phase of that strategy involves his creation of a speaker who seems, initially, like a minor version of Du Bellay's Rome but who turns out to have a life and a voice of her own. The lady who pathetically describes herself as a "princesse" of a small Northern world once ruled by a Roman empress, is not content for long to remain a dependent relation. The very fact that she exists in a poem that refuses to remain within the bounds of Du Bellay's sonnet form testifies to Spenser's desire to make a declaration of independence from his erstwhile source, who inspired him to make poems that were not, in fact, nearly so good as their French originals.[36] He begins to make that declaration of independence through Verlame: loquacious, slightly hysterical, logically inconsistent and theologically suspect, she sounds more like Chaucer's Creseyde or Wife of Bath than like anything in Du Bellay; indeed Du Bellay's personifications of Rome never speak at all.[37] Like Chaucer's women, Verlame is capable of marvelous discourse on her adversities. One of the best moments occurs when she breaks her just-given vow to remain silent about her former riches. It would be labor lost to describe them, she says, but goes on to do just that:

> High towers, faire temples, goodly theaters,
> Strong walls, rich porches, princelie pallaces,
> Large streetes, brave houses, sacred sepulchers,
> Sure gates, sweete gardens, stately galleries,
> Wrought with faire pillours, and fine imageries,
> All those [O pitie] are now turnd to dust,

And overgrowen with blacke oblivions rust.
(11.92–98; Works 8:39)

This stanza, as Lawrence Manley has noted, is an example of
synathroesmus, the figure of "collection" or, as Puttenham called it,
"the heaping figure."[38] It epitomizes Verlame's own role as an emblem
of rhetorical abundance.[39] Her abundance, however, is problematic-
ally chaotic—immature, one might say, reading the poem as an allegorical drama of literary and ethical development. Verlame, from this
perspective, represents a stage or state of being the poet must pass
through before he can achieve a full imaginative renewal, which would
involve not only rhetorical copia but the power to order it, to discriminate more finely between truth and error than Verlame is able
to do.[40] Her tendency to see the world in extremes of all or nothing-
ness becomes almost comical in the lengthy laments for Walsingham,
the Dudleys, and Sidney that occupy the middle part of the poem:
of Leicester she says, for instance, repeating her favorite word "all,"

> He nowe is dead, and all his glorie gone,
> And all his greatnes vapoured to nought
> That as a glasse upon the water shone,
> Which vanisht quite, so soone as it was sought.
(11.218–21)

A few stanzas later, she swings to the opposite extreme, proclaiming
absolutely eternal life for Ambrose Dudley; "Thy Lord," she assures
his widow,

> Shall never die, the whiles this verse
> Shall live, and surely it shall live forever;
> For ever it shall live, and shall rehearse
> His worthie praise, and vertues dying never.
(11.253–56)

Verlame's absolutist statements are not absolutely wrong, Spenser
implies, but partly so; they need tempering, like grief itself. Verlame,
however, is incapable of reform; she is too tied to the past, and to
Rome—or more precisely, to an anachronistic view of Rome as an
"empresse" whose dominion included England. If Verlame's verbal
energy constitutes a symbolic defense against the English poet's sense

of failed inspiration, that defense is finally an inadequate one. After her departure, the narrator finds himself with "no word to say" (1.474).

The poem does not end, however, with Verlame's departure. It concludes with a series of visions that again recall Du Bellay's *Songe* but also signal Spenser's emergent sense of independence from his source. Du Bellay and Verlame are both supplanted by a new figure of inspiration, Philisides or Sir Philip Sidney. Philisides ("lover of a star") was a name Sidney derived from his own and used to represent himself in the *Arcadia*.[41] Spenser at once pays homage to the dead Sidney and gives him a new fictional life by making Philisides into a muse who is, like Milton's *Lycidas*, at once English and Protestant. No longer suffering from a hopeless passion for a lady, as he did in the *Arcadia* and as his fictional double did in *Astrophil and Stella,* Spenser's Philisides himself becomes a star capable of leading others to virtue. By giving us a reformed or perfected image of Sidney (one which differs significantly from the gently critical portrait of the fallen hero presented in *Astrophil*), Spenser not only pays tribute to Sidney's literary effort to reform England, his Queen, and his own imagination, but also defines poetic imitation itself as a process of creative reformation, an art which, as Sidney argued in the *Defense of Poesie,* makes "things either better than nature bringeth forth, or quite anew," with the end of leading readers to "well doing and not . . . well knowing only."[42] Spenser confirms Philisides's new role of guide to heavenly felicity through a description of the dead poet's Orphic harp, an instrument so eloquently moving that even beasts and trees follow it. The dreamer first sees this harp "swimming" in a river; he then sees it rise miraculously above the clouds, to become a constellation (11.603–16). Evidently an emblem for a *translatio* that moves both westward to England (from Orpheus's Greece) and upward to heaven, the harp alludes, as well, to Sidney's own translation of David's Psalms.[43] What is most remarkable about the image of the harp is that it retroactively gives new meaning to a biblical allusion buried, as it were, in the opening lines of the poem, where Verlame sat weeping by the Thames as the psalmist had wept by the waters of Babylon. Verlame, however, like her literary prototype in Du Bellay's

Songe, resembles the psalmist only in outward form; she weeps for
her own ruined city whereas the psalmist wept not for Babylon but
for his exile from Sion; and his mourning included a prayer that his
tongue might cleave to the roof of his mouth if he forgot Sion or
did not prefer her above all others.

At the end of *The Ruines of Time,* Spenser symbolically renews
his allegiance to Sion, which he had been in danger of forgetting in
his fascination with Du Bellay's Rome. The spirit of Sidney as Spenser has re-created it seems to guide him toward Sion and away from
his fears that his erring has been punished with voicelessness—the potential fate of the translator and also of the Christian who forgets his
duty to God. The imaginative journey from Rome to a reformed England which Spenser has taken in this poem brings him, finally, to an
Envoy that contrasts strikingly with the final sonnet of *Ruines of
Rome.* Here Spenser pairs Sidney with his sister Mary, as Donne will
later do in a poem praising them for their translation of the Psalms.[44]
Mary, a female figure with impeccable spiritual qualifications (Donne
compares her to Moses' sister Miriam), becomes in this Envoy an English version of Du Bartas's heavenly Muse, supplanting Du Bellay's
Rome and Sidney's own Stella. And Sidney, or rather Spenser's reformed vision of him, occupies the place given to Du Bellay in the
earlier sonnet:

> L:Envoy
> Immortall spirite of *Philisides,*
> Which now art made the heavens ornament
> That whilome wast the worlds chiefst riches;
> Giue leave to him that lov'de thee to lament
> His losse, by lacke of thee to heaven hent,
> And with last duties of this broken verse,
> Broken with sighes, to decke thy sable Herse.
>
> And ye faire Ladie th'honor of your daies,
> And glorie of the world, your high thoughts scorne;
> Vouchsafe this moniment of his last praise,
> With some few silver dropping teares t'adorne:
> And as ye be of heavenlie off-spring borne,

> So unto heaven let your high minde aspire,
> And loath this drosse of sinfull worlds desire.

These stanzas suggest that Spenser's act of original translation in *The Ruines of Time* has produced a marvelous compromise solution to the problem of choosing between pagan Rome and Christian Jerusalem. By creating, in Sidney and his sister, a set of intermediary English deities who symbolically constitute a new family for the grieving poet, Spenser finds a way to serve heaven while continuing to pursue his desires for poetic growth and fame. He is, however, too shrewd a critic of fantasies to leave the one created by this poem untouched by doubt. His final lines enjoining the Countess of Pembroke to scorn "the glory of this world" and loathe "this drosse of sinful world's desire" invite us to ask whether the poem itself should be included among the objects to be abandoned. The syntax allows for that possibility without insisting on it, suggesting that a final choice between Rome and Sion has been yet once more deferred.

Family romance stories seem destined to lack closure, and an attempt to analyze them may all too easily suffer the same fate. To avoid this fate—in a quantitative if not a qualitative way—I shall make my discussion of Stevens brief: a coda or Envoy, as it were, to this paper. Linking Stevens to two Renaissance poets may appear perverse, but I include him because his poem about Santayana is not only a rhetorically gorgeous fantasy but also a peculiarly American version of a family romance with Rome. In dramatic contrast both to Du Bellay and Spenser, Stevens associates Rome's immense attraction with its status as a religious capital. The religion that draws Stevens imaginatively to Rome, and specifically, to George Santayana's sparely furnished room in a Roman convent, is not, however, Catholicism per se. Rather, it is a religion of art and philosophy, which seems miraculously compatible with traditional Catholicism. This compatibility is symbolized, in Stevens's poem, by Santayana's harmonious relation to the nuns he lives with. Although Santayana was by no means a believing Catholic, he respected the rituals of the Church and praised Catholicism for fostering such great works of the imagination as Dante's *Commedia*.[45] Spenser would have called him an idolator, but for Stevens, Santayana was a hero of the modern world. Or rather, he was a modern hero precisely because he had in some sense *renounced* the world, like the nuns who tended him.

A clue to understanding Stevens's admiration for Santayana, which includes a strong dose of anxious envy, occurs in a passage from an essay entitled "Imagination as Value," which Stevens presented in 1948 to the English Institute.[46] During a discussion of aesthetic value as it occurs not only in art and letters but also in the conduct of life itself, Stevens invokes Santayana to illustrate the thesis that "there can be lives that exist by the deliberate choice of those who live them" (p. 147). In such lives, he says, the imagination functions no less powerfully than it does "in any deliberate work of art or letters." Think, for example, of Santayana, and in particular, of "the present phase" of his life, "in which, in old age, he dwells in the head of the world, in the company of devoted women, in their convent, and in the company of familiar saints, whose presence does so much to make any convent an appropriate place for a generous and human philosopher. To repeat: there can be lives in which the value of the imagination is the same as its value in arts and letters, and I exclude from consideration as part of that statement any thought of poverty or wealth, being a *bauer* or being a king, and so on, as irrelevant" (p. 148).

This final sentence seems to me a curious instance of mystification, for real poverty and wealth are anything but irrelevant to the question of aesthetic value as Stevens himself defines it here—as a phenomenon that exists in life as well as in art. Nor are considerations of social class irrelevant. Santayana was able to *choose* his style of life in part because he had inherited enough money from his mother's family to leave his job at Harvard in 1912 and live, from then on, in Europe, devoting himself entirely to his writing. He was not enormously wealthy, but he had, in addition to his dividends, royalties from his books—something that Stevens, like most American poets, lacked.[47] What fascinated Stevens most about Santayana, however, was that the philosopher *felt* himself to be rich enough to choose a life of comfortable asceticism. Real money made this choice possible,

but Stevens focuses, both in his essay and in his poem about Santayana, on the results rather than on the enabling conditions of that
choice. He presents Santayana as a man who, like the nuns, has renounced the world and the flesh, to live a purified life of the mind in
Rome, "the head of the world." In Stevens's idealized economic system, such renunciation brings magnificent rewards: Santayana possesses not only inspirational riches but also loving attention from
women who neither speak nor make any sexual demands on the old
man who lives like a biblical patriarch in their midst.

"To an Old Philosopher in Rome," published four years after the
English Institute essay, when Stevens was over seventy years old, is a
hauntingly beautiful pre-elegy not only for Santayana but also for
Stevens himself. Unlike other poems in *The Rock*, the concluding
section of Stevens's *Collected Works*, this one has a solemnly joyous
tone throughout; and well it should, for it is about a journey to a
mythical homeland where one may at once die majestically and con-
ceive of that death as a rebirth. Rome, Stevens writes, is a "threshold," and beyond it there is "a more merciful Rome, the two alike
in the make of the mind."[48] The human mind, not the Christian
God, is the object of this poem's worship, and in his own mind's
eye, Stevens enters Santayana's room and finds symbols of beatitude:

> The bed, the books, the chair, the moving nuns,
> The candle as it evades the sight, these are
> The sources of happiness in the shape of Rome,
> A shape within the ancient circles of shapes,
> And these beneath the shadow of a shape
>
> In a confusion on bed and books, a portent
> On the chair, a moving transparence on the nuns.

These lines depict what might be called a transcendental primal
scene, a scene in which consciousness is at once dying and coming to
life "in a confusion on bed and books."[49] The poem goes on to en-
vision Santayana himself in this threshold state, and here we may see
the workings of Stevens's aesthetic inversion of capitalist economy,
an inversion which makes an idealized poverty into the source of
imaginative wealth:

Your dozing in the depths of wakefulness,
In the warmth of your bed, at the edge of your chair, alive
Yet living in two worlds, impenitent
As to one, and, as to one, most penitent,
Impatient for the grandeur that you need

In so much misery; and yet finding it
Only in misery, the afflatus of ruin,
Profound poetry of the poor and of the dead,
As in the last drop of the deepest blood,
As it falls from the heart and lies there to be seen,

Even as the blood of an empire, it might be,
For a citizen of heaven though still of Rome.
It is poverty's speech that seeks us out the most.
It is older than the oldest speech of Rome.
This is the tragic accent of the scene.

And you—it is you that speak it, without speech,
The loftiest syllables among loftiest things,
The one invulnerable man among
Crude captains, the naked majesty, if you like,
Of bird-nest arches and of rain-stained-vaults.

I cannot offer a full interpretation of these lines in this paper, but
I do want to suggest that those "crude captains" whom Santayana sur-
passes include the captains of American industry, among whose ranks
Stevens himself was enlisted. Unlike Stevens, Santayana was invulnerable to the lure of American enterprise and a secure life as a vice-
president of a Hartford insurance company; Santayana is rewarded
by an old age that brings no diminution of inspirational power.
Neither the ruins of Rome nor the ruin of his own body prevent him,
in Stevens's eyes, from achieving

a kind of total grandeur at the end,
With every visible thing enlarged and yet
No more than a bed, a chair, and moving nuns,
The immensest theatre, the pillared porch,
The book and candle in your ambered room
Total grandeur of a total edifice,
Chosen by an inquisitor of structures

For himself. He stops upon this threshold,
As if the design of all his words takes form
And frame from thinking and is realized.

Stevens himself was also an inquisitor of structures, but he felt, at times at least, as if he had achieved totality neither in his style of life nor in his art. As he grimly says in another poem in *The Rock,* entitled "The Plain Sense of Things," "the great structure has become a minor house/No turban walks across the lessened floors."

By imaginatively identifying with Santayana, however—making him both a heroic father and an alter ego—Stevens gains for himself some of the power he associates with Santayana: a power, preeminently, of choice. To choose a total grandeur, and to be able to stop, as if by an act of will, on a threshold between life and death, is to make the mind triumph magnificently over matter. In envisioning such a triumph, Stevens erects a barrier against the idea of death, which corresponds to the barrier against the idea of social and economic determinants that he erected in the essay on "Imagination as Value." If both barriers draw on a peculiarly American myth of free will, the former creates, in addition, a modern American version of a myth that Du Bellay and Spenser also use to defend themselves against fears of literal and metaphorical death. The myth consists in finding reassurance about the continued existence of one's own poetic powers through a re-creative vision of another's ruin—a ruin that is made an occasion for the exercise of one's own eloquence. Du Bellay and Spenser present darker versions of this myth than Stevens does because they dramatize the dangers that attend an encounter with a foreign or past culture and its textual remains. For them, the achievement of an individual accent involves a struggle against the seductive and threatening power of others' voices. Stevens, in contrast, neither dramatizes nor textually enacts such a struggle; he presents the idea of merging his voice with Santayana's in a wholly benign light: "each of us," he writes, "Beholds himself in you, and hears his voice/In yours, master and commiserable man." Like Christ, Santayana is a man-god full of pity, and Stevens welcomes the erasing of difference between himself and the philosopher; the two men, like Rome and "that more merciful Rome/Beyond," become "alike in the make of the mind." This fantasy of union serves to counter Stevens's perception of a real difference between his and Santayana's life choices; it also counters the idea that death may be an experience truly different from life.

Stevens, it would seem, is writing against a different set of fears than those which preoccupied Du Bellay and Spenser. Nonetheless, he does share their concern with the problem of literary secondarity and he seeks, as they do, to establish the authority of his own voice. His concept of "poverty" allows him to do this with remarkable ease:

> It is poverty's speech that seeks us out the most.
> It is older than the oldest speech of Rome.
> This is the tragic accent of the scene.
>
> And you—it is you that speak it, without speech,
> The loftiest syllables among loftiest things.

These lines provide a clue to the strange serenity of Stevens's imagined family reunion in Rome, a reunion in which the poet plays the role of son to Santayana but is most definitely not speechless [*infans*]. It is the "voice of poverty" that allows Stevens to appear so unthreatened by whatever temporal priority (or authority) Santayana might be thought to possess. Santayana is said to "speak without speech" and in fact he is voiceless in this poem, so "like" Stevens that the poet can confidently speak *for* him. And Rome too is rendered unthreatening. Even her "oldest speech" is less old than the voice of poverty, which becomes, through Stevens's elegant transvaluation of values, a veritable source of imaginative wealth. Poverty, one might say, is Stevens's muse or interior paramour here; and if she is older than Rome, she is also newer, since she abides in Hartford, Connecticut, with Stevens himself. In his imaginative quest for "the sources of happiness," he has taken a journey to the Eternal City and has found, there, something he possessed all along. Rome herself—her ruins, her Latin poets, her political history—is strangely absent from Stevens's poem. The city is as silent as her nuns, merely a decorative backdrop for a fantasy about a religion of art whose real capital is the American poet's mind.

NOTES

1. Harold Bloom, *Wallace Stevens: The Poems of Our Climate* (Ithaca: Cornell University Press, 1976), p. 369.

2. See Sigmund Freud, "Family Romances," in *The Standard Edition of the Complete Psychological Works of Sigmund Freud* (hereafter cited as *SE*), ed. James Strachey et al., 24 vols. (London: Hogarth Press, 1953–74), 9:237–41.

3. For Freud's account of the series of dreams he had about Rome, see *The Interpretation of Dreams* (1900), chap. 5 (*SE* 4:193–98). In a letter to Wilhelm Fliess, Freud characterized his longing to visit Rome as "deeply neurotic" and said it was closely linked to his "school-boy hero worship of the Semitic Hannibal" (*The Origins of Psychoanalysis: Letters to Wilhelm Fliess,* ed. Marie Bonaparte et al., trans. Eric Mosbacher and James Strachey [New York: Basic Books, 1954], p. 236). Freud's lifelong fascination with "the Eternal City" is also closely linked to his admiration for Winckelman, the founder of classical archeology; see the passage in *Civilization and Its Discontents* (1930) where Freud compares Rome and her layers of ruins to the psyche (*SE* 21:69–71). There is to my knowledge no detailed study of Freud's ambivalent romance with Rome, although Leonard Schongold makes some brief remarks about this topic in "The Metaphor of the Journey in *The Interpretation of Dreams,*" *Freud and His Self Analysis,* ed. Mark Kanzer and Jules Glenn (New York: Jason Aronson, 1979), pp. 51–65.

4. For the story of Francus, see Jean Lemaire de Belges, *Les Illustrations de Gaule et Singularitez de Troye* (1500), bk. 1, chap. 1 (*Oeuvres de Jean Lemaire de Belges,* ed. J. Stecher [Louvain: Lefevre, 1882], 1:12–13). As Stecher notes in his Introduction (p. xlvi), the Valois kings eagerly proclaimed their noble Trojan ancestry; Louis XII adopted Vergil's phrase *"ultus avos Trojoe"* for his motto after the Battle of Ravenna in 1512. A quarter-century earlier in England, the first Tudor monarch began to exploit the legend of the Trojan Brutus, mythical founder of Albion. Soon after his accession to the throne, Henry VII commissioned a genealogical report that stated that he was "son to Brute in five-score degrees" (quoted from Charles Millican, *Spenser and the Table Round* [Cambridge: Harvard University Press, 1932], p. 16). Henry's successors continued to promulgate their connection to the Trojan hero who, according to Geoffrey of Monmouth, founded the city of "Troynovant" on the Thames (see S. K. Heninger, Jr., "The Tudor Myth of Troy-Novant," *South Atlantic Quarterly* 61 [1962]:378–87). I am indebted for this reference to my colleague Lawrence Manley.

5. For an account of the biblical and classical sources for medieval formulations of the *translatio imperii* theory, see Werner Goez, *Translatio Imperii: Ein Beitrag*

Zur Geschichte des Geschichtsdenkens und der politischen Theorien im Mittel-alter und in der frühen Neuzeit (Tübingen: J. C. B. Mohr, 1958), chaps. 1 and 2. On the origins of the theory of *translatio studii,* see Etienne Gilson, *Les Idées et les lettres* (1932; 2nd ed., Paris: Libraire Philosophique J. Vrin, 1955), 183–85.

6. For a useful discussion of the "westering theory" in relation to the idea of the Roman Empire as a providential preparation for the age of Christ, see M. D. Chenu, *Nature, Man, and Society in the Twelfth Century: Essays on New Theo-logical Perspectives in the Latin West,* trans. Jerome Taylor and Lester K. Little (original French ed., 1957; Chicago: University of Chicago Press: 1968), pp. 184–87.

7. On Protestant critiques of the papal notion of *translatio imperii* and on their own use of the theory, see Goez, *Translatio Imperii,* pp. 281–304.

8. On Catholic attacks on the "vulgar tongue," see Ferdinand Brunot, *Histoire de la langue française des origines à nos jours,* 13 vols. (Paris: Armand Colin, 1905–79), 2 (1967):6–26.

9. For a fuller discussion of the *Deffense,* see my *Trials of Desire: Renaissance Defenses of Poetry* (New Haven: Yale University Press, 1983), pp. 18–53); see also Thomas M. Greene, *The Light in Troy: Imitation and Discovery in Renais-sance Poetry* (New Haven: Yale University Press, 1982), pp. 189–96; and Terence Cave, *The Cornucopian Text: Problems of Writing in the French Renaissance* (Oxford: Clarendon Press, 1979), pp. 59–77.

10. For an account of Joachim's relations with his brother René, see Henri Chamard's biography, *Joachim Du Bellay, 1522–1560* (1900; reprint, Geneva: Slatkine, 1969), pp. 21–24; Chamard discusses Du Bellay's relations to the cardi-nal on pp. 274–79.

11. On Du Bellay's ambivalent attitude toward the cardinal and his fears that clerkly labor may represent a "derogation" to the "noble estate," see *Trials of Desire,* pp. 20–21, 48–50.

12. Quoted from *La Deffense et illustration de la langue françoyse,* ed. Henri Chamard (Paris: Didier, 1948), p. 25. All quotations are from this edition; trans-lations are my own.

13. See the *Quintil Horatian,* a vitriolic commentary on Du Bellay's *Deffense* published (anonymously) by Barthélemy Aneau in 1550 and reprinted in its en-tirety in Chamard's notes to the *Deffense;* the quotation is from p. 43, n. 2.

14. Although Du Bellay does argue that the French language is "not so infertile that she cannot herself produce some fruit of good invention" (*Deffense,* p. 29), he generally conceives of invention as if it were a piece of property belonging to the ancients: "Just as it was most praiseworthy in the ancients to invent well," he writes in bk. 1, chap. 8, "so it is most useful for the moderns to imitate well; it is especially useful for those whose language is not yet very copious or rich" (pp. 45–46).

15. In 1550, for instance, Guillaume d'Autelz took Du Bellay sharply to task for his theory and practice of imitation: "I do not share the opinion that the Frenchman can do nothing by his invention that is worthy of immortality, without the imitation of others," wrote Autelz in his *Replique aux furieuses defenses de Louis Meigret* (quoted in Grahame Castor, *Pléiade Poetics: A Study of Sixteenth-Century Thought and Terminology* [Cambridge: Cambridge University Press, 1964], p. 115).

16. See *Deffense,* pp. 168, 178–79.

17. From 1553 to 1557 Du Bellay served as a secretary and major-domo in the Roman household of the Cardinal Jean du Bellay; on his duties there see G. Dickenson, *Du Bellay in Rome* (Leiden: E. J. Brill, 1960), pp. 92ff.

18. *Les Antiquitez de Rome* 3; all quotations of Du Bellay's poetry are from *Les Regrets et autres oeuvres poétiques,* text established by J. Joliffe, Introduction and Commentary by M. A. Screech (Geneva: Droz, 1966). Spenser translates the lines as follows:

> Thou, stranger, which for *Rome* in *Rome* here seekest,
> And nought of *Rome* in *Rome* perceivs't at all,
> These same olde walls, olde arches, which thou seest,
> Olde Palaces, is that which *Rome* men call.

(*Ruines of Rome* 3, quoted from *The Works of Edmund Spenser: A Variorum Edition,* ed. Edwin Greenlaw, C. G. Osgood, F. M. Padelford, 9 vols. [Baltimore: Johns Hopkins, 1935–49], 8:142. All quotations of Spenser are from this edition.)

19. Du Bellay describes his linguistic sin of adultery in the *Poëmata,* one of the four volumes he published after his return from Rome; see his *Poésies latines et françaises,* ed. E. Courbet (Paris: Garnier, 1918), p. 453.

20. See *Regrets,* pp. 87–90 (on witches); pp. 91–95 (on courtesans and the dangers of syphilis); p. 96 (on fortune); pp. 97–98 (on Rome's demonic *genius loci*), and p. 93 (addressed to the "doulce mère d'amour, gaillarde Cyprienne").

21. See Wayne Rebhorn, "Du Bellay's Imperial Mistress: *Les Antiquitez de Rome* as Petrarchist Sonnet Sequence," *Renaissance Quarterly* 33 (Winter, 1980):609–22.

22. See, for instance, the opening lines of *Antiquitez* 5, which directly echo Petrarch's praise of Laura in *Rime* 358; Rebhorn discusses the parallel on p. 613.

23. On Spenser's translations for the English edition of van der Nood's *Theatre* (which appeared in Flemish and French versions in 1568), see Anne Lake Prescott, *French Poets and the English Renaissance* (New Haven: Yale University Press, 1978), pp. 44–47. The "Sonets" from *Songe,* along with Spenser's other translations for the *Theatre* and the accompanying illustrations, are reprinted in the *Works of Edmund Spenser* 8:5–25.

24. When Spenser reworked the *Songe* sonnets, he gave them a Surreyan

rhyme scheme and added the four poems van der Nood had omitted in the *Theatre*.

25. Van der Nood's introductory epistle to Elizabeth praises Du Bellay as a "Gentleman of France" who "goeth about to persuade, that all things here upon earthe, are nothing but wretched miserie, and miserable vanitie" (quoted from Prescott, p. 45). On van der Nood's theological views and use (or abuse) of Du Bellay, see Prescott, p. 45, and Carl Rasmussen, "'Quietnesse of Minde': *A Theatre for Worldings* as Protestant Poetics," *Spenser Studies* 1 (1980):3–27.

26. For examples of this analogy in the Geneva Bible, Luther's writing, and van der Nood's own prose commentary in the *Theatre,* see James Nohrnberg, *The Analogy of the Faerie Queene* (Princeton: Princeton University Press, 1976), pp. 238–40.

27. Du Bellay himself hints at the possibility of sin in his admiration for pagan Rome; see, for example, *Antiquitez* 5, which refers to the "idole" of Rome that her literature preserves and allows to wander ("errer") through the world. For a useful survey of critical debates about Du Bellay's theological perspective in the *Antiquitez,* see Rebhorn, "Du Bellay's Imperial Mistress," pp. 616–18. No one, to my knowledge, has discussed the problem of idolatry in *Songe;* such a discussion might begin with a look at the four sonnets van der Nood omitted from his *Theatre* (6, 8, 13, 14), in all of which the speaker shows a marked sympathy for the emblems of Rome he is ostensibly defining as images of vanity.

28. The quoted phrase is from *Songe* 14 (*Les Regrets et autres oeuvres poétiques,* p. 320). On Du Bellay's use of Petrarch's canzone, see Margaret B. Wells, "Du Bellay's Sonnet Sequence *Songe,*" *French Studies* 26 (1972):1–8; and Gilbert Gadoffre, *Du Bellay et le sacré* (Paris: Gallimard, 1978), pp. 153–54.

29. See *The Faerie Queene* 1.1.45, for the description of Redcrosse's attempt to awaken Duessa; see also Nohrnberg, *The Analogy of the Faerie Queene,* p. 223.

30. Annabel Patterson has pointed out to me that Spenser and Du Bellay both appear to be obsessed by the image of once great forms reduced to ashes, tiny fragments within which a spark of flame may nonetheless survive. In *Ruines of Rome* 1, Spenser repeats the word "ashes" in line 4, where there is no French equivalent.

31. Greene, *The Light in Troy,* p. 222.

32. *Aeneid* 6.267 (trans. Greene).

33. *The Ruines of Time,* which Spenser chose to place first in his *Complaints* volume, was almost certainly written later than the translations of *Antiquitez* and *Songe,* although Spenser may, of course, have revised those translations—and added the "Envoy" to *Ruines of Rome*—shortly before publishing the *Complaints* in 1592. See Harold Stein, *Studies in Spenser's Complaints* (New York: Oxford University Press, 1934), pp. 31–34, for a discussion of the evidence for dating *The Ruines of Time* between 1589 and 1591.

34. See *The Shepheardes Calendar*, "Ianuarye" 1.72, and Louis Adrian Montrose's shrewd discussion of the breaking of the pipe as a sign of Colin's "failure to accomplish a critical vocational transition from the pastoral already mastered and outgrown to the higher poetic calling which remains above his reach" ("'The Perfecte patterne of a Poete': Courtship in *The Shepheardes Calendar*," *Texas Studies in Language and Literature* 21 (Spring 1979):39).

35. See *Works* 8:63–69. It is significant that *Teares* frequently and ironically echoes Du Bellay's *La Musagnoemachie*, a poem that Prescott accurately describes as a "victory song" celebrating the rout of the forces of ignorance by Renaissance French poets and their royal patrons. Spenser's poem, in contrast, is a "pessimistic vision of the sleepy yet destructive powers of ignorance in England"; see Prescott, *French Poets*, p. 52.

36. W. L. Renwick nicely epitomizes the problem in his comment on *Ruines of Rome* 1, where Spenser translates the French "mon cri" as "my shrieking yell." Spenser's style in his early translations, Renwick says, is "noisy" (quoted from the Variorum *Works* 8:380).

37. Carl Rasmussen notes the parallel between Verlame and Chaucer's "wife" in "'How Weak Be the Passions of Woefulness': Spenser's *Ruines of Time*," *Spenser Studies* 2 (1981):159. He also notes Verlame's affinities with the Whore of Babylon.

38. See Lawrence Manley, "Spenser and the City: The Minor Poems," *Modern Language Quarterly* 43 (Sept. 1982). See also Millar MacLure's discussion of this catalogue stanza in "Spenser and the ruins of time," *A Theatre for Spenserians*, ed. Judith M. Kennedy and James A. Reither (Toronto: University of Toronto Press, 1973), pp. 7–8.

39. Alfred Satterthwaite cites Veré Rubel's observation that *The Ruines of Time* "is outstanding among all the poems in the *Complaints* for its rhetorical tropes" and lists the panoply of tropes Verlame employs, among which are repeated *ploce* and *traductio* on the words *live* and *die* (*Spenser, Ronsard and Du Bellay: A Renaissance Comparison* [Princeton: Princeton University Press, 1960], p. 96).

40. Manley comments astutely on one of Verlame's most interesting failures to discriminate between truth and error, namely her account of the supposed change in the course of the River Thames (11.141–47). She laments the Thames's desertion of her, but the myth that the Thames had once flowed by Verulamium had been thoroughly discredited, as Manley observes, by Camden and other Elizabethan historians.

41. In his edition of *The Poems of Sir Philip Sidney* (Oxford: Clarendon, 1962), p. 378, William Ringler describes Philisides (Phil[ip] Sid[ney]) as a "fictional self portrait" and notes that Sidney heightens Philisides's similarity to Astrophil (also "star lover") in the *New Arcadia*, where Philisides is said to love "a star" (bk. 2, chap. 21); in the *Old Arcadia* (Fourth Eclogues), Philisides

describes his unrequited love for Mira and his decision to "choke his ill fortunes" by "perpetual absence" from her.

42. Quoted from *Miscellaneous Prose of Sir Philip Sidney,* ed. Katherine Duncan-Jones and Jan van Dorsten (Oxford: Clarendon Press, 1973), pp. 79–83. For Spenser's critique of Sidney's "proud desire for praise," see *Astrophel* 11.85–90.

43. Sidney's translation of the psalms, left unfinished at his death, was completed by his sister Mary and is included in Ringler's edition of *The Poems of Sir Philip Sidney,* pp. 265–337.

44. See Donne's "Upon the Translation of the Psalms by Sir Philip Sidney and the Countess of Pembroke his Sister," in *The Divine Poems,* ed. Helen Gardner (Oxford: Clarendon Press, 1959), pp. 33–35.

45. See Santayana's *Interpretation of Poetry and Religion* (New York: George Scribner's Sons, 1900), where he judges religions according to what he calls "poetic standards" and finds Catholicism "infinitely superior" to Protestantism (p. 113). On Santayana's life among the nuns whose faith he admired but did not share, see Daniel Cory, *Santayana: The Later Years* (New York: George Braziller, 1963), pp. 304–5 and passim.

46. The essay was published in the 1949 volume of *English Institute Essays* and reprinted in Stevens's *The Necessary Angel: Essays on Reality and Imagination* (New York: Random House, Vintage Books, 1951), pp. 133–56. My quotations are from this edition.

47. On Santayana's inheritance and royalties, see Cory, *Santayana,* pp. 246, 251.

48. Quotations from *The Collected Poems of Wallace Stevens* (New York: Alfred A. Knopf, 1969), pp. 508–11.

49. See Bloom, *Wallace Stevens,* pp. 362–63, on the allusions in these lines to Emersonian Transcendentalism; and see also Helen Hennessey Vendler, *On Extended Wings: Wallace Stevens' Longer Poems* (Cambridge: Harvard University Press, 1969), p. 310, for a fine discussion of Stevens's imaginative returns to "infancy" in his late poems.

 *Robert S. Miola*

Cymbeline: Shakespeare's Valediction to Rome

Like Petrarch, Dante, Tasso, Du Bellay, Montaigne, Spenser, and other Renaissance figures, Shakespeare spent his artistic life conversing with Latin authors in the shadows of ancient Rome. Since T. W. Baldwin's thorough study of Elizabethan school curricula and their relation to Shakespeare, it is clear that his Latin was "small" (and his Greek "lesse") only in comparison with that of a scholar like Ben Jonson.[1] The average schoolboy's classical learning included training in a wide range of ancient authors—Terence, Plautus, Cicero, Quintilian, Ovid, Vergil, Horace, Juvenal, Persius, Seneca, possibly Lucan and Catullus, and others. This training was fortified by an emphasis on rhetoric and by the prevailing practice of *imitatio* that, sometimes reverently, sometimes irreverently, appropriated classical texts as models.[2] Shakespeare knew the standard authors in the original and in translation and engaged them throughout his career. At first the dialogue was ostentatious and youthful, then ironic and silent, and finally defiant and dialectical.[3]

Ancient Rome, of course, was a central focal point of Shakespeare's engagement with the classical world. In addition to the many scattered allusions and references throughout the canon, Shakespeare depicted Rome in one narrative poem, *The Rape of Lucrece* (1593–94), and in five plays: *Titus Andronicus* (1593–94), *Julius Caesar* (1599), *Antony and Cleopatra* (1606–7), *Coriolanus* (1607–8), and *Cymbeline* (1609–10). For the most part, Shakespeare's Rome is a tragic place wherein ancient Romans struggle to live and die honorably for the rewards of fame, honor, and glory. Because *Cymbeline* little resembles its somber, tragic predecessors and because most of the action takes place in Britain, it has attracted little attention as Shakespeare's last Roman play.[4] Yet Rome is a major locality in the play and opposes Britain. Moreover, Shakespeare draws upon his entire Roman canon in *Cymbeline* to create a pastiche of Roman elements, scenes, characters, and speeches. The play evokes and acknowledges the grandeur that was Rome but celebrates the advent of a new dispensation, one in which Roman pride, courage, and constancy are balanced by humility, kindness, and a capacity for flexibility and change. Not only Shakespeare's last Roman play, *Cymbeline* is also his valediction to Rome and Roman values.

We may begin with act 1, scene 4 of *Cymbeline,* a scene that has aroused much controversy as commentators have described it in light of the traditional wager motif.[5] Few have noticed, however, that the wager strongly resembles the contest recalled in the Argument of *Lucrece.* There Collatine praises the "incomparable chastity of his/ wife Lucretia" (Arg. 12–13) and skeptical Romans test the boast by a late-night visit. Lucrece is celebrated as "priceless wealth the heavens" lend (17); Imogen, similarly, is called "only the gift of the gods" (85). The report of stainless chastity arouses both evil interlopers—Tarquin and Iachimo.[6]

Tarquin's encounter with Lucrece serves as a model for Iachimo's encounter with Imogen. The imagery of siege and invasion defines character and action in both instances. Tarquin appears as a "foul usurper" (412) who makes a "breach" in Lucrece's defenses and enters the "sweet city" (469). Similarly, Iachimo brags that an "easy battery" will lay Imogen's judgment flat and that he can "get ground" of her (1.4.22, 104). Both women are described as a walled fortress and a sacred temple (*Luc.* 1170–76; *Cym.* 2.1.63–64). The sight of the victims astonishes both invaders. "Enchanted Tarquin" gazes in "silent wonder" (83–84); Iachimo exclaims in a breathless aside: "All of her that is out of door most rich!/If she be furnish'd with a mind so rare,/She is alone th'Arabian bird" (1.6.15–17). Both women admit the invaders for their husbands' sake. Lucrece explains later: "for thy [Collatine's] honor did I entertain him;/Coming from thee, I could not put him back" (842–43); and Imogen, in a revealing divergence from the traditional plot, follows Posthumus's written instructions to welcome Iachimo and treat him kindly (1.6.22–25). Both invaders praise the absent husband. Tarquin "stories to her ears her husband's fame" (106); Iachimo, after the initial slander, reports of Posthumus:

He sits 'mongst men like a descended god;
He hath a kind of honor sets him off,
More than a mortal seeming.
                    (1.4.169–71)

The actual invasion scene in *Cymbeline* (2.2) is a palimpsest of Roman elements. The language closely parallels that of *Lucrece.* Images of locks and treasures appear in the poem (16) and in the play (41–42), and both sleeping victims are described as flowers (*Luc.* 395–97; *Cym.* 15). The eyes of both victims are "canopied" in darkness (*Luc.* 398; *Cym.* 21); and both have "azure" veins (*Luc.* 419; *Cym.* 22), a characteristic unique to them in all of Shakespeare's canon. Both women have the look of death in their sleep (*Luc.* 402–6; *Cym.* 31). Iachimo's hope that Imogen's sense remains a "monument,/Thus in a chapel lying" (32–33) echoes the description of Lucrece as "virtuous monument" (391). Little wonder that Iachimo, upon emerging from the trunk, declares:

> Our Tarquin thus
> Did softly press the rushes ere he waken'd
> The chastity he wounded.
>   (12–14)

The possessive pronoun, of course, gives the entire game away. Iachimo fancies himself another Tarquin and Shakespeare delights in fostering the illusion. All the while, however, the disparity between the brutal rape and the sneakily malicious note-taking comes into focus. Tarquin violates Lucrece, her household, family and city; Iachimo merely plays a cheap trick.

The sophisticated playfulness of allusion here appears also in Shakespeare's reference to Tereus and Philomela. This myth, of course, surfaces in *Lucrece,* once in the narrator's description of the victim (1079–80), and again in her own complaint (1128ff.). More important, this myth underlies much of the action in *Titus Andronicus.* [7] Like Lucrece, Lavinia appears as a figure of Philomela; like Tarquin, Demetrius and Chiron appear as figures of Tereus. Iachimo's discovery of the leaf-turned book in Imogen's chamber unmistakably recalls the incident in act 4, scene 1 of *Titus Andronicus,* where

Lavinia opens a copy of Ovid's *Metamorphoses* to the tale of Tereus
and Philomela. Recollection of Shakespeare's models again illuminates
ironically the present scene. For Iachimo is no Tereus, Tarquin,
Demetrius, or Chiron; and Imogen, to be sure, will prove no Philomela, Lucrece, or Lavinia.

Here Shakespeare irreverently shifts the tragic Roman scene,
occasion for the expulse of the Tarquins, the end of Roman monarchy, and his own early poem, into prurient, almost comic, melo-
drama. In part, the shift indicates impatience and dissatisfaction with
Romans, those austere warriors who let their own blood and that of
others for abstract ideals like honor. This impatience and dissatisfaction is also evident in Shakespeare's portrayal of Posthumus. Perhaps
modeled on the historical Germanicus, valorous and well-respected,
Posthumus is recognizably Roman.[8] He resembles Lucius of *Titus
Andronicus,* who likewise suffers banishment and returns home with
an invading army. Like Lucius, Posthumus is the son of a famous
warrior:

> his father
> Was call'd Sicilius, who did join his honor
> Against the Romans with Cassibelan,
> But had his titles by Tenantius, whom
> He serv'd with glory and admir'd success:
> So gain'd the sur-addition Leonatus.
>
> (1.1.28–33)

The First Gentleman's account of the Leonatus genealogy strikes
other familiar Roman notes. We hear the Latinate names, Sicilius,
Tenantius, and Leonatus, the last an agnomen like "Coriolanus." The
name "Posthumus" obviously derives from unhappy circumstances
of birth, but it may owe something as well to Raphael Holinshed's
mention of Posthumus, son of the first Roman, Aeneas, and Lavinia.[9]
There is also here the characteristically Roman emphasis on fame
achieved by military exploits, on "honor" (29), "titles" (31), "glory
and admir'd success" (32).

Like many of Shakespeare's Romans, Posthumus is heir to a tradition of honor and military excellence. Demonstrating his mettle early,
he confronts Cloten and advances "forward still" (1.2.15) toward

the enemy's face. Both Imogen and the Frenchman refer to Posthumus as an "eagle" (1.1.139: 1.4.12), a metaphor here as in *Coriolanus* associated with the Roman eagle, symbol of the city's strength, courage, and superiority. Confident in Posthumus's martial skill and courage, Imogen wishes that he and Cloten could fight it out in "Afric" (1.1.167–69). Volumnia, of course, expresses similar confidence in Coriolanus against the tribunes: "I would my son/Were in Arabia, and thy tribe before him,/His good sword in his hand" (4.2. 23–25). Posthumus hopes to make Iachimo answer with his "sword" (1.4.163) and the words *"honor"* and *"constancy,"* evoking two central Roman virtues in Shakespeare's conception, ring throughout the wager scene. Upon hearing the report of Imogen's infidelity, Posthumus decides to vindicate his honor by her death.

This resolve, like the larger Roman ethos of battlefield heroism, from whence it springs, proves to be ignoble and untenable. Posthumus later repents his rash judgment and vows to perform penance:

> Let me make men know
> More valor in me than my habits show.
> Gods, put the strength o' th' Leonati in me!
> To shame the guise o' th' world, I will begin
> The fashion: less without and more within.
>
> (5.1.29–33)

At first glance, Posthumus's resolution to fight, to live up to his noble ancestry, seems a most Roman way of making reparation, reminiscent, perhaps, of Antony after flight at Actium, of Coriolanus after yielding at Rome. Yet, Posthumus is un-Roman in a number of important particulars. Disguised as a British peasant, he does not seek in battle self-aggrandizement, but self-abnegation. Posthumus hopes to die not for country, but for his wife.

Posthumus's intention to "shame the guise o' th' world" by starting a new "fashion" aims directly at overturning the Roman military ethos that encourages destruction of life for fame and glory. The difference between Posthumus and his Roman predecessors, Roman enemies, and former Roman self becomes evident in the ensuing battle. After vanquishing and disarming Iachimo, he leaves him unharmed, pointedly refusing to exalt himself over the body of an enemy.

Posthumus, in contradistinction to Titus and Coriolanus, rejects the Roman vanity of personal honor for the exercise of British mercy and compassion. After the battle, Posthumus refuses to receive public recognition. Instead, he disguises himself, suffers capture, and endures imprisonment. The Briton who exercised Roman virtue in British costume, finally, in Roman costume, shows a British capacity for humility and spiritual growth.[10]

The rejection of Roman values implicit in Posthumus's character development appears also in Shakespeare's treatment of stage bloodshed. In the Roman works blood flows copiously as Romans struggle to punish their enemies, demonstrate their *vertu,* and justify their deeds.[11] There are many bloody scenes of mutilation and death: mourners carry Lucrece's corpse through Rome to arouse the people against the Tarquins; Titus cuts off his hand to save his son and slits the throats of his enemies for revenge; the conspirators stab Caesar and smear themselves with his blood to vindicate the murder; Scarus jokes about the shape of his wounds to show his courage. Coriolanus appears "flea'd" (1.4.22) and later displays his wounds in the marketplace. In Rome the shedding of blood is liturgical: it confers identity and sanctifies action.

In *Cymbeline,* however, the blood on stage works to different purposes. The goriest incident in the play begins with Imogen's waking next to Cloten's headless corpse. Mistaking Cloten for Posthumus, she exclaims: "Give color to my pale cheek with thy blood,/That we the horrider may seem to those/Which chance to find us" (4.2.330–32). The smearing of Imogen's face with blood here neither asserts her worth nor justifies her deeds. Instead, it is a rousing stage trick that illustrates her misapprehension and confusion. Having no other purpose than to look "horrider," Imogen seems childlike and worthy of bemused sympathy.

Reciting a soliloquy parallel to Imogen's (4.2.291ff.), Posthumus appears on stage *"with a bloody handkerchief"* (4.1. s.d.):

> *Posthumus:* Yea, bloody cloth, I'll keep thee, for I wish'd
> Thou shouldst be color'd thus. You married ones,
> If each of you should take this course, how many

Must murther wives much better than themselves
For wrying but a little!

(5.1.1-5)

This confession and cherishing of the bloody handkerchief also contrasts sharply with the various blood rituals of the Roman works. The closest Roman analogue, namely the imagined dipping of napkins in Caesar's sacred blood (3.2.130ff.), illustrates the uniqueness of Posthumus's action. In *Cymbeline* the bloody handkerchief is a martyr's relic that privately mortifies the possessor; the blood does not glorify the aggressive and destructive impulses, but permanently indicts them. The spilling of blood is a reminder of sin, not a proof of virtue. Human life, Posthumus asserts, is more precious than honor.

Related to the shedding of blood, another expression of *Romanitas* conspicuous in Shakespeare's vision is suicide. Many important Romans—Lucrece, Portia, Cassius, Brutus, and Antony—take their own lives. For each the action is an escape from shame that bestows honor and restores reputation. For each the suicide is a solemn expression of *vertu,* the ultimate proof of a self-control that vindicates and glorifies personal identity. The suicide scene in *Cymbeline* (3.4.) evokes these familiar images and themes. About to be slain for infidelity Imogen hopes to clear her name by assisting in her own death:

Look
I draw the sword myself, take it, and hit
The innocent mansion of my love, my heart.
(66-68)

She offers her chest and encourages the executioner:

Prithee dispatch,
The lamb entreats the butcher. Where's thy knife?
Thou art too slow to do thy master's bidding
When I desire it too.

(95-98)

The action on stage, of course, resembles the similar episodes

enacted by Cassius and Pindarus, Brutus and Strato, Antony and
Eros.

The expected end to this Roman scene, however, never takes
place. Instead of participating in a suicide ritual for honor and fame,
Pisanio and Imogen resort to disguise and deception. Instead of
boldly asserting her identity by death and consecrating her name for
all posterity, Imogen decides to lose both identity and name. She
bids easy farewell to the old self, restricted by responsibility and burdened by sorrow, and takes on a new one, Fidele. The conventions of
comedy—flexible and life-affirming—completely reverse the tragic
Roman momentum here. They do so again later in the play. The last
word on suicide in Shakespeare's Roman vision belongs to the humorous, homely British jailer of Act 5. After noting Posthumus's
desire for death, he reflects:

> Unless a man would marry a gallows and
> beget young gibbets, I never saw one so prone. Yet,
> on my conscience, there are verier knaves desire
> to live, for all he be a Roman; and there be some of
> them too that die against their wills. So should I, if I
> were one. I would we were all of one mind, and one
> mind good.
>
> (5.4.198-204)

Again, Roman pride seems brittle and destructive in comparison with
British flexibility and natural instinct. Life is better than death, even
for proud Romans.

The confrontation with Rome implicit in individual characters and
incidents becomes explicit in the larger action of the play. Afer recalling Julius Caesar's conquest, Romans invade Britain again, only to
find a people who can outmatch them on their own testing ground—
the battlefield. British warriors, however, show themselves to be distinctly different from Roman ones. The best of them—Belarius,
Guiderius, Arviragus, and Posthumus—fight under an assumed name
and identity for love of country.

Britons exhibit as well an Anglicized version of *pietas* that mani-
fests itself in intuitive sympathy and emotional love for family members. In the other Roman works *pietas* often takes the form of

unnatural familial violation: Titus murders his son and daughter; Portia acts the soldier instead of the wife and ends in despair and death; Brutus and Cassius slay the *pater patriae;* Volumnia declares that she would rather see Coriolanus dead than defeated. Here, however, Guiderius and Arviragus instinctively love their disguised sister; the Leonati plead with Jupiter for the sorrowful Posthumus; Posthumus offers his life to the gods in exchange for Imogen's; Cymbeline happily recovers his son and daughter. Instead of witnessing Roman will and Stoical suppression of emotion, the audience rejoices in the capacities of the human heart.

Not surprisingly, the final victory in *Cymbeline* (5.1.) evokes a Roman analogue in order to demonstrate the unique qualities of the British.[12] The kinsmen of the slain demand the lives of the Roman captives so as to appease the souls of the dead "with slaughter" (72). The scene closely parallels the opening of *Titus Andronicus,* wherein victorious Romans butcher Alarbus "*ad manes fratrum*" (1.1.98). Despite the agonized pleas of Tamora, the Andronici perform the barbarous rite—the hewing of limbs and the burning of flesh. Significantly, however, the sacrifice of the Romans in *Cymbeline* never takes place. Inspired by Posthumus's forgiveness of Iachimo, Cymbeline pardons all the prisoners. The contrast between the early and late sacrifice scenes graphically illustrates the differences between Roman and British civilization, the one founded on self-assertion, revenge, and bloodshed, the other on forgiveness and mercy. Even the Roman Lucius appears in *Cymbeline*'s final comic circle. After defeating Rome, Cymbeline reconciles the warring factions of the larger, extended Roman family to create blessed peace and harmony.[13] In Shakespeare's Rome the family, country, and gods make up a series of concentric and increasingly important values. Romans like Titus, Brutus, Caesar, Portia, and Coriolanus must subordinate private feelings to public concerns. In Shakespeare's Britain the smallest circle, the family, expands outward to include the rest and to eliminate the possibility of conflict. Private and public obligations become one and the same.

The differences between Roman Britain in *Cymbeline* and the Romes of Shakespeare's other works come into clear focus upon further reflection on *Titus Andronicus,* a play much in the dramatist's mind during the construction of his last Roman effort. In that early tragedy private emotion sharply conflicts with public obligation, and the resulting battle rages through scenes of ghoulish bloodletting and barbaric ritual. On stage and in language the pastoral world, symbolic of the non-urban, un-Roman, and therefore private sphere, is repeatedly violated, its innocent life hunted and maimed, its branches lopped, its green shade turned red with blood.[14] In *Cymbeline,* however, the pastoral world withstands the Roman invasion unscathed. Indeed, the air itself subdues the enemy:

> *Iachimo:* The heaviness and guilt within my bosom
> Takes off my manhood. I have belied a lady,
> The Princess of this country; and the air on't
> Revengingly enfeebles me.
>
> (5.2.1–4)

Noble pastoral residents conquer the would-be destroyers and proceed to take their place in a new civilization, wherein natural and Roman, private and public join in accord. The conflict between the two worlds results not in mutilation but in magical restoration and growth. The lopped branches of the stately cedar revive, become joined to the old stock, and freshly grow.

Cymbeline, no one will deny, differs considerably from Shakespeare's other Roman works. Yet this play embodies the disenchantment with Rome evident in the works immediately preceding.[15] In *Coriolanus,* for example, Shakespeare seems uncomfortable or impatient with the Roman hero, rigid, martial, and absolute. Coriolanus embodies various elements of *Romanitas* but these do not cohere. His yielding to his mother effects finally a disintegration of character, not a development. Antony, for another example, pointedly renounces Rome and Roman ideals for love of Cleopatra. In life as well as in death he refuses to subordinate himself and his desires to Roman ideals. His end, a Phyrrhic but resplendent victory, points the way to *Cymbeline,* wherein love dissolves rather than resolves all difficulties. In *Cymbeline* Shakespeare calls attention to the marmoreal rigidity of Roman pride, the vanity of their high seriousness, and the inhumanity of their military values. The play presents his final critique of Rome, the city that long engaged his intelligence and his imagination. Perhaps it is enough simply to remember the soothsayer in the play. In his as well as in Shakespeare's Roman vision, the eagle flies westward and vanishes in British sunlight.

NOTES

1. *William Shakspere's Small Latine & Lesse Greeke,* 2 vols. (Urbana: University of Illinois Press, 1944).

2. For studies of Renaissance *imitatio,* see G. W. Pigman III, "Versions of Imitation in the Renaissance," *RenQ* 33 (1980):1–32. Thomas M. Greene, *The Light in Troy: Imitation and Discovery in Renaissance Poetry* (New Haven: Yale University Press, 1982).

3. For a study of this dialogue, see my "Vergil in Shakespeare: From Allusion to Imitation," in the Vergil Bimillennial Volume (Berkeley and Los Angeles: University of California Press), forthcoming.

4. The exceptions are Hugh M. Richmond, "Shakespeare's Roman Trilogy: The Climax in *Cymbeline,*" *Studies in the Literary Imagination* 5 (1972):129–39, and David M. Bergeron, "*Cymbeline:* Shakespeare's Last Roman Play," *SQ* 31 (1980):31–41. Some have made in passing suggestive comments on *Cymbeline* as a Roman play: Roy Walker, "The Northern Star: An Essay on the Roman Plays," *SQ* 2 (1951):287–93; A. P. Rossiter, *Angel with Horns* (New York: Theatre Arts, and London: Longmans, 1961), p. 252; J. L. Simmons, *Shakespeare's Pagan World: The Roman Tragedies* (Charlottesville: University Press of Virginia, 1973), pp. 10, 165–66. Walker speaks of Shakespeare's Rome as devolving to degenerate Italian brilliance, Rossiter of *Cymbeline* as an escape from the darkness of history evident in *Coriolanus,* and Simmons of the providential Roman peace with which the play ends.

5. For references to Shakespeare I have used throughout G. Blakemore Evans, ed., *The Riverside Shakespeare* (Boston: Houghton Mifflin, 1974). On the wager scene, see William Witherle Lawrence, *Shakespeare's Problem Comedies* (New York: Macmillan, 1931), pp. 174–205; Homer Swander, "*Cymbeline* and the Blameless Hero," *ELH* 31 (1964):259–70.

6. I follow the First Folio and read "Iachimo" for Evans's "Jachimo."

7. See Ann Thompson, "Philomel in 'Titus Andronicus' and 'Cymbeline,'" *ShS* 31 (1978):23–32, who argues that the symbolic power of the allusion is latent in *Titus Andronicus* and fully realized in *Cymbeline.* I think just the

reverse is true. Some of the allusions in *Cymbeline* are ornamental; others, like this one, are mildly ironic. On the ironic ones see R. J. Schork, "Allusion, Theme, and Characterization in *Cymbeline*," *SP* 69 (1972):210–16.

8. See Bergeron, *"Cymbeline,"* p. 37.

9. "The First Booke of the Historie of England" in *The First and Second Volumes of Chronicles* (1587), p. 7. There is also a "Posthumus" in Ben Jonson's *Sejanus* (1603).

10. On the importance of costuming to the play see John Scott Colley, "Disguise and New Guise in *Cymbeline*," *ShakS* 7 (1974):233–52.

11. See "Shakespeare's Stage Blood and Its Critical Significance," *PMLA* 64 (1949):517–29; Brents Stirling, "Or Else This Were a Savage Spectacle," *PMLA* 66 (1951):765–74.

12. First to notice the parallel, I believe, was George Lyman Kittredge, ed., *The Complete Works of Shakespeare* (Boston: Ginn and Co., 1936), p. 1332.

13. The myth of Britain's Trojan ancestry, of course, was a commonplace, appearing in Holinshed's *Chronicles* as well as in another source for the play, Higgins and Blenerhasset's additions to *The Mirror for Magistrates*.

14. See Albert H. Tricomi, "The Mutilated Garden in *Titus Andronicus*," *ShakS* 9 (1976):89–105.

15. Doubtless, contemporary theatrical conditions and tastes also contributed to Shakespeare's disenchantment with Rome. An essay on such external influences might well consider Clifford J. Ronan, "The 'Antique Roman' in Elizabethan Drama," Diss. University of California, Berkeley, 1971, before analyzing the surviving Elizabethan and Jacobean Roman plays.

Patricia B. Craddock

Edward Gibbon and the "Ruins of the Capitol"

The image of Rome most firmly associated with Edward Gibbon is that of the great pagan city, once the *caput mundi*,[1] reduced to magnificent ruins or supplanted by inferior Christian structures. The physical and political reduction of the city of Rome is the subject of the final chapter of the *Decline and Fall*, and both in the history itself and in his memoirs, Gibbon credits the "ruins of the Capitol" with inspiring his writing of Rome's history.[2] A careful examination of Gibbon's several accounts of that experience suggests that the image of ruins is itself complex, and that in an extended and metaphoric sense, "ruins" are an emblem for Gibbon's view of Rome, an emblem that enables his reader to reconcile Gibbon's cautiously progressive philosophy of historical change with his elegiac and even tragic tone.

The ruins Gibbon considers are not limited to broken fragments incapable of serving useful purposes. His ruins include buildings wrested from their original purposes, materials reused for new buildings, sites retaining old functions but bearing new structures, incorrect or inappropriate restorations of old monuments, as well as remnants and fragments of the originals. Such ruins, whether they are material or metaphorical, have the interesting property of representing—re-presenting—a lost order within its successors or supplanters. They require both continuity and change for their very existence. A Rome that had been totally destroyed or one that had never fallen was not Gibbon's subject. It was important to him that he wrote not only of a "revolution which will ever be remembered," but also of one that "is still felt by the nations of the earth" (1:1, chap. 1). Each ruin could represent any relationship between past and present except irrelevance. If the earlier state had been a golden age, then the ruins would have represented tragic loss—desolate broken fragments. If the new order were consistently an improvement, with promise of more improvements to come, then the ruins would be only the temporary debris incidental to progress. But the ruins Gibbon examines represent both building (or preservation) and destruction, flaws or limitations in the original structures as well as malice or folly in subsequent destroyers, activity or neglect by the possessors far more than attacks of enemies or natural forces.

In 1966, historians at a conference reconsidering "Gibbon's problem after 200 years" decided that the principal difference between themselves and Gibbon was that he regarded the events he described as the "decline and fall" of a society; they regarded those events as a transformation of one society into another.[3] Ten years later, another historian at a similar conference reminded us that Gibbon knew many things he chose not to emphasize, including, clearly, the fact that the decline and fall of the Roman world was equally the rise and emergence of modern Europe.[4] I suggest, indeed, that Gibbon's very reason for choosing Rome, as indicated rhetorically by his presentation of the emblematic image of its ruins, was its capacity to show that transformation *is* destruction—and vice versa. The succession of Romes opened to him the question of the transfer of power, the replacement of progenitors by successors who, whatever their faults or merits or intentions, are inevitably unfaithful to the filial ideal because they fail to duplicate their originals.[5] Yet Rome, as city, political entity, and idea, had never been destroyed utterly. Gibbon is not recreating a state like the kingdoms of Ozymandius or Priam, preserved only in the images of artists. The images of the republic, the empire, even the Germanic kingdom of Rome and the papacy, survived in the more substantial form of their influence on new Romes.

The myth of origin that Gibbon so carefully provided for the *Decline and Fall* itself, in both the history and his memoirs, emphasizes the ironic complexity of the "ruins" that inspired him. In mid October, 1764, sitting in the ruins of the Capitol, he heard the Franciscan friars sing Vespers in a Christian church on the site of the ancient Temple of Jupiter and thought of writing the history.[6] His repetition of this story shows how important it is to him that we attribute the very existence of the *Decline and Fall* to this scene.

Modern biographers and critics, however, aware that the details of
the story vary in the several versions (was he inside or outside the
church, for example), have often been distracted by the issue of its
factuality from the question, vital to its interpretation, of its content.
Most often overlooked is the fact, which no cultivated eighteenth-
century reader could have missed, because all of them would have
taken the Grand Tour or at least enjoyed it vicariously in the im-
mensely popular genre of travel books, that there were no ruins on
the Capitoline Hill.[7] One summit was dominated by the Campidoglio,
the other by the Church of Sta. Maria in Aracoeli—both in excellent
repair. Here is the description Gibbon recorded in his Italian journal
(December 1764):

> The modern Capitol is still grand. You ascend by a great flight of steps to a
> large court. The palace of the Senator is at the end. That of the Conservators,
> the modern Consuls on one side, and the Museum on the other. The second
> is the work of Michael Angelo, and the last built on the same model. Their
> architecture is large & bold, the piers ornamented with corinthian pilasters
> and the architrave supported by Ionick columns: the intervals are so great
> that it contracts [i.e., acquires] a weak and meager look.[8]

Whether he was inside or outside the Aracoeli, then, the ruins amid
which he sat were metaphorical. They consisted in the transfer of the
functions, site, and power of the old Roman world to the new. Similarly, though the appropriately autumnal season was determined by
biographical accident, perhaps we should recognize in the singing of
Vespers, the valedictory chant appropriate for both the day and the
age, a deliberate figure. Such rhetorical ornament is entirely consistent with historical truth, in Gibbon's view. It helps his reader to perceive an important philosophical truth, that the transformed remains
of the Roman idea are summed up in the modern prospect of the
Capitol. In short, while Gibbon certainly expected his readers to
visualize the scene most of us have supplied mentally as we read the
famous passage—dusk, fragments of shadowy marble columns, the
writer seated on a flight of broken steps amid encroaching vines and
underbrush, while brown-robed, hooded figures chant plaintively in an
ostentatious church nearby—he expects us also to remember that
without the process that he associates with those and other ruins, that

is, a combination of looting, reusing materials, preserving, imitating, attempting to supplant, and attempting to restore the remains of a past order, much that is could not have come to be.

His account of the fate of the city, in the concluding chapter of the *Decline and Fall,* is similarly complex. It begins with Poggio's fifteenth-century portrayal of desolation. It surveys the causes for the lost and damaged structures, the diminished extent and population of the city. Of these causes, by far the most potent, Gibbon finds, were "the domestic hostilities of the Romans themselves" (7:313, chap. 71). But the monuments have not all been lost, and the modern city is far from a mere relic. While "in the gradual destruction of the monuments of [ancient] Rome Sixtus the Fifth may *alone* be excused for employing the stones of the Septizonium in the glorious edifice of St. Peter's" (7:312, chap. 71, emphasis added)—most often we destroy our past without using its materials to construct something better—even the popes have protected or restored the monuments of the past, often by the very means of reusing them for a new purpose. In fact, "the beauty and splendour of the modern city may be ascribed to the abuses of the government, to the influence of superstition" (7:324, chap. 71). The significance of the *ruins* of the Capitol, then, is not that civilization is displaced by barrenness, but that it is displaced by alternative civilizations, better in some ways, inferior in others.

For the classically minded reader, the history of the Temple of Jupiter epitomized the complex significance of ruins with particular nicety. The first temple of Jupiter on the Capitoline Hill had been built by the last king of Rome, but dedicated in the first year of the republic. Thus it immediately represented a transfer of power within the continuity of religion and culture. Its social function did not change, but its political spirit was intimately associated with the new form of government. "At all periods, the hill was less an inhabited part of the city than a citadel and religious center. Here the consul took vows before going to his province and here he returned in triumph."[9] Bronze tablets, recording military achievements and senatorial decrees alike, hung within it.[10] The republican temple was a central symbol of military expansion, shared political authority, and the civic functions of religion.

The large but simple temple built by Tarquin but maintained by the republic lasted for some five hundred years, until it burned in 83 B.C., in the last age of that republic. It was rebuilt by Sulla and by Quintus Lutatius Catulus, one of his supporters, and dedicated in 69 B.C.[11] Gibbon noted that Catulus was criticized for ostentation because he had covered the Capitol with "tuiles de bronze"[12]—an ominous sign that the grand simplicity of the republic had been corrupted. Thanks to the prudent repairs of Augustus, this temple lasted until 69 A.D., when it burned. Vespasian replaced it, but his temple burned in 80. It was in turn replaced by the final temple of Jupiter on the site, erected, at a "cost of 12,000 gold talents," by a tyrant, Domitian.[13] His temple, a "richly decorated marble structure with gilded tiles and gold-plated doors,"[14] endured until 455, when it was plundered by the Vandal, Gaiseric, to whom Rome "fell." The events of Gibbon's first three volumes—the decline and fall of the Western empire—are contemporary with Domitian's temple.

At no period had the buildings of the Capitol been left in lonely, useless fragments, and none had left ruins visible to Gibbon, though the platform of the earliest temple has been recovered by nineteenth- and twentieth-century archaeology. Gibbon could see, however, the remains of the facade of the Tabularium (the state record repository) of 78 B.C., because they had been incorporated in Michelangelo's designs for the Capitoline Palace. Visible only to the historian's imagination was the twelfth-century Senators' Palace, which had made the Capitoline Hill, whence once the world was governed, the center of municipal government for the then small city of Rome. But he could see the thirteenth-century church in which the friars sang, with its fine mosaic pavement "using porphyries and marbles robbed from classical buildings" and ideas copied from classical models, and the fourteenth-century steps, magnificent produce of "superstitious" fervor—they had been built as a "thank offering after a plague."[15]

Thus the ruins of the Capitol summed up many Romes: the republic, threatened by militarism, civilized sloth, and tyrants; the Augustan

age, characterized by the founder's "tender respect . . . for a free
constitution which he had destroyed" and designed to "deceive the
people by an image of civil liberty, and the armies by an image of
civil government" (1:70, 71, chap. 3); the two hundred years between Augustus and Commodus, when "the dangers inherent to a
military government were, in a great measure, suspended" by Augustus's successful deceit and by the practice of associating each successor with the power of his predecessor before the latter's death
(1, 72, 73, chap. 3); the reign of Domitian, final prelude to the osten-
sible golden age to which the first three chapters of the *Decline and
Fall* are devoted, the reign of five successive good monarchs; four
hundred years of declining empire; the coming of the barbarians; civil
strife and superstition in the Dark and Middle Ages; Renaissance re-
building.

A principal reason for ending his account of Rome with a description of its "ruins" that recognizes the poignant combination of loss
and achievement in the transfer of power is, I suggest, to show that
the history also begins with such an account of the ruins of a Rome.
The magnificent valedictory survey of the city, the elegiac coda that
ensures that the final effect of the tragedy will be cathartic, not
merely destructive, is matched by the three introductory chapters.
Notoriously, Gibbon says that the reigns of Nerva, Trajan, Hadrian,
and the two Antonines were the "period in the history of the world
during which the condition of the human race was most happy and
prosperous" (1:78, chap. 3). But this praise is only relative, after all,
and the first three chapters do not portray an idyll or a golden age. Instead, they show that, in exactly the same metaphorical way that the
"cross was erected on the ruins of the Capitol,"[16] the empire was
erected on the ruins of the republic. The "age of enlightenment"[17]
with which the history begins is both the product of pillaged ruins
and the fragile precursor of other ruins. The subtext of the first
three chapters constantly reiterates this theme: the happy state of
the empire under these princes is based on the looting or supplanting of the accomplishments of the republic, on an illusion of constitutional law, a reality of inescapable power. The dignity and authority
of Rome itself, the desirability of citizenship and the controlled

power of the military, are only the residue and image of the Roman republic. The grandeur of a world state, the efficiency of a common culture, language, and commerce, the blessings of universal law, peace, and religious tolerance are real effects of empire, but they are both vulnerable and flawed. It is highly surprising that such a happy period should have existed, even briefly, and at its best

> this long peace, and the uniform government of the Romans, introduced a slow and secret poison into the vitals of the empire. The minds of men were gradually reduced to the same level, the fire of genius was extinguished, and even the military spirit evaporated. . . . Their personal valour remained, but they no longer possessed that public courage which is nourished by the love of independence, the sense of national honour, the presence of danger, and the habit of command. (1:56, chap. 2)

Thus there was much in the most golden of ages that deserved to be lost.

Nor did Gibbon subscribe to the view that the republic it supplanted was ideal. As Michel Baridon has perhaps most fully shown, an idealized image of the republic already enjoyed powerful mythic status when Gibbon began to write, especially among "Polybian Whigs." The republic, "vertueuse, . . . conquerante, civilisatrice,"[18] was held to have a constitution under which personal freedom was limited by laws, not tyrants, and whose laws were determined not by the anarchy of a pure democracy, but by a balanced government. Gibbon describes this constitution. The consuls "represented the dignity of the state" and controlled finances, and "though they seldom had leisure to administer justice in person, they were considered as the supreme guardians of law, equity, and the public peace," and in emergencies, "exercised, in the defence of liberty, a temporary despotism." The tribunes were "suited rather for opposition than for action. They were instituted to defend the oppressed, to pardon offences, to arraign the enemies of the people, and when they judged it necessary, to stop, by a single word, the whole machine of government" (1:64–65, chap. 3). The powers of these officers were limited by annual election, by the fact that there were two consuls and ten tribunes to share their respective rights, and by the natural opposition of the two groups of officials. The senators, though not directly elected, were appointed by elected magistrates and, whether they came of patrician or plebeian families, had to have formerly served as magistrates to qualify for the senate. Membership, once achieved, was de facto perpetual.[19] Thus under the republic, aristocracy and commoners, legislators and executives, temporary and permanent members of government, all played their parts. Military leaders were awarded despotic powers, but for use in foreign wars, and for limited periods only.

The legends of Roman invincibility were of course to some extent self-fulfilling prophecies, and military virtues "did not abandon the Romans until long after all their sisters."[20] Under the republic, "the use of arms was reserved for those ranks of citizens who had a country to lose, a property to defend, and some share in enacting those laws which it was their interest, as well as duty, to maintain" (1:9, chap. 1). Military service, legislative power, and sacrosanct property rights had once characterized free Roman citizens, making Roman citizenship well worth aspiring to. Peace and a standing army freed Romans from the burden of the first and deprived them, eventually, of the other two.

But the republic Gibbon presents had a darker side. "The perfect settlement of the Roman empire was preceded by ages of violence and rapine" (1:39, chap. 2). Freedom, "the first wish of our heart . . . the first blessing of our nature,"[21] was denied, he points out, by that republic to at least three groups: women and children, conquered peoples, and slaves. As early as his "first serious production in [his] native language," an abstract of Blackstone's *Commentaries on the Laws of England,* Gibbon had demonstrated his preoccupation with the terrifying powers accorded by the Roman republic to the *paterfamilias.*[22] Furthermore, in its expansive period, its republican greatness, Rome dedicated itself to ending the freedom of other peoples. In a note, Gibbon has a little argument with his admired Tacitus on the subject of Augustus's decision to "confine the empire within those limits, which Nature seemed to have placed as its permanent bulwarks and boundaries":

Incertum metu an per invidiam (Tacit. Annal. 1.2.) Why must rational advice be imputed to a base or foolish motive? To what cause, error, malevolence or flattery shall I ascribe this unworthy alternative? Was the historian dazzled by Trajan's conquests? [23]

Gibbon sees Augustus's decision as preferable to the republican desire (here shared by Trajan) to expand indefinitely; he agrees with Montesquieu that "immoderate" size contributed to the doom of Rome, but argues that this weakness originated in the republican idea, not the empire. For all its vaunted freedom, in "the age of Roman virtue" only the citizens enjoyed the rule of law; "the provinces were subject to the arms . . . of the republic" and "destitute of any public force or constitutional freedom. . . . [Even] the free states and cities which had embraced the cause of Rome were rewarded with a nominal alliance, and insensibly sunk into real servitude" (1:35, chap. 2).

Moreover, Rome's prosperity as a republic required the misery of a body of "men who endured the weight without sharing the benefits of society," the slaves. Ironically, it was in the "free states of antiquity" that "the domestic slaves were exposed to the wanton rigour of despotism" (1:39, chap. 2). Gibbon is careful to indicate that the "ruins" of the republic that underlie the state of Rome with which he begins are, like the other ruins he will treat, ambiguous. In the case of these darker legacies, inherited and transformed by the empire, to ruin the republic is to better the state of human beings. The mortal weaknesses of a parent state permit transfer of power to its heirs. The republic, a state in which individual freedom, virtuous actions, world leadership, safety from foreign enemies, and the diffusion of arts, sciences, public works, and luxury were accompanied by constant wars of conquest, domestic tyranny, and chattel slavery, fell, victim in part of its own success, on the paradoxical principle described by Machiavelli, that the "forces that buil[d] up human personality [are] identical with the forces that undermine it."[24] Yet it was also a victim of the evil genius of Augustus. Each new wielder of power may justify the destruction the change of rule represents only by creation of new orders that correct the weaknesses and preserve the virtues of the old. The Augustan scheme improves on the republic in some respects, but it represents on the whole the looting of the republic, only gradually recognizable as such, thanks to the magnificent preservation of the republican facades.

The clearest improvement is the blessing of peace. So great a blessing was this that, as Gibbon points out, when the Augustan scheme was operating under the control of wise and beneficent individuals, the subjects of the empire, provincials as well as citizens, overcame the natural propensity of mankind "to exalt the past and to depreciate the present" in appreciating the civilized blessings of their own time—"laws, agriculture, and science" (Gibbon adds a fourth blessing, world-wide trade) (1:56, chap. 2). The empire extended the advantages of citizenship to the former enemies, now provincials, of the republic. To avoid rival despotism, the emperors "introduced some relaxation of the laws governing paternal rights over children [and women]."[25] By ending wars of conquest, the empire even improved the lot of the slaves, for when there was no longer a continuous new supply from conquered enemies, masters were encouraged to be humane for their own self-interest. "The progress of manners was accelerated by the virtue or policy of the emperors; and by the edicts of Hadrian and the Antonines the protection of the laws was extended to the most abject part of mankind." Moreover, slaves had a very real hope of manumission, as "the benevolence of the master was . . . frequently prompted by . . . vanity and avarice"; so frequently that laws had to be made to prevent too easy access to the benefits of citizenship for freedmen (1:40–41, chap. 2). In all these respects, the transfer of power from the republic to the empire represented real improvement, even in the very freedom for which the republic was most renowned.

Like the republic, the empire was a source of civilization. Its citizens "celebrate[d] the increasing splendour of the cities, the beautiful face of the country, cultivated and adorned like an immense garden." Moreover, the "love of letters, almost inseparable from peace and refinement, was fashionable among the subjects of Hadrian and the Antonines. . . . It was diffused over the whole extent of their empire" (1:56–57, chap. 2). With the decreasing distinction between Romans and provincials, it was virtually a world government. Though Gibbon carefully acknowledges the existence of "outlying countries . . . left in the enjoyment of a barbarous independence," he betrays a tendency to feel, like the ancients, that "the empire of the Romans filled the world" (1:27, chap. 1; 1:81, chap. 3). World government, the diffusion of language, culture, and riches, led to the diffusion of the monuments that most seized Gibbon's imagination—the great roads, the postal system, the pirate-free seas, the aqueducts and other useful public works—which left their literal and metaphorical ruins throughout the Roman world.

Moreover, in its happiest period, the empire enjoyed some unique blessings. The reign of the Antonines was "possibly the *only* period in which the happiness of a great people was the sole object of government" (1:76, chap. 3, my emphasis). For nearly a century, the "profane virtues" (as Gibbon called them) of order, lucidity, reason, and humanity characterized the exercise of absolute power.[26] Finally, the empire maintained the republican blessing of universal religious toleration. "It is not by rapidity or extent of conquest that we should estimate the greatness of Rome. . . . [Provincials and conquered peoples] enjoyed the religion of their ancestors" (1:28, chap. 2). For Gibbon, of course, religion was only a matter of opinion and therefore useful, like other prejudices, for controlling the masses, but, like questions of taste, not worth fighting for. Hence he was incapable of understanding the significance of religious belief in the lives of those for whom it was a matter of ultimate truths, but he was also keenly sensitive to the horrors of religious persecution and intolerance. The ruin of this tolerance therefore seemed to him a clear change for the worse, when the power of the pagan empire was transmitted to its christianized successor.

Yet the first age of the empire, the period of the five good emperors, is not portrayed as a golden age. If it was the happiest period in man's history, it was still radically flawed. As the empire is to the republic, so successor states will prove to be to the age of the Antonines: products, for better and worse, of ruins. The crucial ruin, in the change from republic to empire, is the loss of shared sovereignty, the balance of power among numerous offices and persons. Under the empire, all happiness rested on the fragile foundation of the life and virtue of one man. The actions and ideas of Augustus pervade

Gibbon's portrayal of the speciously golden age that begins the *Decline and Fall,* and as Howard Weinbrot has fully demonstrated, Gibbon was no admirer of Augustus.[27]

Augustus made of the Roman world, Gibbon said, "an absolute monarchy disguised by the form of a commonwealth" (1:68, chap. 3). Gibbon enumerates the ancient offices Augustus chose to hold— and his destruction of the crucial constitutional limitations those offices once held. The military leaders of Rome had always had "almost despotic" power over "the soldiers, the enemies, and the subjects of the republic" (1:62, chap. 3). But this power was temporary, while Augustus was made permanent military leader and allowed to maintain a standing army in the capital itself. Even more invidiously, Augustus disguised the military source of his power by seeking the civil offices that had traditionally governed the republic. Augustus, of course, was both consul and tribune, held both offices perpetually, and combined them with the offices of military leader, supreme pontiff, and censor. His extraordinary powers extended beyond his lifetime, being transmitted to his successors. Like the Romans who used the stones of the Colosseum to build their own houses, he accelerated the ruin of the republic by taking its materials for his own purposes, and in this instance, too, the new building was far inferior to the old.

The preservation of the facade of the republic, however, was a most successful ruse. For some two hundred years, "the dangers inherent to a military scheme were, in a great measure, suspended." Civil war and revolutions, except for the overthrow of Nero, did not occur. "The emperor was elected by the *authority* of the senate, and the *consent* of the soldiers" (Gibbon's emphasis), that is, the transfer of civil authority to the army was not complete and was not recognized (1:72–73, chap. 3). In this instance, the ruin is like the hollow fabric of a once substantial building, appearing as strong as ever, but ready to crumble at a touch. Augustus knew, says Gibbon, "that mankind is governed by names; nor was he deceived in his expectation that the senate and people would submit to slavery, provided they were respectfully assured that they still enjoyed their ancient freedom. A feeble senate and enervated people cheerfully acquiesced in the pleasing illusion, as long as it was supported by the virtue, or even by the prudence, of the successors of Augustus" (1:71, chap. 3).

Some, however, like the historian in 1764, were not deceived by names. The penalty for their wisdom was the bitter consciousness that ruins lay around them, and that the new edifices had dangerous flaws. Though "oppressed beneath the weight of their own corruption and of military violence," some citizens of the empire—educated, after all, just as Cato and Cicero had been

> for a long while preserved the sentiments, or at least the ideas of their free-born ancestors. . . . From Grecian philosophy they had imbibed the justest and most liberal notions of the dignity of human nature and the origin of civil society. The history of their own country had taught them to revere a free, a virtuous, and a victorious commonwealth; to abhor the successful crimes of Caesar and Augustus; and inwardly to despise those tyrants whom they adored with the most abject flattery (1:85, chap. 3).

Clearly they were conscious of having lost both dignity and courage. The effects extended even to the very arts of peace for which the ending of the wars of expansion was necessary. No longer a soldier, the citizen might detest war, with Marcus Antoninus, "as the disgrace and calamity of human nature." He had time to cultivate arts and sciences and did so. Yet the arts and sciences did not flourish in the highest degree. In his summary of the civil state of the empire under the good emperors, Gibbon emphasizes this debilitude. His praise is meager; his peroration exalts not the artists of the empire, but their eventual conquerors and successors:

> The sciences of physic and astronomy were successfully cultivated by the Greeks [Galen and Ptolemy]; but if we except the inimitable Lucian, this age of indolence passed away without having produced a single writer of original genius. . . . "In the same manner," says [Longinus], "as some children always remain pigmies, whose infant limbs have been too closely confined; thus our tender minds, fettered by the prejudices and habits of a just servitude, are unable to expand themselves, or to attain that well-proportioned greatness which we admire in the ancients, who, living under a popular government, wrote with the same freedom as they acted." . . . The Roman world was indeed peopled by a race of pigmies, when the fierce giants of the north broke in and mended the puny breed. They restored a manly spirit of

freedom; and, after the revolution of ten centuries, freedom became the happy parent of taste and science. (1:57–58, chap. 2)

The Roman people themselves, no longer lawgivers or conquerors, cease also to be originals. Their moral degeneration is a cause of the replacement of the republic by the empire, a reason that the good emperors cannot restore the republic, and the precondition for their own ruin, which will prove to be, like the use of the stones of the Septizonium for St. Peter's, an instance in which ruin is constructive, at least for freedom, taste, and science.

Most ironic of the weaknesses of the empire, perhaps, is its great strength, its unification of the world. This grandest of ideas and ideals gave the state a terrible power over those of its own people who transgressed or offended its authority:

> The slave of Imperial despotism, whether he was condemned to drag his gilded chain in Rome and the senate, or to wear out a life of exile on the barren rock of Seriphus, or the frozen banks of the Danube, expected his fate in silent despair. To resist was fatal, and it was impossible to fly. On every side he was encompassed with a vast extent of sea and land. . . . Beyond the frontiers, his anxious view could discover nothing, except the ocean, inhospitable deserts, hostile tribes of barbarians . . . or dependent kings. . . . "Wherever you are," said Cicero to the exiled Marcellus, "remember that you are equally within the power of the conqueror." (1:82–83, chap. 3)

Like cultural uniformity, then, this greatness of political unity had to be ruined if individual liberty were again to be possible. Gibbon is quite explicit about the merits of the breaking and fragmentation of this aspect of imperial greatness. Earlier, he had pointed out to us that the very "broken fragments" of the ruined empire have formed many "powerful kingdoms" (1:26, chap. 1). That mere fragments could be kingdoms is an impressive image of greatness lost. But destruction is also transformation, and individual freedom has emerged from these shards:

> A modern tyrant . . . would soon experience a gentle restraint from the example of his equals, the dread of present censure, the advice of his allies, and the apprehension of his enemies. The object of his displeasure, escaping from the narrow limits of his dominions, would easily obtain . . . a secure refuge. (1:81, chap. 3)

Grandeur is gone, but the unrestrained tyranny it permitted has gone with it.

The complexity and ambivalence of the relationship established here between the early empire and its predecessor, the republic, and foreshadowed for the empire even as it is presented, proves paradigmatic for the portrayal of transfers of power in the *Decline and Fall*. Since to transform is to destroy, the maker of changes has a heavy responsibility for preserving the prior good and for replacing the bad with something better. Very few persons or groups are successful in doing so, but some deserve great credit for trying, while others are blameable for the stupid or cynical way in which they hasten to avoidable loss. The villains of the *Decline and Fall* deliberately contribute to the destruction of something good; they divide the empire, eliminate toleration, reward irrationality, fanaticism, or withdrawal from the world, and the like. The heroes, such as Julian, Mohammed, and even Athanasias, try to construct or preserve or restore one or more of the virtues of the past order. Only Julian, however, tries to restore the whole of the older order, and he fails in large part because of his own tragic flaw, his failure to distinguish the weaknesses of the past from its strengths. Without the correction of its errors, the previous order is an experiment that has already failed.

Much of the *Decline and Fall* is devoted to the somber narrative of the process of ruin inherent in each Rome in its very nature, and criminally accelerated by various unworthy exercisers of power. But destruction is transformation just as transformation is destruction. Ironically or heroically, sometimes a better monument replaces the one destroyed. The heroic conflict in the *Decline and Fall* occurs when someone exercises the human power to make order out of destruction or chaos. As David Jordan well puts it, "Institutions are but the framework in which men must live. . . . Historical necessity . . . direct[s] the energies of men into specific channels, but [does not destroy] a human nature which can create order out of chaos."[28] Gibbon admires the exercise of such energy even when it is, in his view, misdirected; he reveres it when it attempts, however unsuccessfully, to conserve in a new order what deserves to survive from the past.

In the course of the *Decline and Fall,* new political structures several times take or attempt to take the name, power, or territory once held by the Roman Empire. Christianity, for example, superimposes a rival political and social order on the empire; Gibbon respects it for correcting the moral corruption and indifference to domestic suffering that had characterized the Rome of the late republic and the empire, and perhaps for preserving the empire's virtue of strong political union.[29] But it is erected on the ruins of the empire's fostering of the good things of this world: arts, public works, the virtue of "honor" that replaced patriotism as a motive for military achievement,[30] economic and cultural unity based on the great model of the republic, and most of all, religious toleration and individual intellectual freedom. The division of the empire into East and West and the creation of new bureaucratic structures reestablished civilian authority, but at the cost of political, economic, and military fragmentation and of the entire loss of the Latin, senatorial model for culture and individual behavior. Gibbon appears reasonably confident that the modern world is less faulty in that it is less subject to total destruction, and even to the partial destruction represented by ruins, than the world it replaces.[31] Nevertheless, he chooses to mark his subject with the image of ruin, an image to which our first response is a sense of loss, an image inconsistent with smug self-satisfaction, despite the undoubted blessings of our mercantile, power-balanced, relatively humane, enlightened modernity.

The *Decline and Fall* resists systematizing abstractions. Perhaps Gibbon's recognition of the paradoxical combination of good and ill effects in every historical process should have made him a doctrinaire fatalist or driven him to make of the Roman Empire an exemplum for his own age.[32] Instead, he seems to see the enduring qualities of the Roman idea in various tragically missed opportunities for preservation or restoration and also in various admirably seized opportunities either for new building or for preservation. "The same chapter in which Gibbon describes the unraveling of the web of civilized life at the hands of the monks ends with a warm appreciation of how the Christian Gothic Bishop Ufilus and the later Catholic bishops of the West patiently took up again those tattered shreds to weave, albeit unconsciously, yet another web of civilized living around the barbarians of the north."[33] Paraphrasing Walpole's famous *mot,* we might say that the ruins of Rome are a tragedy to those who feel, but a sublime comedy to those who think. Gibbon, of course, did both.

In his final chapter, Gibbon quotes an anonymous thirteenth-century writer, according to whom, "The Capitol . . . is so named as being the head of the world; where the consuls and senators formerly resided for the government of the city and the globe. . . . Below the citadel stood a palace, . . . whose value might be esteemed at one third of the world itself. . . . If the province rebelled against Rome, the prophet of the Capitol [magical belled statues] reported the prodigy, and the senate was admonished of the impending danger" (7:321, chap. 71). Thus in the thirteenth century, people at last believed (as Bede, for instance, in the eighth century, did not) that Rome had in fact fallen, but the images of the empire preserved in their myth—wealth, world power, invincibility, and the effective magic of the pagan religion—stood. Gibbon's professed contempt for the legend does not prevent his exploiting it to indicate the power of the empire's ruins.

It has often been observed that Gibbon is not really interested in abstract historical, political, or sociological theory. But he was interested in the transfer of power through time, both by violence and by natural succession. As sons can be good or bad, but can neither replicate nor escape the influence of their fathers, so builders can undermine or restore the monumental legacy of the past, but they can never re-create a city of the past. As a narrative artist, Gibbon knew what as philosophic historian he never articulated: all change, including growth, implies death. Death may not be followed by immortality, but immortality never occurs, in history, until after death. The immortal Romes of the senators and the emperors were ultimately significant not in their fleeting triumphs, but in their declines and falls, in the lasting stones and shadows of their ruins.

NOTES

1. According to G. Giarrizzo, Rome's role as *caput mundi* was the deepest ground for Gibbon's attraction to Imperial Rome; "Roma è allora la sede di un dialogo universale in cui ognuno versa il proprio ingegno e il proprio sapere, e si nutre dell'ingegno e del sapere degli altri." Giuseppe Giarrizzo, *Edward Gibbon e la cultura europea del settocento* (Naples: Edit. Istit. italiano per gli studi storici, 1954), pp. 103–4.

2. Edward Gibbon, *Memoirs of My Life,* ed. Georges A. Bonnard (London: Thomas Nelson and Sons, 1966), p. 136, hereafter cited as *Memoirs,* and Edward Gibbon, *The History of the Decline and Fall of the Roman Empire,* ed. J. B. Bury (London: Methuen, 1909–1916), 7:325, chap. 71, hereafter cited in text as the *Decline and Fall.*

3. Lynn White, Jr. "Conclusion: The Temple of Jupiter Revisited," in *The Transformation of the Roman World: Gibbon's Problem after Two Centuries,* ed. Lynn White, Jr. (Berkeley and Los Angeles: University of California Press, 1966), p. 301. Hereafter, *Transformation.*

4. Peter Brown, "Gibbon's Views on Culture and Society in the Fifth and Sixth Centuries," in *Edward Gibbon and the Decline and Fall of the Roman Empire,* ed. G. W. Bowersock, John Clive, and Stephen Graubard (Cambridge: Harvard University Press, 1977), p. 74. Hereafter, *Edward Gibbon and the Decline and Fall.*

5. For an extensive exploration of the *Decline and Fall* in the terms of this metaphor, see Lionel Gossman, "The Plenitude of Paternal Power," in his *The Empire Unpossess'd* (Cambridge: Cambridge University Press, 1981), pp. 25–47.

6. For a balanced discussion of the evidence against the authenticity of this anecdote, see David P. Jordan, *Gibbon and His Roman Empire* (Urbana: University of Illinois Press, 1971), pp. 18–21.

7. G. A. Bonnard's note to this passage in the *Memoirs* (p. 305) remarks upon this fact, but Bonnard does not discuss its implications. Lynn White, in his preface to *Transformation,* comments, "In the 1530s . . . Michelangelo redesigned the Campidoglio, the piazza of the Capitoline. . . . Glorying in the magnificence of the ancient Roman tradition, nevertheless he drastically reoriented the Campidoglio away from . . . the Forum to the east, toward . . . the shrine of St. Peter to the west. He removed to the Campidoglio the great equestrian statue of Constantine . . . and since then the first Christian emperor, turning his back upon paganism, has ridden majestically toward the Vatican" (p. v). But White does not even question the factuality of Gibbon's anecdote, much less analyze the significance of its figures.

8. *Gibbon's Journey from Geneva to Rome,* ed. G. A. Bonnard (London: Thomas Nelson and Sons, 1961), p. 239.

9. "Capitol," *Oxford Classical Dictionary,* 2d ed. (Oxford: Clarendon Press, 1970), pp. 202–3.

10. Rodolfo Lanciani, *Pagan and Christian Rome* (1892; reprint, New York: Benjamin Blom, 1967), p. 87.

11. Ibid., p. 86, date from *Oxford Classical Dictionary,* p. 203.

12. Edward Gibbon, "Nomina Gentesque Antiquae Italia," in his *Miscellaneous Works,* ed. John, Lord Sheffield (London: John Murray, 1815), 4:214.

13. *Oxford Classical Dictionary,* p. 203.

14. John B. Ward-Perkins, "Rome," *Encyclopedia Britannica* (Chicago: William Benton, 1968), 19:571.

15. Ibid., 19:575–76.

16. "On erige la croix sur les debris de Capitole." British Library Additional Manuscripts 34880, folio 155r; see my *Young Edward Gibbon: Gentleman of Letters* (Baltimore: Johns Hopkins University Press, 1982), pp. 129–30.

17. Jordan, *Gibbon and His Roman Empire,* p. 216.

18. Michel Baridon, *Edward Gibbon et le mythe de Rome* (Paris: Editions Honore Champion, 1977), p. 392.

19. "Senatus," *Oxford Classical Dictionary,* pp. 973–74.

20. See British Library Additional Manuscripts 34880, folios 152–53.

21. *Memoirs,* p. 45.

22. *Memoirs,* p. 148, and *The English Essays of Edward Gibbon,* ed. Patricia B. Craddock (Oxford: Clarendon Press, 1973), p. 85.

23. Craddock, *English Essays,* p. 338.

24. J. G. A. Pocock, "Between Machiavelli and Hume: Gibbon as Civic Humanist and Philosophical Historian," in *Edward Gibbon and the Decline and Fall,* p. 137.

25. Gossman, "Plenitude of Paternal Power," pp. 64–65. Gossman comments that the discussion of the family "makes it clear that while the empire may represent in Gibbon's history a decline from the earlier heroic age of Rome and the feminization of the manly Republic, the latter is by no means unequivocally presented as an ideal."

26. See Jordan for a discussion of the celebration of these virtues as the real theme of the history, pp. 152–53.

27. In his *Augustus Caesar in "Augustan" England* (Princeton: Princeton University Press, 1978), especially pp. 101–8.

28. Jordan, p. 121.

29. For Gibbon's appreciation of some aspects of Christianity, see Gerhart B. Ladner, "The Impact of Christianity," *Transformation,* pp. 59–91; and Deno J.

Geanakoplos, "Edward Gibbon and Byzantine Ecclesiastical History," *Church History* 35 (1966):170-85.

30. See *Decline and Fall,* 1:10, chap. 1, and Pocock, *Edward Gibbon and the Decline and Fall,* p. 1-9.

31. Gibbon's fullest expression of this premise, however, is in the early "General Observations on the Decline of the Empire in the West," written, he stated, by 1774, though published as the conclusion of his third volume in 1781. Leo Braudy, in "Gibbon, Public History and the Shaping Self," gives a more optimistic account; see his *Narrative Form in History and Fiction* (Princeton: Princeton University Press, 1970), pp. 213-68.

32. Andrew Lossky, "Introduction: Gibbon and the Enlightenment," *Transformation,* asks the significant question, "why Gibbon did not choose to dazzle us with the glories of ancient Rome rather than dwell upon the decay of the City. Is this morbid taste? Or does he tell us a cautionary tale? Neither of these explanations is satisfactory" (p. 3).

33. Brown, "Gibbon's Views," p. 80.

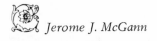 *Jerome J. McGann*

Rome and Its
Romantic Significance

I

Why should the subject of Romantic Rome have anything more than a passing interest for critics and scholars? Imagination, Nature, the Self: these are the crucial elements of the Romantic experience. Rome is not. Wherein lies its scholarly significance?

The answer to this question begins to emerge when we recall certain facts about the Romantic experience. First, most Romantics did not like cities, which seemed to them the emblems of a debased social life. In this respect cities represent a defining limit of the Romantic experience in its own predominant self-conception. How Victorian ideology separates from Romanticism can be seen, in part, through the deliberate interest which Victorian writers took in cities and the urban experience.

Only one city escaped the judgment of Romanticism, and that was Rome. The obsession of Napoleon and Chateaubriand, the grave of Keats, Rome attracted to herself—to the idea of herself, perhaps we should say—nearly all the great figures of the Romantic movement. Body or soul, she came to possess most of these people. Even Wordsworth would eventually visit Rome and memorialize his experience and thoughts in verse we are spared from having to remember.[1]

The Rome that focused Romantic attention was a far different place from either Renaissance or Counter-Reformation Rome, which together comprise what we now call papal Rome in the age of its vigor, or Rome between the reigns of Martin V (1417–1431) and Clement XIII (1758–1769). The end of this great period in the history of Rome should probably be dated from 1773, the year in which Clement XIV agreed, under pressure from Paris and Madrid, to suppress the power of the Jesuits. But the decline and fall of Counter-Reformation Rome signaled the emergence of Romantic Rome, and it was the great art historian Winckelmann who presided over its birth. Winckelmann went to Rome in 1755 and joined the circle of scholars who gathered around Cardinal Albani.[2] The recent excavations at Herculaneum and Pompeii were the impetus for a renewed interest in the ancient world. Rome was a museum in which historical scholarship could inaugurate systematic investigations into the antiquities of the West.

As the city of ruins, then, Rome would receive the investments of Romantic ideology to an extent that was not possible for any other city, not even Venice. This historical fact is a peculiar gift to subsequent critical scholarship, since in it we shall find an opportunity for tracing a special and important history: the history whereby Romanticism came to discover the limits of its own ideological experience.

We may begin with one of the most famous Romantic passages dealing with the Roman experience, Chateaubriand's short piece of poetic prose called "Promenade dans Rome au clair de lune."

> Rome is asleep in the midst of her ruins. This orb of the night, this sphere which is supposed to be extinguished and unpeopled, moves through her pale solitudes, above the solitude of Rome. She shines upon the streets without inhabitants, upon enclosed spaces, open squares, and gardens in which no one walks, upon monasteries where the voices of monks are no longer heard, upon cloisters which are as deserted as the arches of the Colosseum.[3]

This solitude is an emblem that a living culture has departed; the people whom Chateaubriand cannot see are not the actual inhabitants of early nineteenth-century Rome—they are there, of course, but they do not engage his feelings. The inhabitants he looks for in vain are those who once gave life to the empty places and ruins of the present.

What is crucially Romantic about this scene, however, that which sets it apart from a Renaissance, or Baroque, or even neoclassical view of Roman ruins, is its melancholy sense that time has not only borne down the Rome of the ancients, it has also overcome the Rome of the popes, the greatness of the Church. Traces alone remain of what Chateaubriand calls "the two Italies" with their "two glories." In this night of Rome Chateaubriand can see, by the light of the Romantic imagination, that "pagan Rome is plunging deeper and deeper into her tombs, and Christian Rome once again descends, little by little, into the catacombs whence she originally came."[4]

Chateaubriand's Romantic vision of Rome is born not merely of a sense that time overcomes the works of human greatness, but that its power can be seen to move even in the midst of this very life in the works and days of one's own world and culture. The passage is dominated by a historical sense, which scholarship like Winckelmann's had helped to create; but Chateaubriand's sense of the triumph of time has moved beyond Winckelmann to a consciousness that his own culture was as historically fragile as that of pagan Rome.

The picture of a Rome dominated by ruins and monuments but deserted by people is typically Romantic, and is often delivered to the reader (or viewer) under that most explicit of Romantic signs, the moonlight. The greatest English text offering such a scene is of course *Childe Harold,* canto 4.[5] This Byron text is as central as it is, in the iconography of Romanticism, because its emblems belong to more than one form of Romantic consciousness. Before we can understand the peculiar arrangements that Byron's poetry makes with Rome, however, we must retreat to a period before Chateaubriand wrote his prose poem—specifically, to a moment between the time when Winckelmann came to Rome and the outbreak of the French Revolution.

II

Late in September 1786, having just passed his thirty-seventh birthday, Goethe left behind the bourgeois life he had been leading for the previous ten years—left behind Frau Von Stein, his state duties in Weimar, and his friend the duke—and entered Rome. He would spend fifteen months in the city (until June 1788) and he would be utterly changed by this, the single most important experience of his life. "I reckon my second life, a very rebirth, from the day I entered Rome," he wrote at the time in his *Italian Journey.*[6] The record of his first months at Rome shows that he deliberately took Winckelmann as his mediator and guide. Soon after he arrived

he bought the new edition of Winckelmann's *History* translated by
Carlo Fea, he read Winckelmann's letters from Italy, and he recurred
to the great scholar's experiences as to a model for his own rebirth: [7]

> This morning I came by chance on the letters which Winckelmann wrote
> from Italy, and you can imagine with what emotion I have started to read
> them. Thirty-one years ago, at the same time of year, he arrived here, an even
> greater fool than I was. But, with true German seriousness, he set himself to
> make a thorough and accurate study of antiquity and its arts. How bravely he
> worked his way through! And, in this city, what it means to me to remember
> him! (P. 137)

The intellectual legacy bequeathed by Winckelmann to Goethe was
that, in the study of antiquity and the arts in general, "judgment is
impossible without a knowledge of historical development" (p. 156).
But Winckelmann's work also taught Goethe how such historical
knowledge could offer to the contemporary European a program of
spiritual liberation. Because Winckelmann showed how to trace
"the history of styles in their gradual growth and decadence" (pp.
155–56), he opened an avenue back to what Goethe called "the
Everlasting Rome, not the Rome which is replaced by another every
decade" (p. 142).

Winckelmann helped Goethe explain to himself why he felt, when
he came to Rome, that "the noble objects with which I am surrounded never lose their freshness for me" (p. 135). Again and again
Goethe is struck by the apparent perfection in the arts of the Greeks,
the Romans, and even of the more recent artists of the Italian Renaissance. And this experience leads him to his true, immediate interest,
his personal need: "But can we, petty as we are and accustomed to
pettiness, ever become equal to such noble perfection?" (p. 135).
The answer emerges from Goethe's meditations on Winckelmann's
historiography. To understand the cycles of art's growth and decay
in Greece, in Rome, and finally in the Italian Renaissance—to understand, even more, the relations in which these cycles stand to each
other—is to place one's self at the beginning of yet another cycle.
The German scholar and poet came to Rome to initiate again the
birth of art's "noble perfection." "At sight of the immense wealth
of this city, even though it consists of scattered fragments, one is

inevitably led to ask when it came into being" (p. 155). Goethe's conclusion is that "Everlasting Rome" comes into being in a cycle of rebirths, and that her latest rebirth is even now taking place at the end of the eighteenth century through the agency of people like Cardinal Albani, Winckelmann, and, of course, Goethe himself.

This insight, or conviction, informs the entire cycle of the *Roman Elegies*,[8] and it appears explicitly in Elegy 15 when Goethe invokes the sun and its everlasting knowledge of perpetual cyclic renewal: "And out of the ruins once more an even greater world!" This general theme will eventually be linked to the power of poetry itself ("Ünd ihr, wächset und blüht, geliebte Lieder," Elegy 20), and specifically to Goethe's own love elegies as these incarnate the living freshness of antiquity.

In his *Roman Elegies* Goethe deliberately sets out to enshrine in his own verse the vital spirit immortalized in the Latin love elegy, especially in the elegies of Propertius. The peculiar character of these great poems appears most forcibly when we compare the Faustina of Goethe's work with Propertius's cruel and imperious mistress. Indeed, Goethe's poetic mistress could scarcely be more unlike any of the famous women whose names and characters appear through the agency of Catullus, Propertius, and Tibullus—the three "Triumvirs" who are explicitly acknowledged in Goethe's elegies.

That Propertius's Cynthia should not resemble the voluptuous and compliant innocent of Goethe's cycle is of course exactly what we should expect. For if Faustina corresponds to any Roman girl whom Goethe knew, or to Christiane Vulpius, or perhaps if she is an imaginative creature drawn from several life originals, that fact is ideologically subordinated in the poems.[9] Faustina is not a woman, a fictive representation of a particular human being, she is the embodiment of Goethe's idea of Rome: that is to say, of human life as perpetually fresh, perpetually young, perpetually being reborn. As Amor says to Goethe in Elegy 13: "I, your teacher, am always young, and I'm fond of young people. I don't like you when you're precocious. Awake! Understand me! Antiquity also was new when those blessed ones lived! Happily live your life so the past may live in you!"

Being a god, Amor speaks of such matters with an ease born of a certain distance—as it were, in a "naive" rather than in a "sentimental" mode of discourse. This tone corresponds to Goethe's not only in the *Italian Journey,* so notable for its lack of self-absorption, but in the *Roman Elegies* as well. The famous Elegy 5 epitomizes what being "in love" means in this cycle of poems: that is, it means being young in the antique manner, being "naive." "Inspired on classical ground," Goethe means to reincarnate the classical spirit. His success in this effort is achieved in the manner of Winckelmann rather than in the manner of Propertius. Like the Roman relics and ruins lying open to Winckelmann's passionate interest, Faustina lies in bed next to Goethe, and as his hands "glide down her hips" he thinks: "at last I can understand sculpture." More than this, however, through her he rediscovers the youthful spirit of the ancient world. Self-conscious without also being self-absorbed, Goethe recovers the spirit of the ancients as it were by art rather than by nature or circumstance. Nothing reveals this aspect of the elegies so well as the scholarly mind that works through them; and perhaps no detail reveals the presence of that scholarly mind better than the unexpected appearance of the word *"Quiriten"* at the end of Elegy 18; "Grant me, O Romans [*"o Quiriten"*], my happiness." Before this passage the inhabitants of Rome are always referred to in the usual form *"die Römer,"* as to those who visibly inhabit the actual city of Goethe's sojourn. In the final elegies he resorts to the verbal form, which calls up the idea of a primitive and (as it were) absolute Rome, the city and people that he called "Everlasting" in his *Italian Journey.*

Because Goethe imagined that he and his world stood at the beginning of a new historical cycle, that an Everlasting Human Life was actually in process of being born again, his Roman experience constitutes a challenge and a call, rather than, as with Chateaubriand, a mood of melancholy nostalgia. This difference is nicely displayed when we compare Chateaubriand's moonlight meditation among the Roman ruins with the corresponding meditations in Goethe's *Italian Journey.* For Goethe, "each day [is] spent in distractions mingled with sadness," but when he walks out "quite alone" in the moonlight to the Capitol the experience is like entering "an enchanted palace in a desert" (p. 496). Goethe is transported out of the present by the great Roman presences from the past, is transported with the sense that he is now at last moving "into another simpler and greater world," that a splendid vision of futurity can be glimpsed in the noble remains of this past. He describes the experience as "awe-inspiring," he narrates the fear that this past greatness induces, and he even confesses to a failed effort to match the greatness of the ancients. "Aroused" to "a mood I might call heroic-elegiac," Goethe recalls an elegy from the third book of Ovid's *Tristia,* but when he tries to compose his own elegy he cannot do it. The book therefore closes with a quotation from Ovid rather than from Goethe, but the effect of this, paradoxically, is to reveal not the failure of Goethe's poetic powers, but their desire, their energy, and their promise. At the end of the *Italian Journey* Goethe has placed himself at the beginning of a world-historical cycle, a young man whose future is beginning to unfold as he "ventures upon something unusual."

III

To explain the different effects of the experience of Rome on Goethe and Chateaubriand is beyond the scope of this paper and my own competence. Nevertheless, the intervention of the years 1789–1803 is manifestly significant. Both men were deeply influenced by the recently developed theories of historical periodicity, and in *Le Génie du Christianisme* Chateaubriand had offered a theory of the Christian religion that challenged the views of the *philosophes.* Bonaparte's accession to power had opened a space in France for the development of conservative ideology. The Concordat was signed in 1801, Chateaubriand's celebrated book appeared in 1802, and in 1803 the event that Chateaubriand had hoped and even angled for finally came about. He was sent to Rome as the secretary to the legation. He initially saw Bonaparte as the engine that would bring about the renascence of the Christian world. Only a few months would pass, after he arrived in Rome so full of hopes and plans, before his vision of a reborn era of Christianity would collapse, before he would write passages like the one quoted above, as well as its famous companion piece, the letter to Fontanes on the Roman campagna (10 January 1804). We do not need to rehearse the well-known events of late 1803, when Chateaubriand revealed a sort of sublimity in political incompetence, to realize that his vision of a new Christian era did not collapse through mismanagement of his worldly affairs, or because Bonaparte was unequal to such a glorious mission. Christianity was a once and future kingdom and as such it stood outside the cycles of historical change and repetition. Similarly, the two Romes—pagan and papal—were once but not future kingdoms, and so Chateaubriand's historical sense finally returned him to the essential truth of his imagination: that papal Rome, like the city of the republic and the empire, was born to perish, and that Chateaubriand, for his part, was born to minister at her going. This is the central message of the *Memoires*, just as it is the inspiration of his prose-poetic moonlight meditations on the ruins of Rome. "Grief is my element," he said at the time; "it is only when I am unhappy that I really find myself."[10]

For the liberal and Jacobin consciousness, the course of the French Revolution from 1789–1802 taught another, if equally disheartening, lesson. Goethe's sense that a new day was dawning has its English counterpart in Blake's *Marriage of Heaven and Hell,* but the confidence and exuberant hope of the *Elegies* and the *Marriage* was to succeed, following the Terror and Bonaparte, to the melancholy of works like *The Prelude.* When, in 1818, Byron sets forth his great, extended meditation on Rome and her ruins, he explains what the revolution meant to those who identified with it:

> There is the moral of all human tales;
>   'Tis but the same rehearsal of the past,
> First Freedom, and then Glory—when that fails,
>   Wealth, Vice, Corruption,—barbarism at last.
> And History, with all her volumes vast,
>   Hath but *one* page,—'tis . . . written here.
>   (Chap. 4, stanza 108)

Set against the background of his Roman reflections on the Revolution in France (stanzas 89–98), the "*one* page" to which Byron refers involves a dismal interpretation of Goethe's cyclic vision. The interpretation is typical of the postrevolutionary Romantic consciousness.

The liberal and humanist Romantics will not, however, use this interpretation to fashion an ideology of reaction based upon a Christian or transcendental historical renunciation. Their problem was—to adapt a phrase from Blake—to keep the human vision in a time of trouble, to preserve a historical hope, a civilized ideal. The figures who struggled hardest and most successfully in this task were Shelley, Byron, and Stendhal. Of these three I shall here consider only the last two, principally because only Byron and Stendhal used Rome to focus and elaborate their literary programs. Rome was, for Shelley, the inspiration of *Prometheus Unbound,* but it figured only incidentally in the structure of that work. For Byron and Stendhal, however, Rome is central: to canto 4 of *Childe Harold's Pilgrimage,* on the one hand and on the other to Stendhal's pair of great Italian travel books, *Rome, Naples, et Florence* (1817, 1826) and *Promenades dans Rome* (1830).[11]

But before we can turn to them we must pause to consider Madame de Staël's *Corinne,* published in 1807; for if Stendhal composes his works in the context of Byron's famous poem, Byron wrote his own work against the background of *Corinne.* And the background of de Staël's novel is her exile from France, her struggle against Napoleon, and her central position among the expatriate French ideologues. All this combined to make her perhaps the single most important European liberal of the period, the point of focus for a ragged and disparate band of angels.

IV

In the first book of *Corinne* the novel's heroine conducts Lord Nelvil on a tour of the Capitol in Rome. This is his first view of "the vestiges of ancient Rome" and it inspires him to the following meditations:

> The reading of history, and the reflections to which it gives rise, operate less forcibly on our minds, than these stones in disorder, than these ruins

interspersed with new habitations. . . . Without a doubt we are annoyed by all
the modern buildings, which interfere with the ancient ruins. . . . Everything
is common, everything is prosaic in the exterior of most of our European
cities, and Rome more than any other presents the mournful appearance of
misery and degradation; but all at once, a broken column, a half-destroyed
basrelief, stones united by the indestructible means of the ancient architects, remind us, that there is in man an eternal power, a spark of divinity,
and that we must not omit to excite it in ourselves, and to re-animate it in
others. [12]

The conceptual basis of this passage is very close to the ideas we have
already seen in Goethe's *Roman Elegies,* but the tone is entirely different. That De Staël's awareness of Winckelmann is no less acute
than Goethe's is apparent throughout the novel—as we see, for example, at the end of Nelvil's and Corinne's tour of the Capitol. "In
Rome," Nelvil observes, "there are many distinguished men whose
sole occupation is to discover a new connection between history and
the ruins." He praises the "animating" powers of this scholarly
activity: "We might say, that we gave a second life to all that we discovered, and that the past re-appeared from under the dust where it
had been buried" (p. 212). Though Nelvil here invokes the theme of
rebirth through a historical consciousness, his remarks betray a divergence from Goethe's thought, which helps to explain the melancholy
nostalgia of De Staël's novel. In this book, the greatness of the past
does not live again in the present, does not appear incarnate in the
novel and its characters. Corinne is not the ancient Tanagran poetess
redivivus; she possesses that name as a memorial to one splendid but
scarcely remembered "spark of divinity" from the past. Corinne's
function—her novel's function—is to reanimate that spark in others,
which is to say that her life's purpose is oriented toward the past and
the future. The present—and we must remember that the action of
the novel is set between the years 1794 and 1807—is seen as a time
of darkness and loss, a time when the spark of divinity is cherished
for a new birth of freedom that is to come. The novel's promise falls
not to Nelvil or to Corinne, whose love is star-crossed, but to Nelvil's

daughter, born of another woman but, at the novel's conclusion, educated by Corinne.

Corinne is a very brainy book (possibly too brainy, but quite befitting so resolute an intellectual as De Staël). Indeed, it is an allegory, a part at least of which we now easily decode. The heroine is Italy epitomized as the imaginative spirit of Rome, and she focuses the attention of the two chief male figures in the book, Lord Nelvil (a Scotsman who stands for Britain) and the Count D'Erfeuil (who represents the interests of France). A fervent admirer of British political institutions and democracy, De Staël presents Nelvil as Corinne's natural mate and lover; D'Erfeuil is, beside Nelvil, too self-centered, too deficient in moral seriousness, to be worthy of Corinne. In the end, neither man will enjoy or be truly worthy of Corinne's love, and the promise of civilized life that she holds out will remain unrealized.

Like Chateaubriand, De Staël saw the historical promise embodied in the French revolution collapse in the actual historical events that that revolution unfolded. Chateaubriand's reaction against Napoleon was to the right and out of time, a not untypical Romantic move into religion and the ultramontane. For her part, De Staël refused the illusory promises of a Napoleonic present in favor of a future hope, when the historical ideal of the revolution would achieve the actuality it could not live without.

The liberal, humanist future embodied in De Staël's picture of Rome in the European context of 1807 carries over to Byron's treatment of Rome in 1817 and 1818. Byron's Roman meditations culminate the fourth canto of *Childe Harold* (stanzas 78–175), and De Staël's book guides much of Byron's thought. Central to both texts is the conviction that Rome's is a tragic history of lost promises and betrayed greatness, so that in her melancholy precincts we too, contemporary sufferers, "may be consoled even for the sorrows of the heart" (p. 86). This theme—along with the related one of the revivifying power of art—dominates Corinne's famous improvised poem in book 1, chapter 3, the "Extempore Effusion of Corinne in the Capitol." Byron's Roman stanzas are written in conscious recollection of this text, as we can see even in the opening passage of Byron's Roman stanzas:

> Oh Rome! my country! city of the soul!
>   The orphans of the heart must turn to thee,
> Lone mother of dead empires! and controul
>   In their shut breasts their petty misery.
> What are our woes and sufferance?
>
>   (stanza 78)

In following this theme, however, Byron necessarily introduces a profound mutation of its form. De Staël's Rome provides the sorrowful and melancholy soul, such as Lord Nelvil's, with a model of suffering that should lead him to see that his own happiness depends upon the depth of his love and commitment to Corinne and to Rome (who are the psychological and the political forms of a single ideal). Rome and Corinne, for De Staël, have an objective existence toward which one can move. In Byron's poem, however, Rome is a private and interiorized locale: "*my* country," Byron calls the great city, a metropolis of "the soul." Like everything else in Byron's poem, Rome is an expression and extension of himself, a model that Byron receives from De Staël only to appropriate in a gesture of Romantic, even Napoleonic, imperialism. Byron ridicules the "petty misery" of the ordinary person, but he does not enter Rome to discover that his own miseries are of this sort. On the contrary, to his initial, ambiguous question—"What are our woes and sufferance?"—Byron will eventually answer, at least for himself, that they are so great, so terrible, so barely to be borne, that the history of Rome becomes an emblem of his heart.

In this respect Byron has returned to the stylistic posture that we observed initially in Goethe. The future perfect tense, which dominates and gives such a sentimental nobility (if the oxymoron be permitted) to De Staël's novel, appears in Byron's poem as it does in Goethe's elegies, merely to establish a limitless range of experience, a something evermore to be. Goethe and Byron both establish their works at the outset of a historical cycle whose end they cannot foresee; but whereas Goethe's is a cycle of new and exuberant life, Byron's is a cycle of high-energy trials and suffering. And, unlike De Staël, what Byron anticipates for the future is not the eventual realization of a civilized and human way of life, it is a perpetuity of energetic struggle: "Then let the winds howl on! their harmony / Shall henceforth be my music" (stanza 106).

Like Goethe, then, Byron comes to incarnate in himself an idea of Rome, which—to adapt a line from Wordsworth—"having been must ever be." But the mode of both his Romanticism and his Romanism is tragic and desperate rather than comic and hopeful because—unlike Goethe's—the history he has inherited includes the crucial years of 1789–1817, when western civilization suffered what he brilliantly called "man's worst, his second fall." A promise given twice and lost twice means for Byron a history in which the promise will never fail to be given and will never succeed in being realized. Byron believes in what De Staël calls "the long dream" of the civilized imagination (p. 88), but it is a faith bereft of any correspondent hope; "A faith," in short, "whose martyrs are the broken heart" (stanza 121).

V

With Stendhal the Romantic morphology of Rome achieves a final, ironic shift. Byron's work is Stendhal's immediate precursor, but Stendhal is a Byron with no faith at all in the political ideal of intellectuals like De Staël. Again and again Stendhal heaps ridicule on "the North" and its "metaphysical" predispositions. "The South," and preeminently Italy, guides its life by feeling and passion rather than by brain and superego. It is a Tom Wolfe of Restoration France who declares: "I almost think that one can say that the North feels only by thinking: to such people one must speak of sculpture only by borrowing the forms of philosophy." As far as Stendhal is concerned, Byron's admiration for the intellectual idealist De Staël is thoroughly misguided and Stendhal can think of nothing truer (or more devastating) to say of his French compatriots than this: "to bring the general public in France to a feeling for the arts it would be necessary to give to language the poetic bombast of Madame de Staël's *Corinne*."[13] So much for De Staël's sentimental brainstorming along with its correspondent breeze, that peculiarly French form of sublimation called the life of the mind.

Like Byron, Stendhal transforms Italy into a geopolitical myth through which he can criticize the deficiencies of contemporary Europe, on the one hand, and intimate more generous and vital forms of human civilization on the other. Moreover, he too associates different Italian cities with variant specific forms of a central Italian ideal. The two most important books in which Stendhal represents his idea of Rome are, as I have already noted, his *Promenades* and *Rome, Naples, and Florence.* The latter is a drastic reworking of a text he had published earlier as *Rome, Naples, et Florence en 1817* and in which he first presented his theory of Italy, as it were. The 1817 book is a thinly veiled *cri de coeur* over what he saw as the tragedy of the restoration of the thrones following Waterloo and the Congress of Vienna. Stendhal journeys to Italy in 1817 as to the shrine of a lost ideal embodied in Napoleon. This is the ideal of the energetic, spontaneous, and passionate life.

We shall find it useful to keep in mind the 1817 text of *Rome, Naples, and Florence* because it is so different from the 1826 text that they illuminate each other brilliantly. For my present purpose the 1826 version is the important one, since that book not only elaborates the theory of Italy set forth in the early work, it proposes as well—something not possible in the 1817 text—what has been aptly called "a hope for the future as well as a message of solidarity addressed to the victims of police repression."[14]

The book's title is as misleading as its travelogue form. Stendhal organizes his book as a traveler's journal for 1816–17, but of course the series of entries correspond in no way to any journey Stendhal actually took. Furthermore, the itinerary does not move Rome/ Naples/Florence, nor are Naples and Florence nearly so important in the book as Milan. Stendhal's travelogue begins in Milan, the city that, for him, most perfectly exhibits his theory of Italian spontaneity. It ends—or rather, it culminates—in Rome, the city where the promise of the future is most appropriately located. Indeed, the most significant formal change made between the texts of 1817 and 1826 involves the reconstitution of Stendhal's view of Rome, which also involves, necessarily, a reconstitution of his view of himself. In the 1817 text Rome is Stendhal's initial Italian subject, and as such she is made to illustrate the peculiarly degraded condition into which Italy—and with her, all of Europe—has fallen. In 1826, on the other hand, the travelogue reaches its climax and conclusion in Rome, just as Byron's pilgrimage had done earlier.

Both versions of Stendhal's work are as personally constructed as Byron's poem had been, but the 1826 work has these additional affiliations with Byron's poem: it too associates a European renascence with an Italian *risorgimento,* it too presents Rome as the key to Italy's future promise, and—most important of all—it relates these political changes to a renovation that takes place within the author himself. In Byron this is largely a psychological renovation, whereas in Stendhal it involves so drastic a shift in his political opinions that his entire character and fundamental self-conception are altered as well.

This change begins, according to the narrative of 1826, in the three hours that Stendhal spends in Rome on 6 February [1817] as he journeys from Florence to Naples. His initial impression of the city is not at all favorable, and when his progress is interrupted by a military procession honoring the appointment of the Minister of War to "the dignity of Archbishop," Stendhal's liberal, republican, and anticlerical attitude erupts into a short prose invective. But as he is leaving the city via the Campagna, the ancient ruins induce in him a profound sense of awe, which leaves him "all on edge" and forces him to reflect seriously upon some of his most cherished ideas. He suddenly realizes that his liberalism, his republicanism, and even his anticlericalism are all compromised by other, conflicting tendencies: "aristocratic leanings" and "a certain predilection for . . . the Christian Establishment." In fact, Stendhal's burst of contempt was a piece of self-delusion generated by his near-sighted view of Rome's present condition. The truth is that Rome is as much his dream and ideal as it was the dream of Napoleon.

> And yet, in spite of so many grievances, my heart still sides with Rome. . . .
> [I]n every page of history, I behold the deeds and see the life of Rome; and
> what the eye cannot see, the heart cannot love. Thus do I account to myself

for my obsession with those vestiges of Roman grandeur, those ruins, those inscriptions. Nor is this the limit of my weakness: for I even detect in certain churches of remote antiquity the pale reflection of still older pagan temples. Christianity, triumphant at the last after so many years of persecution, would fall with implacable rage upon a shrine of Jupiter, and rend it stone from stone; yet hard beside the old foundations, there would arise a new Church of St. Paul. (P. 346)

Here Stendhal observes the scene with an eye schooled by Winckelmann, in a prose that recalls the passage from *Corinne* quoted above, and in a frame of mind exactly analogous to Byron's in the famous Colosseum stanzas (canto 4, stanzas 138–47), when he is forced to reconsider his call for revenge against the bloody tyrants of Imperial Rome.

In the final pages of his book Stendhal accepts the contradictions of Rome. From the first, Stendhal's Romanticism had been tied up with his irony, just as Byron's Romanticism reached its culmination and apotheosis in irony. But Stendhal moves past the final form of Byronic and his own earlier Romanticism by reducing the size and pretensions of his own most cherished illusion, the ideal of Romantic irony. This event comes at the end of his book when Romantic irony is revealed in its true significance and its purest form. Stendhal's entry for 10 October is an enthusiastic report of an "evening spent in the company of the marionettes of the *Palazzo Fiano*"; as such, it is also a literal representation of the importance, as well as the triviality, of his Romantic irony—indeed, of the importance of that triviality.

The very fact that he could produce such a narrative is significant, for in Stendhal's initial, contemptuous remarks about Rome (journal entry for 6 February) he had singled out "the wooden limbed marionettes" (p. 343) of Rome as an especially notable example of the debased condition of the city and its culture. Such remarks were, of course, made out of ignorance and self-satisfied prejudice. Stendhal's encounter with Rome and the Romans has cleared his mind of some of its worst cant, so that now, at the conclusion of his trip, he can not only appreciate the puppet theatre of Rome, he can understand its cultural and political significance.

I doubt whether there be any race in Europe with a greater fondness for the bite and ingenuity of satire than the worthy citizens of Rome; so acute and subtle are their minds, that they will pounce with eager delight even upon the remotest of allusions. The element which raises the level of their happiness so infinitely far above that which prevails, say, in London, is their acquaintance with *despair*. Accustomed now for three whole centuries to regard the evils which it endures as inevitable and eternal, the Roman *bourgeoisie* feels no desire to pour forth the seething rage within its heart against the Minister; it has no wish to bring about his death; it knows full well that *this* particular incarnation of authority will merely be replaced by another, not a whit less evil-minded. Consequently, what the people of Rome desire above all else is to show their strong contempt for the powers that control their destiny, and to laugh at their expense; hence the dialogues between *Pasquino* and *Marforio*. . . . [I]n Rome, the censorship is more meticulous than in Paris, [so that] comedy in the live theatre is nothing but a string of unspeakable platitudes. True laughter has sought refuge among the marionettes. (Pp. 472-73)

The puppet theatre of Rome produces its satiric political allegories in so miniaturized and trivial a form that its work escapes the censor's power. Furthermore, the puppet theatre is a model of artistic integrity. The chief target of its satire is the "oligarchic Court . . . [where] power tends to accumulate in the hands of old age" (p. 474). Nevertheless, the miniaturized form in which the satire is delivered tells an equally profound truth about the subversive elements of Roman culture in 1826. As Stendhal observes, this is a comedy born of despair.

For all its limits, however, this Roman culture seems to Stendhal, in the larger European context, one of the few places where one can still find a society which prizes truth and exhibits vitality and energy. Stendhal's myth of Italy and Rome is produced in relation to his contempt for the convention-bound and hypocritical societies of France, England, and Germany in 1826.

The imaginary travelogue that Stendhal published in 1826 would be succeeded three years later by an equally extraordinary book, the *Promenades dans Rome* (published in two volumes). This work appears to be the diary of a visit to Rome undertaken between August 1827 and April 1829. In fact, it was written in a hotel room in Paris in 1828 to 1829 partly from Beyle's recollections (his last visit to Rome was in 1824), but largely from books and notes supplied to him.[15] The *Promenades* represents itself as an on-the-spot report of immediate experiences and spontaneous reactions; it is, in reality, an imaginary voyage to a Rome constructed in Stendhal's brain out of a heterogeneous collection of second-hand materials.

What is especially interesting about the Rome of Stendhal's *Promenades* is the manner in which he has incorporated, and finally transformed, the earlier Romantic imaginations of the city—including his own earlier presentation set forth in 1826. The *Promenades* resumes the images, attitudes, and forms we have already seen, but with the heroic element definitively removed. The contrast with his book of 1826 is especially notable. There, his final eulogium of the Roman character included the following prophetic declaration:

> Do but grant him [the Roman citizen] a Napoleon for the space of twenty years, and you will see him rise, beyond question, to be the foremost race in Europe. (P. 472)

In 1829, however, Stendhal takes a much more problematic view of the matter. When he discusses the disappearance of banditry in the papal states, he not only associates the phenomenon with a general decline in the level of Italian "energy," he connects this deplorable loss of the Italian national character with the emergence of Napoleon as a force in Italian culture (pp. 282–83, 287). By a supreme sort of paradox, Stendhal's Romantic model of the energetic hero becomes the instrument that is destroying his Romantic model of the energetic society, the society defined by erotic love, an appreciation of the fine arts, and fierce independence:

> The cannon of the bridge of Lodi (May, 1796) began the awakening of Italy. Generous souls were able to forget love and the fine arts; something newer was offered to their imaginations.
>
> I repeat: in 1829 there are no more organized bandits between Rome and Naples; they have entirely disappeared. (P. 283)

But this new thing offered to the imagination of the generous soul would itself be taken away, from Stendhal as well as from Italy, and in the remaining void would appear the volatile and ironic consciousness that we associate with Stendhal and that he associated with Rome.

Stendhal's Rome, then, locates the same kind of nostalgia epitomized in Chateaubriand, except that Stendhal's presentation is not itself nostalgic. Stendhal also exhibits the despair that Byron made immortal, as well as the future perfect promise defined by De Staël; but Stendhal's is a despair without a sense of desperation, and a hope for the future that need not take itself seriously. He is, in fact, precisely like those he represents at the Roman puppet theatre: a man who sees the evils of his society as "inevitable and eternal," and who responds to his situation with irony and contempt. But he is also a man with "no wish to bring about" practical changes, because he has no belief that change can mean anything but superficial alteration. For Stendhal, change is repetition in disguise.

VI

Goethe wished to experience a spiritual rebirth at Rome, a change that would transform his immediate historical life into a deathless form correspondent to the Eternal City he identified with. The same pursuit dominates the Romanism of Chateaubriand, De Staël, and Byron, as we have seen, and in Stendhal it achieves its ironic conclusion. When Alberto Moravia, himself a Roman, praises Stendhal's work for its modernity, he helps to explain the significance of Stendhal's attitude toward Rome:

> [N]o more than in Stendhal's time has novelty in modern Rome succeeded in transforming, or making an impression on, or in any way modifying, the unalterable core of Roman "indifference." As in 1827, so today, everything that is done and happens in Rome, happens and is done without any real participation on the part of the people. . . . With the people of Rome, participation is conditioned and restricted by a deep, yet at the same time discouraging (at least as regards political effects), sense of eternity; hence the all-embracing unreality of life in Rome, which is like a magnificent stage for performing tragedy, comedy, farce, or plain drama, without it making any difference.[16]

Here is a revelation of the "eternity" of the Eternal City, which will not be found in Goethe or the Romantic writers we have considered. Here is an "eternity" generated when social life is consciously pursued and maintained under retrograde and inveterate circumstances. Change takes place but makes no difference in Stendhalian Rome; and that famous Roman "energy" that Stendhal celebrates is actually, Moravia says, "a sort of irritation or exasperation" (p. 162), that erupts like heat lightning in an oppressive climate.

Moravia will not implicate Stendhal in the reactionary world he represented: "It was the Italy he described with so much enjoyment that was reactionary, not the man who described it" (p. 163). This is generous, but misleading. Stendhal's Rome is as much a project of his own imagination as it is a fictional model or representation of an actual human world. The contradictions that appear in Stendhal's representation of the Rome he knew reflect the Roman culture of the period as well as Stendhal's own ideological contradictions; they do so, however, because the subject of Stendhal's books is neither of these particular sets of contradictions, but the meaning—the significance—of their nexus. Stendhal the writer was a political liberal with a host of imbedded reactionary commitments; Rome, on the other hand, was a center of ultramontane and conservative power, which exhibited as well various contrary impulses and ideologies. The works that Stendhal produced are important because they opened an engagement between these two worlds, and because, in doing so, they illuminated each of these worlds in a critical way, as well as the larger European world that they shared.

With Stendhal the Romantic experience of Rome, as well as the Romantic understanding of itself through that experience, achieves its most profound level; which is to say that Romanticism here encounters and acknowledges the limits of its own ideology. Not even the Byron of *Childe Harold,* canto 4, was able to drive through his Romantic agony to this kind of objectivity and cool self-knowledge. What we distinguish here are the Romantic *experience* of itself and the Romantic *understanding* of itself. Byron's is perhaps the supreme example of Romantic experience in a Roman mode, though one might also recall Shelley's *Adonais,* whose desperate heart breaks in a Rome symbolized by the grave of Keats. At Rome Shelley and Byron lament that their highest hopes have departed from all things here. In this gesture they demonstrate a refusal to part with their most cherished forms of Romantic illusion and displacement.

With Stendhal it is different, which is why Stendhal, like Heine, should be so important to later scholars and critics of Romanticism. For in Stendhal—and preeminently in Stendhal's experience of Rome—the Romantic movement has summed itself up: has weighed itself in the balance of love and desire, and has found itself, as it had found all other things, finally, wanting.

NOTES

1. *Memorials of a Tour in Italy, 1837,* published in 1842.

2. For Cardinal Albani's circle, see Lesley Lewis, *Connoisseurs and Secret Agents in Eighteenth-Century Rome* (London: Chatto and Windus, 1961).

3. From *Voyages et Mélanges Littéraires,* in *Oeuvres Complètes,* 12 vols. (Paris: Garnier Frères, 1872), 9:253–54 (hereafter cited as *Oeuvres*); see also the letter to A. M. de Fontanes, dated "Rome le 10 janvier 1804" (*Oeuvres,* 9:269–85); and *Les Martyrs,* bks. 4, 5.

4. *Oeuvres,* 9:253–54.

5. See also the prose fragment by Shelley commonly known as "The Colosseum."

6. J. W. von Goethe, *Italian Journey (1786-1788),* trans. W. H. Auden and E. Mayer (New York: Pantheon Books, 1968), p. 136.

7. *Storia della arti del desegno presso gli Antichi . . . ,* ed. C. Fea (Rome: Dalle Stamperia Pagliarini, 1783–84).

8. *J. W. von Goethe's Roman Elegies and Venetian Epigrams,* trans. L. R. Lind (Lawrence: University of Kansas Press, 1974).

9. See the discussion by Lind in ibid., pp. 12–15, 219–22.

10. Quoted in André Maurois, *Chateaubriand,* trans. Vera Fraser (New York: Blue Ribbon Books, 1940), p. 121.

11. The 1817 and 1826 versions are radically different; for 1817, not yet translated into English, see *Rome, Naples, et Florence,* ed. Victor del Litto (Lausanne: Editions Rencontre, 1961); for 1826, see *Rome, Naples, and Florence, by Stendhal,* trans. Richard N. Coe (London: John Calder, 1959); for the *Promenades,* see *A Roman Journal, by Stendhal,* ed. and trans. Haakon Chevalier (New York: Onion Press, 1957).

12. Madame de Staël, *Corinne,* 3 vols. (London, 1807), 1:86–87.

13. Stendhal, *Rome, Naples, and Florence* (1826), p. 187.

14. *Rome, Naples, et Florence* (1817), p. 16.

15. See Chevalier's Introduction to *A Roman Journal*, pp. XIX-XX.

16. Alberto Moravia, "Roman Walks," in *Man as an End*, trans. Bernard Wall (New York: Farrar, Straus and Giroux, 1966), p. 161.

William L. Vance

The Colosseum:
American Uses of
an Imperial Image

Near the end of *The Portrait of a Lady* (1881), Henry James makes the Colosseum the object of an excursion intended to amuse Isabel Archer's sister-in-law, the Countess Gemini. The countess, James tells us, "had not the historic sense, though she had in some directions the anecdotic," and when she visited antiquities "her preference was to sit in the carriage and exclaim that everything was most interesting." On this occasion, however, her niece, Pansy Osmond, persuades her to enter the monument and "to climb to the upper tiers." Isabel remains below, and James sketches a portrait of Isabel alone in the Colosseum. In doing so, he associates his heroine with the conventional Romantic image of the Colosseum that derives from Goethe, Mme. de Staël, Byron, and Stendhal:

> She had often ascended to those desolate ledges from which the Roman crowd used to bellow applause and where now the wild-flowers (when they are allowed) bloom in the deep crevices; and today she felt weary and disposed to sit in the despoiled arena. . . . The great enclosure was half in shadow; the western sun brought out the pale red tone of the great blocks of travertine—the latent colour that is the only living element in the immense ruin. Here and there wandered a peasant or a tourist, looking up at the far skyline where, in the clear stillness, a multitude of swallows kept circling and plunging.[1]

This is one of many juxtapositions in nineteenth-century American literature and painting of a representative American character and a classical architectural image, of which the Colosseum is by far the most commonly chosen. The Colosseum had by this time a complex accumulation of meanings in European architectural history, literature, art, and folklore.[2] The American writers and painters naturally exploited the traditional understandings of the Colosseum's significance, but they also sometimes raised—more sharply than did their

European predecessors and contemporaries—questions of the meanings of the Colosseum for a modern, Christian, and democratic culture. James's image of the once willful Isabel Archer sitting alone in the ancient arena is the last in a series of four passages that together chart her changing relation to classical Rome. It may serve as a preliminary indication of how, in an extended context, the Colosseum as backdrop may be used to define character and in turn be itself redefined. The great amphitheater contributes to the general symbolic classical setting, while certain of its own particular attributes receive metaphorical stress.

The first two of James's passages show Isabel long before her disastrous marriage to Gilbert Osmond: "She had an imagination that kindled at the mention of great deeds," James says of her first acquaintance with Rome; and it responded readily to "the terrible human past." But it required something "altogether contemporary" to "give it wings." James then shows Isabel in the Forum, where even her keen interest in the "rugged relics" does not keep her mind from wandering soon to "regions and objects charged with a more active appeal"—namely, Isabel Archer's future: it is over that "nearer and richer field" that her imagination "hovered in slow circles." Now, at the end, in the Colosseum, while the swallows circle and plunge above her, she sits in the despoiled arena. The displacement of imagery of flight by imagery of ruin measures the alteration in Isabel's vision of her own reality. In the preceding chapter, James had shown her in the Campagna and had generalized that "in a world of ruins the ruin of her happiness seemed a less unnatural catastrophe":

> She rested her weariness upon things that had crumbled for centuries and yet still were upright; she dropped her secret sadness into the silence of lonely places, where its very modern quality detached itself and grew objective, so that as she sat in the sun-warmed angle on a winter's day, or stood in a mouldy church to which no one came, she could almost smile at it and think of its smallness. Small it was, in the large Roman record, and her haunting sense of the continuity of the human lot easily carried her from the less to the greater.

In these passages James establishes with characteristic tact Isabel's changed understanding of the less and the greater, and the diminishment of her egoism only increases our regard for her. The destiny of a contemporary American is linked to the grand historical images without the cynicism or satire of the mock-heroic tradition, without the naively self-aggrandizing equations of the neoclassicists, and without the self-pity and rage of Byronic Romanticism, all of which we find in other American instances. The image of the Colosseum in James's sequence from Forum to Campagna is the most sharply expressive of "the terrible human past," and several different aspects of the structure's traditional meanings are evoked: above all, its monumentality and beauty as architecture; secondly, the memory of it as a place of barbaric entertainment (the crowd bellowing applause)—a negative image, which has, however, its positive side, since the same entertainment was the occasion for heroic trials of skill and courage, and also afforded so many glorious martyrdoms; and finally —in sharp distinction from the preceding—its nineteenth-century character as a magnificent but melancholy imperial ruin covered with flowers, visited by wandering peasants, pilgrims, and tourists. James's use of the Colosseum in its relation to both present image and historical associations to his character's personal experience and knowledge is unobtrusively yet profoundly expressive. The same cannot be said of all the selective collocations of the Colosseum's meanings in American art and literature. Yet many others, both individually and cumulatively, have substantial significance and are of notable diversity.

THE COLOSSEUM AS LANDSCAPE

Nineteenth-century paintings of the Colosseum alone (that is, without significant figures) are a version of landscape in obvious contrast to the close architectural studies made in the Renaissance, but also differing from the precise yet visionary works of Piranesi in which Nature is not the essence but the embellishment. The Colosseum had first appeared capriciously as a part of the natural landscape in the idyllic world of Claude Lorrain (d. 1682), where it was as likely to appear by the seashore as in its proper place at the end of the "Cow

Pasture" (the Campo Vaccino, the ancient Roman Forum).[3] Nine-teenth-century painters do not use the image with such ahistorical freedom. Their works are closer to the eighteenth-century souvenir paintings of Bellotto and Panini, picturesque but relatively literal. Yet the best of the later artists brought to the Colosseum their own particular genius (or at least point-of-view). With Turner and Corot, for example, one perceives the results in the first instance as paintings *by* Turner and Corot rather than as paintings *of* the Colosseum, some-thing that cannot be said of their predecessors.

Of the many American artists, mostly forgotten, who painted landscape views of the Colosseum, Thomas Cole is the most impor-tant. In Cole, too, the informing idea—his concept—matters more than the object, but the concept is more thematic than formal, and his theme is common to his paintings of the Campagna as well: the transmutation of man-made objects by Time and Nature. By virtue of becoming a ruin, a building is improved: it becomes a part of Na-ture. Cole considered the Colosseum to be the most affecting of the "wondrous things" he had seen in Rome, and he made sketches of its interior,[4] where the architectural elements are most thoroughly eroded. The verbal description in his notebook of 1832[5] opens with the same perspective adopted in the small canvas probably painted in the same year (fig. 1):

> It is stupendous, yet beautiful in its destruction. From the broad arena within, it rises around you, arch above arch, broken and desolate, and mantled in many parts with the laurustinus, the acanthus, and numerous other plants and flowers, exquisite both for their color and fragrance. It looks more like a work of nature than of man; for the regularity of art is lost, in a great mea-sure, in dilapidation, and the luxuriant herbage, clinging to its ruins as if to "mouth its distress," completes the illusion. Crag rises over crag, green and breezy summits mount into the sky.

"To walk beneath its crumbling walls," he concludes, is "to lapse into sad, though not unpleasing meditation." Several aspects of the painting itself encourage this attitude: the sense of an enclosed space is created by the curving wall that stretches from edge to edge; the lower broken buttresses are in deep shadow while the jagged ridge of the highest stones catch the light; the conspicuousness of the Stations

FIG. 1. Thomas Cole, *The Coliseum, Rome.* ca. 1832. Oil on canvas. 10 1/8 x 18 3/8 in. Courtesy of Albany Institute of History and Art.

of the Cross, and the presence of the cross itself, relate the scene to those picturesque paintings of enclosed mountain spaces in which religious shrines define the proper feeling for Nature itself. In its organization the painting is close to one of Piranesi's views, but the execution in oil blurs the outline and details that Piranesi stressed. Green vegetation sprouts along the crown of the earth-colored slopes.

Coles's notebook description in a second paragraph goes where painting finally cannot follow. It shifts to a view from a high terrace from which by moonlight the Colosseum is metamorphosed into Vesuvius, that other favorite Romantic object of contemplation. Gazing into the "abyss," Cole finds that the "mighty spectacle, mysterious and dark," becomes "more like some awful dream than an earthly reality,—a vision of the valley and shadow of death, rather than the substantial work of man." The volcanic metaphor briefly suggests the "terrible fires" that once "blazed forth with desolating power" in this "crater of human passions"—an association to which Gérôme's historicism would later give literal embodiment. Here it serves chiefly to heighten by contrast the quietude of the present, where a union of Nature and religious feeling is evident in the harmony of the only sounds—warbling birds and chanting monks.

Others too saw the Colosseum, if not as Vesuvius, as essentially a mountain. Henry James, in "A Roman Holiday" (1873), even says that "the roughly mountainous quality of the great ruin is its chief interest."[6] Years earlier (1845) the young Bayard Taylor, having just descended from the Alps and Apennines with knapsack on his back— long before he provided America with its standard translation of Goethe's *Faust*—was already sufficiently under Goethe's influence to race to the Colosseum on his first night in Rome to see it by moonlight, only to discover that there was no moon. Taylor settled for a sunset view, also recommended by Goethe, and wrote: "A majesty like that of nature clothes this wonderful edifice. Walls rise above walls and arches above arches from every side of the grand arena like a sweep of craggy, pinnacled mountains around an oval lake."[7]

It is easier to appreciate the early nineteenth-century image of the Colosseum as a work of Nature if we recall that one of the touristic tragedies of the late nineteenth century occurred when the archeologists of the New Italy after 1870 thoroughly carried out what the French under Napoleon had but feebly begun in 1812, the "debushing" or one might well say deflowering of the Colosseum—the ruin of a ruin. The American sculptor William Wetmore Story, through many an edition of his invaluable *Roba di Roma,* had told how practically alone among ancient ruins the Colosseum stood ("despite the assault of time and the work of barbarians, it still stands, noble and beautiful in its decay—yes, more beautiful than ever"), and had lovingly described how when the sunset transfigures the travertine to "brown and massive gold," "the quivering stalks and weeds seem on fire; the flowers drink in a glory of color, and show like gems against the rough crust of their setting." His thirteenth edition, however, adds a long, sour footnote: "The arena, once so peaceful and smoothed over with low grass, has been excavated to exhibit the foundations. . . . [A]ll the charm of the place has been destroyed." Now you may, "if that satisfies you, gaze down into ugly pits and trenches."[8]

The preference for the Colosseum as a "natural" ruin was explicitly stated by many, but by no one more forcefully than George Hillard, author of the very popular guidebook *Six Months in Italy.* After self-righteously, inconsistently, and ungratefully attacking the "rapacity" and "cupidity" of wealthy nobles and cardinals for ruining the Colosseum, he expressed the hope that the current pope's efforts at restoration "may not be carried so far as to impair the peculiar and unique character of the edifice." For if "as a building the Colosseum was open to criticism, as a ruin it is perfect. The work of decay has stopped short at the exact point required by taste and sentiment." In short, the tiresomely classical has been transformed into Nature's superior Gothic: "formal curves and perpendicular lines" replaced by "interruptions and unexpected turns which are essential elements of the picturesque":

> When a building is abandoned to decay, it is given over to the dominion of Nature, whose works are never uniform. . . . Now that it is a vast ruin, it has all the variety of form and outline which we admire in a Gothic cathedral.

Hillard loved the Colosseum as passionately as any Renaissance architect but for exactly the opposite reasons: it expresses no "rule and measure," no "contriving mind," no "hand of man." The original builders seem even to have been granted remarkable foresight in choosing travertine as the material, since it is "exactly fitted to the purposes of a great ruin."[9] These purposes are of course much higher, as we shall see, than the purposes the original designers had more immediately in mind.

THE HISTORICAL ARENA

At the opposite extreme from the perception of the Colosseum as a sublime mountain or as a Gothic cathedral was the later attempt to re-create it, visually and verbally, as it was at the time of the empire: to see it as the pristine and splendorous architectural ground for gladiators and martyrs with a vast audience of humanity—ranging from the imperial family to slaves—united by sensational experience. This romantic historicism (executed with the detail of specious realism) reached its climax in the academic painting of Gérôme. His celebrated *Ave Caesar, Morituri te Salutant* (1859; Yale University Art Gallery) depicts a high moment in the gladiatorial games where the emphasis is on character rather than physical violence. Story, in *Roba di Roma,* uses a lengthy description of Gérôme's painting as the point of departure for his own prose evocation of the activities within the Colosseum at the height of empire. It is only one of the many paintings by Gérôme that were bought by, and in several cases commissioned by, Americans; and through the photogravure reproductions of Gérôme's father-in-law, Goupil, they furnished America in the second half of the nineteenth century with its popular image of imperial Rome.[10] That image is equivocal. The Colosseum is in this painting enormously exaggerated, and the image of splendor provided by the building, with its unfurled velarium, and by the masses of spectators displayed in sunlight, is not diminished greatly by the evident brutality of the games, since the emphasis is on the heroism of the gladiators themselves in declaring and facing their mortality.

The point of view is that of someone *within* the arena, rather than
that of the spectator above. The historical realism Gérôme strove for
as the chief value of his paintings is even more evident in later works
such as *Pollice Verso* (1874; Phoenix Museum of Art), yet Gérôme
also saw the world he re-created as "barbaric, savage, and strange"; a
romantic conception he emphasized not only through the specialized
trappings of the gladiators, so bizarre to modern eyes, but also
through the exaggerated behavior of the crowd, in particular that of
the Vestal Virgins, about whom Victorians seem to have been extremely curious.[11] The young Henry James, who had criticized Gérôme for a "heartlessness" equal to that of Flaubert, nevertheless
responded enthusiastically to his *Chariot Race* (1876; George F.
Harding Museum, Chicago).[12] *The Christian Martyrs' Last Prayer*
(commissioned by Mr. Walters in 1863, finished in 1883; Walters Art
Gallery, Baltimore) supplied the most impressive image of steadfast
Christians facing lions and tigers, and may have been a source for the
novelist Francis Marion Crawford's pathetic depiction of martyrdom
in *Ave Roma Immortalis* (1898).[13]

Gérôme's productions being so satisfactory and so widely dis-
tributed, there was little need for an American artist in his field.
There were, of course, illustrations for such popular works as General
Lew Wallace's *Ben-Hur* (1880), whose events occur before the Colosseum was built but that includes a famous scene in a provincial arena
that belongs to the same genre. There also must have been backdrops
for such stage spectaculars as *The Gladiator* (1831), written by
Robert Montgomery Bird for the great Edwin Forrest, and one of the
actor's most popular productions.[14] But only one American painter
of some importance indulged in Gérôme's kind of unidealized historical re-creation. He was Edwin Howland Blashfield,[15] who began
his career in Paris painting directly under the influence of Gérôme
(and using his props), exhibiting at the Salon in the 1870s works
with titles such as *Roman Ladies: A Lesson in the Gladiator's School*
(1879) and *The Emperor Commodus, Dressed as Hercules, Leaves
the Amphitheater at the Head of the Gladiators* (1878) (fig. 2). Although Blashfield strives for Gérôme's archeological exactitude and
similarly heightens the sense of the arena's drama through sharp

FIG. 2. Edwin H. Blashfield, *The Emperor Commodus, Dressed as Hercules, Leaves the Amphitheater at the Head of the Gladiators.* 1878. Oil on canvas, 44 1/2 x 91 in. Courtesy of Hermitage Foundation, Norfolk, Virginia.

contrast in shadow and light, and by the use of deep perspective to convey the Colosseum's grandeur, viewed from the floor of the arena, his choice of specific subject differs significantly. There is no ambiguity arising from a sense of human fatality, endurance, martyrdom, or athletic skill, as in Gérôme. Departing even further from the neo-classical ethical idealism (typically centering on crises of the republic) that was central to the scenes of ancient Rome painted by Benjamin West and by Copley, Blashfield's emphasis is purely on the decadence of the empire, for which the spectacular architecture provides a congruently luxurious setting instead of a grandly ennobling theater. Blashfield could hardly have chosen a more disagreeable personality to place at the exact center of an enormous canvas than Commodus, half-mad son of the saintly Marcus Aurelius, who patterned himself after Caligula and Nero rather than after his father. His reign has been said to initiate the empire's decline, and he himself was called by a contemporary Greek historian, Dio Cassius, "a greater plague to the Romans than any pestilence or crime." Even as he exalted himself as Hercules reborn (complete with lionskin and club), his participation as a gladiator in the public arena was seen as proof of his depravity. The imperial name was degraded. The common people avoided his shows from shame and fear (members of the audience were sometimes victims of Hercules' rage).[16] This contribution to the image of the Colosseum by Blashfield, who was to become for a time the most successful painter of academic allegories of Law and Justice in American courthouses, was one of moral reprobation, which at the same time exploited a fascination for the historically alien and antithetical re-created in minute and vivid detail. His work in this respect is closer to Couture's *Les Romains de la Décadence* (1847; Louvre), which in spite of its explicit moralism owes its fame as much or more to the vulgar appeal of the sensationally depicted scene. James indirectly alludes to this painting when characterizing contemporary English society in *The Princess Casamassima* (1885): The half-American/half-Italian Christina Light, now married to Prince Casamassima, says to the half-English/half-French Hyacinth Robinson that English society is "a reproduction of the Roman world in its decadence, gouty, apoplectic, depraved, gorged and

clogged with wealth and spoils, selfishness and scepticism, and waiting for the onset of the barbarians."[17]

Questions about motive and interpretation that arise with Couture,
Gérôme, and Blashfield may be found much earlier in Thomas Cole's
Consummation, the central panel of his series, *The Course of Empire*
(1836; New York Historical Society). This depiction of a gorgeous
triumphal arrival at a port from which monumental architecture has
eliminated all natural contours is, of course, romantic fantasy rather
than historical realism. But here it is also impossible to tell whether
this luxurious world is being celebrated or deplored, whether, by implication, it should be the goal or must be the inevitable fate of
America, whether the entire series, which "progresses" from Savagery
to Desolation, is dispassionate historical myth or moral exemplum.[18]
By the end of the century the imperial potentialities of America were
much more fully realized. The "White City" of the World's Columbian
Exhibition in Chicago (1893) employed America's most prominent
designers in the creation of a setting whose central "Court of Honor"
was remarkably reminiscent of Cole's *Consummation.* The planned
ephemerality of Chicago's image of imperial pride, which consciously
echoed Roman design but was made of easily destructible materials,
only added to the irony and presumption of the analogy.[19] Within
the decade Charles Eliot Norton, who could not make up his mind
about the White City (he said that in spite of its incongruities and
vulgarities it "forbids despair"), was unequivocal about the "bastard
'imperialism,' . . . this turn toward barbarism" represented by the
"miserable war in the Philippines." But his word to his fellow citizens was still: *"Nil desperandum de republica."*[20]

Writers of course could not hope to re-create the visual scene in the
Colosseum as vividly as did the historical painters, and their vague
allusions to the Colosseum as architecture amount to little more than
verbal gaping. Their sense of the significance of what transpired
within it, however, can be very explicit, and runs the gamut from
exalted feeling to contemptuous satire. In between these extremes
are relatively neutral and factual descriptions such as those of Hillard
and Story. Guidebooks simply give the facts, with a few quotations

from Gibbon and Byron, while the popular romances and stage productions have it both ways: they combine self-righteous indignation with the thrill of vicariously witnessing the bestiality and suffering they deplore, while taking satisfaction in painless identification with steadfast martyrs or rebellious slaves. The pure (if not more admirable) extremes of unquestioning exultation on the one hand and outright debunking on the other are defined by Margaret Fuller and Mark Twain.

As Margaret Fuller journeyed toward that Rome that was her destination and was to provide her destiny, her anticipation was so great that the splendid ancient amphitheater at Arles was sufficient to evoke a rapture that the Colosseum itself could hardly later surpass: "Here for the first time I saw the great handwriting of the Romans in its proper medium of stone. . . . It looked as grand and solid as I expected, as if life in those days was thought worth the having, the enjoying, and the using." Blessedly released at last from the confinements of Concord and Boston, Fuller exults in a large sense of aggressive life that can include without criticism the "fierce excitement" of "fights of men and lions."[21]

While taking the opposite position, Mark Twain yet chose not to use the gladiatorial games and the persecutions of the Christians as evidence against the "damned human race" as he later used the cruelties of Christians themselves. In *The Innocents Abroad* (1869) the young Clemens can acknowledge that the Colosseum is sacred ground, but as an American he can only make it personal by imagining those who attended the ancient sports as Americans going to the opera or to the circus—to Mark Twain, essentially the same thing. After describing everyone from the "man of fashion with his private box" to the street boy in the gallery with his peanuts, Mark Twain claims to have found two items: a playbill and a review. The playbill ends with the promise of a "chaste and elegant GENERAL SLAUGHTER!" The review parodies American dramatic criticism in all its irrelevancy and sycophancy, with references to the audience and to the decor of the refurbished theater. The description of the performance is ambivalent as satire, since the incongruity between the reviewer's prissy standards and style and the brute action he is describing favorably may turn the balance against either the Americans or the Romans:

> When at last he fell a corpse, his aged mother ran screaming, with her hair disheveled and tears streaming from her eyes, and swooned away just as her hands were clutching at the railings of the arena. She was promptly removed by the police. Under the circumstances the woman's conduct was pardonable, perhaps, but we suggest that such exhibitions interfere with the decorum which should be preserved during the performances, and are highly improper in the presence of the Emperor.

The critic praises the star, "Marcus Marcellus Valerian (stage name— his real name is Smith)," and apologizes for departing from his usual practice of criticizing only the martyrs and the tigers, when he dares to suggest that Smith has one fault: "The pausing in the fight to bow when bouquets are thrown to him is in bad taste," a habit evidently picked up in the provinces and unsuitable to the metropolis. Finally, "The General Slaughter was rendered with a faithfulness to details which reflects the highest credit upon the late participants in it," and the entire performance sheds honor "upon the city that encourages and sustains such wholesome and instructive entertainments." "A matinée for the little folks is promised for this afternoon, on which occasion several martyrs will be eaten by the tigers."

Mark Twain was not really concerned about either the insipidity of Victorian American entertainments or the barbarities of imperial Rome. He was attacking rather the sentimentality and romantic conventions that had attached themselves to the Colosseum. At the end, he congratulates himself on having written about "the gladiators, the martyrs, and the lions, and yet . . . never once [using] the phrase 'butchered to make a Roman holiday.' I am the only free white man of mature age who has accomplished this since Byron originated the expression," he brags. The Colosseum and its bogus historical glamor have been leveled by American common sense.[22]

THE MEASURE OF MAN

For both Margaret Fuller and Mark Twain the Roman arenas provide the measure of man: for one there is an indication of his potential for fullness of life, for the other the universal fraudulence and triviality of his pursuits, his pleasures, and his myths. Historical analogies, biblical and classical, had been a part of American consciousness from the beginning, and the relation of the contemporary world to the classical world was for Americans, as representatives of the most progressive and democratic nation, even more problematic than it was for the French or the English or even the Germans. To the extent that America's westward expansion enhanced the possibilities of imperial power, and this notion superseded the ideal of the republic, it became even more so. Juxtaposition of images of the ancient world with those of contemporary life, which characterizes so much European and English art and literature from the Renaissance onward (to say nothing of Dante), is also a significant element in the cultural self-definition found in American art and literature.

John Adams, indulging in "a piece of Vanity" as he later called it, posed for Copley in London with a classical statue behind him at the very time when he was ransacking the history of ancient Rome for proofs in defense of the American constitutions that provided for a senate in which the *aristoi* would counterbalance the popular assembly, thus safeguarding each party from the avarice and ambition of the other.[23] But a different and more imperial American was seen in 1860 by Adams's great-grandson Henry (a member of the new nobility that John Adams had described as arising naturally in republics) when he placed himself self-consciously upon the steps of the Capitoline where Gibbon had first conceived the idea for the *Decline and Fall of the Roman Empire*. In his old age he recalled how "One looked idly enough at the Forum or at St. Peter's, but never forgot the look, and it never ceased reacting. . . . Rome was actual; it was England; it was going to be America." For Adams the powerful future he prophesied for America was not attractive, but that does not mean that there was anything to be said for the mediocre and secure present, either. "Rome dwarfs teachers," says Adams. "The greatest men of the age scarcely bore the test of posing with Rome for a background. Perhaps Garibaldi—possibly even Cavour—could have sat [Adams here quoted Gibbon] 'in the close of the evening, among the ruins of the Capitol.'" "Tacitus could do it; so could Michelangelo; and so, at a pinch, could Gibbon, though in a figure hardly heroic." But one "hardly saw Napoleon III there, or Palmerston, or Tennyson, or Longfellow."[24]

Yet, no matter what Adams was to think, American artists and writers (including Longfellow), like those of England and France and Germany, were frequently tempted to place themselves, their subjects, or their fictional characters against this backdrop of classical Rome, and chose more often than any other the most famous monument of imperial grandeur, the Colosseum. The consequences, from their point of view, were not always so discouraging as the cynical Adams assumed. This is partly because the Colosseum had other meanings than that of impermanent cultural fulfillment, which Adams assigned to Rome and specifically to the Capitol. (Rome was, he wrote, "above all the monument of the two great failures of Western Civilization," and the "eternal question" was "why?" had they failed. "Substitute the word America for the word Rome," he concluded, and the question becomes "personal.")[25] As we have seen, even in the brief passage in James's *The Portrait of a Lady,* several different aspects of the Colosseum are evoked as relevant to the figure of Isabel. As different artists stress or imply different associations, the image of the Colosseum is altered and with it the contemporary image.

The problem of interpreting the relationship rises in simplest and starkest form in portraits with the arena in the background, the sort to which Adams was referring.[26] The earliest appearance of the Colosseum in an American painting is in the double portrait by John Singleton Copley of Mr. and Mrs. Ralph Izard, painted in Rome in 1775 (fig. 3). It resembles the double portrait of Sir William and Lady Hamilton painted five years earlier in Naples by David Allan, in which Vesuvius fulfills the function of the Colosseum in the Copley.

Fig. 3. John Singleton Copley, *Mr. and Mrs. Ralph Izard*. ca. 1775. Oil on canvas. 69 x 88 1/2 in. Courtesy of Museum of Fine Arts, Boston.

An atmosphere of refined culture (the first Lady Hamilton plays the harpsichord for her relaxed but appreciative husband) prevails in both paintings. In Copley's portrait, the Colosseum itself is hardly more than a tiny place-sign in the center background, far beyond the grand loggia where the Izards inhabit anything but a world in ruin. Yet the sumptuous furnishings and artifacts clearly do not belong to the New World that Copley had just left behind, that simpler world where sufficient accessories had been found in peaches, pet squirrels, and teapots. But neither are the Izards in the "Old" World. They belong instead to a wholly imaginary classical Roman world, that is, to a timeless, unchipped, dustless, connoisseur's world of aristocratical neoclassicism, reminiscent of Winckelmann, but supplied with comfortable sofas. The Izards discuss the sketch of the statue that stands on the table beside them and is reflected in its polished surface; they are far from the contemporary musket-fire on the fields of Lexington and Concord that presaged the new republic on whose behalf Izard, a South Carolinian resident in England, was soon to make futile diplomatic overtures to the Grand Duke of Tuscany, and in whose first senate he was to sit. All this was in the future, but the portrait is consistent with the confident identification with the ancient world that characterized the nascent republic. Here the Colosseum itself appears to be merely a lovely soft element against the theatrically painted sky, the whole a purely artificial and therefore unthreatening backdrop. Copley locates the Izards within the frame in such a way that the great monument, hardly perceptible as a ruin, but near the center, radiates its rich cultural associations upon them. The Izards clearly do not make Isabel Archer's distinction between the personal less and the historical greater.[27]

Nearly a century later, George Healy—the Boston Irishman who had become to the court of Napoleon III what the American Benjamin West had been to the court of George III—the semi-official painter of European monarchy, and the first American to have his self-portrait requested by the Uffizi, jointly produced with two other American painters a work as aesthetically naïve as Healy was socially sophisticated.[28] (fig. 4) Naïveté is not what one would expect from this former student of Couture, and an occasional member of that

FIG. 4. G. P. A. Healy, Frederic Church, and Jervis McIntee, *Arch of Titus*. 1871. Oil on canvas. 73 1/2 x 49 in. Courtesy of The Newark Museum.

colony of American artists resident in Rome (who were, according to James—who seems to have had many candidates for the rôle—themselves the Romans of the Decadence).[29] The painting is sometimes called merely *The Arch of Titus* (1871), but the two stiff little dolls standing beneath the arch are Longfellow, the most respected representative of democratic culture, and his daughter Edith. No wonder Adams thought Longfellow should not risk posing before the ruins of Rome! Even now we feel he *ought* to have looked bigger in 1871. The two are caught in Victorian complacency staring straight into the camera; for the painting is in fact taken from a photograph preserved in the Archives of American Art, still bearing carefully drawn rulings to determine exact perspective and proportions (those most unfortunate proportions).[30] Also, Healy and his colleagues, Frederic Church and Jervis McIntee, have further confused the subject by introducing themselves into the right foreground, one of them sketching the Longfellows, the three of them together forming a pyramid that buttresses the right leg of the arch itself. Beyond and through the arch looms the Colosseum. One may doubt that this is conscious satire. It is rather a glorified and naïve equivalent in oil of the tourist photograph that says, "We were there!" But the naïveté itself is significant.

One wonders, however, whether William Page, who was called the American Titian before either he or any of his admirers had seen a real Titian, might not have been partially conscious of what he was doing when he chose to place his third wife in front of the Colosseum. (This is the only painting of a woman alone at the site.) (See fig. 5.) The historian James Thomas Flexner describes her rather luridly as being in real life a "dragonlike widow and newspaper woman who for the rest of his life warmed Page with the fire from her nostrils and forced her businessmen brothers to keep her genius financially afloat."[31] Page has certainly rendered her forcefulness, and—no Isabel—she stands there like a Victorian female gladiator posing before the scene of her triumphs. The irregular outline of her hood even suggests the impression that she herself might have been ripped from the stones behind her, a notion encouraged by the telling fact that the straight diagonal buttress erected on the south wall of the

FIG. 5. William Page, *Mrs. William Page.* 1860. Oil on canvas. 60 1/4 x 36 1/4 in. Courtesy of The Detroit Institute of Arts. Gift of Mr. and Mrs. George S. Page, Blinn S. Page, Lowell Briggs Page, and Mrs. Leslie Stockton Howell.

Colosseum a half-century before is missing, so that an improbably craggy profile frames one side of her head. Although in Rome, Page has not troubled to paint the actual Colosseum, but has anachronistically copied an eighteenth-century rendition.[32] At any rate, the perspective makes the self-assured Mrs. Page commensurate with the monument, and she appears more sturdy, more noble than the Colosseum itself, and in her own way as beautiful and imposing.

Thus the three most familiar American portraits with the Colosseum have, respectively, aggrandizing, diminishing, and equalizing effects on the American figures who appear in relation to it. In literature the relations are more complex but the figures are from a narrower range.

THE HEROIC PLACE

The Colosseum is the apt setting for madwomen and geniuses in American poetry and fiction at all levels of accomplishment. One Theodore S. Fay, who also wrote a so-called "True Tale of the Coliseum," set in ancient Rome, in 1835 published the first version of his *Norman Leslie,* the most popular novel of the day until Edgar Allan Poe made his critical debut by demolishing it. At its climax Rosalie Romaine, a New York fashion plate and Sunday School teacher who has gone mad as a consequence of being confined to a madhouse by her Neapolitan abductor, is seen leaping about the upper reaches of the Colosseum, from which the villain falls to his death.[33] The painter Washington Allston, in his Gothic romance *Monaldi* (1841, but written twenty years earlier) has one of his two alter-ego heroes (the writer) say to the other (the painter) that he sees his own condition in the "oppressive splendor" of "that proud pile of Titus" (the Colosseum); "so dark and desolate within," it speaks from without "in the gorgeous language of the sun" to his own heart, about himself.[34]

Extreme emotion and great aspiration characterize the typical figure at the Colosseum, the Romantic soul that feels itself misplaced in the nineteenth century, trying to extend its capacities or to understand its limitations, measuring itself against heroic architecture once achieved and powerful feelings once experienced. The artist above all is the appropriate perceiver of the Colosseum, because he alone can adequately feel its meaning as classical symbol and Romantic ruin. The model for this meeting of Colosseum and great soul was set primarily by Byron, who—anticipating Adams's question—thought that there was only one modern man worthy of posing with Rome as a background: George Washington. But he implies a close competitor—himself.[35]

Edgar Allan Poe, who was never in Rome, directly imitated Byron's two celebrated passages—those in *Manfred* (1817) and in *Childe Harold's Pilgrimage,* canto 4 (1818). Poe's poem, "The Coliseum," was originally the final scene from his unfinished verse-drama, *Politian* (1833). In all three works the Colosseum is seen, in Poe's words, as a "Rich reliquary/Of lofty contemplation left to Time/By buried centuries of pomp and power!" Poe specifically isolates the attributes and associations that appeal to him: Size, Age, Memory, Silence, Desolation, Night. For Poe as for Byron the Colosseum instills an essentially modern religious feeling, more potent than that of either paganism or Christianity. Poe's single important revision of this poem—and its only significant departure from Byron—consisted precisely of changing the words "I stand" to "I kneel." Humility is inculcated by the obvious evidence of man's insignificance before Time. Poe lists former and present things in alternation, a method that had long since become conventional in both prose and poetry describing Roman ruins. Here, says Poe, where once there were eagles, gilded hair, and monarchs, there are now bats, thistles, and lizards. But these are not all. To Poe's hero's despairing cries, the stones answer:

> "Prophetic sounds and loud, arise forever
> From us, and from all Ruins, unto the wise,
> As melody from Memnon to the Sun."

The stones of the Colosseum "rule the hearts of mightiest men" and "all giant minds" with their magic, wonder, mystery, and memories. Thus even here, where it seems that the ruin will convey above all a lesson in humility, ultimately—as with Byron—what is enforced is an impression of superior genius, the poetic aristocrats, who alone are capable of hearing the voice that speaks from the stones of human capacity for achievement. More than that, they are the ones who *evoke* the voice that would otherwise be dumb; the analogy with the statue of Memnon, which emitted music when struck by the sun's rays, makes artists the equivalent of the awakening and enlightening sun.[36]

Nathaniel Hawthorne often seems to combine the Romantic aspiration of Poe with the hard-headed (even hard-hearted) realism of Mark Twain. This is evident in *The Marble Faun* (1860), when his group of artists go on their obligatory moonlit visit to the Colosseum. Hawthorne initially sounds like Mark Twain when he points out that there is anything but solitude—the arena is jammed with visitors, and on the "topmost wall" a party of English and Americans are "exalting themselves with raptures that were Byron's, not their own." As for the moonlight, it is too bright; everything is "too distinctly visible." Yet as artists Hawthorne's characters have the capacity to enjoy "the thin delights of moonshine and romance." They are abundantly pleased, claiming—like Hawthorne's friend Hillard—that the Colosseum has only now come into its "best uses"; it was built for their pleasure. That pleasure, in spite of their gaiety and the classical setting, is primarily Gothic, and as they sit imagining ghosts and recalling the demons that Cellini and his necromancer had raised on the spot, Hawthorne's critical humor gradually becomes mixed with horror, preparing for the re-entrance of Miriam's specter of the Catacombs and for the completely Gothic scene in which Miriam is transformed into an almost superhuman madwoman raging "under the dusky arches of the Coliseum." Now all the earlier allusions to martyrdom, demons, gladiatorial combat, and power, contribute to the characterization of Miriam and her situation, even as her behavior reinforces the Gothic and heroic associations of the Colosseum. When Donatello, the innocent "faun" of the title, makes his explicit avowal to die for her, Miriam reasserts much of her imperious superiority: "I used to fancy that . . . I could bring the whole world to my feet." Now she sees only the threatening evil that hangs over her and

Donatello like the crumbling dark vaults of the mighty Colosseum. Like Byron and Poe, Hawthorne finds the classical ruin the apt setting for the doomed but heroic contemporary personality martyred by misplacement in the ignobility and decay of the present.[37]

Unquestionably Hawthorne's use of the Colosseum encouraged that of Henry James, who employed it no fewer than five times at crucial moments in the lives of his characters. In the earliest instance, in the story "Adina" (1874), a Donatello-like character undergoes *his* transformation from innocence to experience at the center of the Colosseum, where he swears revenge upon the man who has wronged him.[38] In his first full-scale novel, *Roderick Hudson* (1875), James much more fully exploits the scene in the book's central chapter, using every aspect of what he saw as the Colosseum's Alpine topography—its ruggedness, its opportunities for lovers' trysts and for eavesdropping, its flowers on high ledges. But all this might have been found in the Baths of Caracalla, of which James was equally fond. The special symbolic appropriateness of the Colosseum is obviously its classical associations with athletic and heroic action: contests of will, questions of strength, even the definition of manliness, all those, moreover, as something observed, witnessed, as Rowland here witnesses Christina Light's tigerish challenges to Roderick, and Roderick's attempts to prove himself. Roderick is the young man who has proposed to become the Whitman of American sculpture, but Christina tells him that he is too weak for "splendid achievement," that he has "not the voice of a conqueror"; on the contrary, he is a drifter, a dodger, a self-doubter, in short, a "scant" person. Roderick takes Christina herself to be a very superior person who judges him by the highest standards of achievement—against the "best"; and by a great effort of will he manages momentarily to control her. But, so shaken is he by this "episode of the Coliseum," that his decadence really begins at this point. He is the genius who fails, and the Colosseum measures his fall.[39]

The important scene in *The Portrait of a Lady,* already discussed with respect to Isabel Archer, goes on to use the Colosseum for comic-pathetic purposes as the backdrop for a young man's declaration of strength. Isabel sees little Ned Rosier, her step-daughter

Pansy's faithful suitor, "planted in the middle of the arena" in a pose "characteristic of baffled but indestructible purpose." He has sacrificed all his bibelots—the chief source of his identity; but he nevertheless cries out, "I feel very safe!" "It evidently made him feel more so to make the announcement in a rather loud voice, balancing himself a little complacently on his toes and looking all round the Coliseum as if it were filled with an audience."

The Colosseum is even used by James in *The Bostonians* (1886) to heighten the effect of the most tumultuous dénouement to any of his novels. Boston in those days lacked an arena naturally associated with violent entertainment for the masses, so James has the aggressively masculine Basil Ransom perceive, on the occasion of his own descent to brute force, a resemblance between the Boston Music Hall and the Roman Colosseum. James draws the parallels in some detail. The fulfillment of the feminist Olive Chancellor's desire for martyrdom is thus implicit when at the end she desperately plunges out onto the stage to face the roaring crowd.

James's most famous use of the Colosseum is that in *Daisy Miller* (1879), his early attempt to see how much dignity and importance could be attributed to the presumptively small and unaware. Almost the last words Daisy speaks to her undeclared suitor Winterbourne are, "Well, I *have* seen the Colosseum by moonlight! . . . That's one thing I can rave about!" The breaking of one convention to conform to another—that of Byronic Romanticism—kills her. Winterbourne, himself a "lover of the picturesque," has found Daisy and the infatuated Giovanelli together in the Colosseum just after he has interrupted his own recitation of Byron's lines from *Manfred* by reminding himself that "the historic atmosphere" is a "villainous miasma," "scientifically considered." Daisy sees him looking at her "as one of the old lions or tigers may have looked at the Christian martyrs!" And he is in fact sacrificing her at the moment he recognizes her. His judgment of her, "I believe it makes very little difference whether you are engaged or not!" parallels her reply, "I don't care . . . whether I have Roman Fever or not!" The relation between her death and her failure to win respect on her own terms is clear. Like Roderick, like Christina, like Ned Rosier, like Isabel herself and the fiercely shy and self-deprecating Olive Chancellor—like all of James's characters who respond to the Emersonian injunction to "descend into the dust of the arena," "She would have appreciated one's esteem."[40]

THE COLOSSEUM AS NEGATIVE MODEL

In the course of the nineteenth century, America developed its own "ancient history," and found in Washington and Franklin, Adams and Jefferson its Cincinnatus, Cicero, and Cato, rendering the originals superfluous. Many of the Founding Fathers themselves, however, had shared the belief that the modern nation could find its model in the Roman Republic, that the contemporary man could rival and surpass the high achievements of even imperial Rome, without—it was hoped—loss of republican virtue. By providing models both of national fulfillment and of individual greatness, then, Rome had a relevance. But, as several intellectual historians have shown,[41] there was always some confusion as to what that relevance was, since there was confusion about America's place within history and disagreement about the meaning of history itself. If history was cyclical, America's own origins combined primitivism with commercial, political, and cultural sophistication in a way that defined the nation equivocally: was it new, its cycle just beginning, or was it a necessarily contemporaneous offshoot of the British Empire, already (supposedly) at its height and corrupt? If America was essentially at its beginning, could it read the history of Rome with sufficient intelligence to slow down or even evade the ultimate implications of cyclical theories, free will overcoming fate as revealed in history? Should it believe, instead, in a millennial interpretation of history, in which America represented the western edge of civilization, progressing toward its perfection, the fulfillment of which was history's purpose? In 1780 David Humphreys had written "On the Happiness of America" thus:

> All former empires rose, the work of guilt,
> On conquest, blood, or usurpation built:
> But we, taught wisdom by their woes and crimes,

Fraught with their lore, and born to better times;
Our constitutions form'd on freedom's base,
Which all the blessings of all lands embrace;
Embrace humanity's extended cause,
A world our empire, for a world our laws. [42]

Such a declaration of political novelty had implications for architecture as well. A passage spoken by the Genius of Long Island
Sound in the final book of Timothy Dwight's *Greenfield Hill* (1794)
(dedicated to John Adams) explicitly attacks imitation in perfectly
conventional heroic couplets. His point is that *everything* is to be
thought of as being "done first" in America—not in Rome. The
image informing his verse is clearly the Colosseum as it had been perceived in the Renaissance, as the architectural ideal of superimposed
orders:

Her pride of empire haughty Rome unfold:
A world despoil'd, for luxury, and gold:
Here nobler wonders of the world shall rise;
Far other empire here mankind surprise:
Of orders pure, that ask no Grecian name,
A new born structure here ascend to fame.
The base, shall knowledge, choice, and freedom, form,
Sapp'd by no flood, and shaken by no storm;
Unpattern'd columns, union'd States ascend;
Combining arches, virtuous manners bend;
Of balanc'd powers, proportion'd stories rise. [43]

A visual representation of Dwight's Mansion of Freedom under Law,
with its "unpattern'd columns" of nameless orders, would have little
resemblance to the edifice eventually constructed at Washington to
house the Congress, and "pompously"—as Tocqueville said—called
the "Capitol." [44]

By the middle of the nineteenth century commercial and terri-
torial expansionism, political corruption, and other signs of luxury
and dissipation made all hopeful views of sequence and of historical
teleology difficult to sustain. In congressional debates of the 1840s
leading up to the Mexican War, imperial Rome as a negative reference
replaced innovations of the Roman Republic. [45] Later, William Dean

Howells, who was convinced that ancient Rome had been architecturally hideous, saw a resemblance between the faces of ancient senators and those of American senators from the South: the common physiognomy of slaveholders.[46] At the turn of the century, Henry Adams could state that Americans "were as familiar with political assassination as though they had lived under Nero. The climax of empire could be seen approaching, year after year, as though Sulla were a President or McKinley a Consul." In 1905, looking down from a window of Fifth Avenue, Adams "felt himself in Rome, under Diocletian, witnessing the anarchy, with no Constantine the Great in sight."[47]

In the second half of the nineteenth century Henry James, alone among American realists, could create a noble character like Isabel Archer for whom the contemporary and the past converge in an awareness of the individual life within the political mutations of history, lending a tragic dignity to both. Otherwise, even as historicism in architecture itself had a final flowering in the classical mode,[48] in literature and art the interests of realism shifted wholly to the contemporary world. There developed a large indifference to the *entire* past, classical or medieval; and humanity, both social and individual, both classic and contemporary, became—in spite of the efforts of Walt Whitman and Winslow Homer—very small. Not only the past, but history itself—and thus the future, too—lost significance. This antihistoricism had actually been expressed in verses by Freneau as early as 1775:

> This age may decay, and another may arise,
> Before it is fully revealed to our eyes,
> That Latin and Hebrew, Chaldaic and Greek,
> To the shades of oblivion must certainly sneak;
> Too much of our time is employed on such trash
> When we ought to be taught to accumulate cash.[49]

THE ABYSS OF TIME

Henry Adams, trying to find relatedness in history, could not imagine Longfellow posed before the ruins of Rome, but he could think of Michelangelo as adequate to the setting. Longfellow himself imagined Michelangelo there, and in a remarkable passage in his unfinished verse drama, *Michael Angelo: A Fragment* (1882), most of the meanings of the Colosseum that we have observed come together. Michelangelo tells his questioning companion Tomasso de' Cavalieri that he has come to the Colosseum to "learn" from "the great master of antiquity" who built it. He sees the structure as "the great marble rose of Rome," its petals torn by the wind and rain of centuries, yet still opening itself to the constellations that hang above it like a swarm of bees. To this image Cavalieri opposes Dante's white rose of Paradise whose petals were saints, while the thousands who once filled out the Colosseum's design "came to see the gladiators die," and "could not give sweetness to a rose like this." But Michelangelo speaks "not of its uses, but its beauty." Even to this, Cavalieri argues that "the end and aim" of a work constitutes its nobility. This arena once served "people/Whose pleasure was the pain of dying men," and even now, as a ruin, it serves robbers and "the ghosts/Of murdered men." For Michelangelo, however, as a ruin it has been reclaimed by its thousands of wild flowers and birds, which are also capable of teaching the artist lessons of beauty.

Yet Longfellow does not stop there, with this summation of the questions about a building's identity—its definition by its various historical uses, by its inherent beauty of design, by its eventual reclamation by Nature, by its accumulated associations. With astonishing eloquence he goes on to a deeper lesson in which Michelangelo converts the Colosseum into a philosophical symbol; implicitly it becomes the image of the skeletal remains of the world:

> All things must have an end; the world itself
> Must have an end, as in a dream I saw it.
> There came a great hand out of heaven, and touched
> The earth, and stopped it in its course. The seas

Leaped, a vast cataract, into the abyss;
The forests and the fields slid off, and floated
Like wooded islands in the air. The dead
Were hurled forth from their sepulchres; the living
Were mingled with them, and themselves were dead,—
All being dead; and the fair, shining cities
Dropped out like jewels from a broken crown.
Naught but the core of the great globe remained,
A skeleton of stone[50]

This reading of the Colosseum, which has distant connections with the cosmic mysteries surrounding it in the Middle Ages, had been adumbrated by Hawthorne at the end of the Colosseum scene in *The Marble Faun,* where he too passed beyond the questions of the classical measure of man and the atmosphere of the gothic ruin toward an apocalyptic vision: His little quartet of artists strolls away from the Colosseum, past the Arch of Constantine, and then along the Via Sacra beneath the Arch of Titus, with the Palace of the Caesars in the background, and Hawthorne imagines a "Roman Triumph, that most gorgeous pageant of earthly pride," coming along the same way. Then he adds quickly:

It is politic, however, to make few allusions to such a Past; nor, if we would create an interest in the characters of our story, is it wise to suggest how Cicero's foot may have stepped on yonder stone, or how Horace was wont to stroll nearby, making his footsteps chime with the measure of the ode that was ringing in his mind. The very ghosts of that massive and stately epoch have so much density, that the actual people of today seem the thinner of the two, and stand more ghostlike by the arches and columns.

This diminishment of the contemporary world reaffirms the stature of the classical one. But then Hawthorne takes the further step into historical nihilism. He has Miriam suggest finally that everything— classical as well as contemporary—is ultimately reduced to insignificance. Kenyon has just cited the heroic act of Curtius riding his horse into a fissure in the earth to save the city, and she replies: "It was a foolish piece of heroism in Curtius to precipitate himself there, in advance; for all Rome, you see, has been swallowed up in that gulf, in spite of him." Into that abyss of Time have gone the Caesars and their palaces, the temples, the statues, the armies, "All the heroes, the statesmen and the poets!" Hawthorne's four characters then turn their backs on the moonlit Colosseum and stride off across the Forum toward the Tarpeian Rock where the tragic crisis of the book will occur. As they go along the Via Sacra they sing, somewhat shrilly, "Hail! Columbia!" Theirs is a desperate triumphal march of the present over the past, replacing the earlier American Republic's identification with it. They trample the proofs of history underfoot, a defiance of Time by the representatives of Columbia, the new republic and the empire to be.[51]

CONCLUSION

Architects and architectural historians, concerned with influences and innovations in form, elegant solutions to specific problems, and the relation of the smallest detail to the grandest design, no doubt reluctantly realize that the general public, including even artists and writers, has only the vaguest notion of these aspects of a building. A building becomes the history of its uses and associations; what the architects made it, to be sure, but also what others make of it. The Colosseum, in nineteenth-century American art and literature, is not finally so much a great work of architecture or a noble ruin, but a multivalent symbol, dreadful and magnificent, the Moby Dick of architecture: sublime and heroic, ravaged yet enduring, by tradition both sacred and malignant, alien and triumphant. In it were reflected a new nation's own sense of material progress, its spiritual emptiness, its aspirations and fears for what it might become, its fluctuating sense of the proper model and measure for both nation and individual, its uncertainty about its own meaning as a modern republic with potential for empire, and its temptation to place all faith in Nature. A building that had stood for absolute power spoke ultimately of impotence. Burdened by too many meanings, its final message, like that of history to the historian Adams, was enigmatic.

NOTES

1. Henry James, *The Portrait of a Lady,* New York, 2 vols. (New York: Charles Scribner's Sons, 1908), 2:339–40 (chap. 50). Subsequent quotations are from 1:413–15 and 2:327–29 (chaps. 27 and 49).

2. See Michela di Macco, *Il Colosseo: funzione simbolica, storica, urbana* (Rome: Bulzoni Editore, 1971); Peter Quennell, *The Colosseum* (New York: Newsweek, 1971); and John Pearson, *Arena* (London: Thames and Hudson, 1973).

3. See Marcel Röthlisberger, *Claude Lorrain: The Paintings,* 2 vols. (New Haven: Yale University Press, 1961); 2, figs. 26, 27, 42, 142.

4. See Howard S. Merritt, *Thomas Cole, 1801–1848* (Rochester: Memorial Art Gallery of the University of Rochester, 1969), 28, 75.

5. In Louis Legrand Noble, *The Life and Works of Thomas Cole,* ed. Elliot S. Vesell (1853; Cambridge: Harvard University Press, 1964), 115–16.

6. Henry James, *Italian Hours* (1909; New York: Horizon Press, 1968), 201–2.

7. Bayard Taylor, *Views A-Foot, Or Europe Seen With Knapsack and Staff* (New York: A. L. Burt, 1848), 327. Cf. J. W. Goethe, *Italian Journey 1786–1788,* trans. W. H. Auden and Elizabeth Mayer (New York: Schocken, 1968), 125, 156, 496–97.

8. William Wetmore Story, *Roba di Roma,* 2 vols., 13th ed. (Boston: Houghton Mifflin Co., 1887), 1:241, 242.

9. George S. Hillard, *Six Months in Italy,* 2 vols. (Boston: Ticknor, Reed, and Fields, 1853), 1:239–41.

10. On Gérôme's Roman paintings, see Gerald M. Ackerman, *Jean-Léon Gérôme (1824–1904)* (Dayton: Dayton Art Institute, 1972), 11–12, 44–45, 62–63, 73–74, and 86–87.

11. See Story, *Roba di Roma,* 1:243.

12. John L. Sweeney, ed., *The Painter's Eye: Notes and Essays on the Pictorial Arts* [by Henry James] (Cambridge: Harvard University Press, 1956), 42. Ackerman, *Jean-Léon Gérôme,* 74, quotes from James's *Parisian Sketches,* ed. Leon Edel and Ilse Dusoir Lind (New York: New York University Press, 1957), 98–99.

13. Francis Marion Crawford, *Ave Roma Immortalis,* 2 vols. (New York: Macmillan Co., 1898), 2:97–100.

14. Byrd's drama, widely reprinted in anthologies of American plays, has as its hero the rebellious slave-gladiator Spartacus. The events, which slightly precede the building of the Colosseum, were seen to have contemporary American relevance.

15. On Blashfield, see Eric Zafran, "Edwin H. Blashfield: Motifs of the American Renaissance," *Arts Magazine* 54, no. 3 (Nov. 1979): 149–51.

16. Moses Hadas, ed., *A History of Rome from Its Origins to 529 A.D. as Told by the Roman Historians* (Garden City, N.Y.: Doubleday, 1956), 140. Passages on Commodus from Dio Cassius and Aurelius Victor in Hadas, 137–40. Blashfield's Commodus is clearly modeled on the statue known as "Commodus as Hercules" in the Vatican, a copy of which is at Versailles. It is possible that his interest in the subject was excited by the much-publicized discovery in 1874 of an antique bust of Commodus as Hercules; see Francis Haskell and Nicholas Penny, *Taste and the Antique: The Lore of Classical Sculpture, 1500–1900* (New Haven: Yale University Press, 1981), 188–89.

17. Henry James, *The Princess Casamassima,* New York ed., 2 vols. (New York: Charles Scribner's Sons, 1908), 2:23 (chap. 22).

18. Critics of the series have largely confined themselves to quotations from Cole's own commentary (reprinted in Noble, *Life and Works*), which does not resolve the question of historical causation and inevitability.

19. Compare Cole's painting with photographs of the Court of Honor such as those reproduced in William H. Jordy, *American Buildings and Their Architects: Progressive and Academic Ideals at the Turn of the Twentieth Century* (Garden City: Doubleday, 1972), 70–71. Jordy comments that: "In its Roman and baroque trappings . . . the imperial flavor of the White City accorded with the imperial flavor of American culture at the end of the century" (p. 79).

20. *Letters of Charles Eliot Norton,* ed. Sara Norton and M. A. DeWolfe Howe, 2 vols. (Boston: Houghton Mifflin Co., 1913), 2:218, 269, 284.

21. Margaret Fuller (Ossoli), *At Home and Abroad, or Things and Thoughts in America and Europe,* ed. Arthur B. Fuller (Boston: Crosby, Nichols, and Co., 1856), 216.

22. Mark Twain, *The Innocents Abroad,* 2 vols. (1869; New York: Harper and Row, 1911), 1:287–96.

23. John Adams, *A Defence of the Constitutions of Government of the United States,* in *The Works of John Adams,* ed. C. F. Adams (Boston: Little, Brown and Co., 1850–56), vols. 4–6; see especially 4:297–98, 439–47, 520–42, and 5:202–3. For the portrait, see Peter Shaw, *The Character of John Adams* (Chapel Hill: University of North Carolina Press, 1976), 192 and fig. 2.

24. Henry Adams, *The Education of Henry Adams,* ed. Ernest Samuels (1918; Boston: Houghton Mifflin Co., 1974), 92.

25. Ibid., 91–92.

26. Space does not permit discussion of European examples of the phenomenon, extending from Marten Van Heemskerck's double *Self-Portrait* with the Colosseum (1530s; Fitzwilliam Museum, Cambridge) to Ingres's *Joseph Antoine Moltedo* (1815; Metropolitan), both of which have significations different from those of any American paintings. For examples of the most common type—the souvenir painting of the eighteenth century—see Brinsley Ford, "The Grand Tour," *Apollo* 114 (Dec. 1981):390–400, figs. 10, 13, 17.

27. On the Izards see Appendix A, Martha Babcock Amory (Copley's grand-daughter), *The Domestic and Artistic Life of John Singleton Copley* (Boston: Houghton Mifflin Co., 1882), 445–49. Allan's painting of Hamilton and his wife (private collection) is reproduced in Ford, "Grand Tour," 391, fig. 4.

28. See G. P. A. Healy, *Reminiscences of a Portrait Painter* (Chicago: n. p., 1894); *A Souvenir of the Exhibition: Healy's Sitters* (Richmond: Virginia Museum of Fine Arts, 1950); and Marie de Mare, *G. P. A. Healy, American Artist* (New York: D. McKay, 1954).

29. Henry James, *Letters,* ed. Leon Edel (Cambridge: Harvard University Press), 2:163.

30. Photograph reproduced in *Exhibit* 74 (May–June 1976). For an interpretation of the painting as a successful expression of Rome's "overwhelming influence on artists and poets," see the exhibition catalog, *The Classical Spirit in American Portraiture* (Providence: Brown University Department of Art, 1976), 99–100.

31. James Thomas Flexner, *That Wilder Image: The Native School from Thomas Cole to Winslow Homer,* vol. 3 of the *History of American Painting* (1962; reprint, New York: Dover Publications, 1970), 161.

32. Dr. Trevor Fairbrother kindly brought to my attention the last photograph of Elizabeth Barrett Browning (1861; published in Peter Quennell, *History of English Literature* [Springfield, Mass.: G. C. Merriam, 1973], 399), which clearly is a studio photograph taken in front of a drop of the unbuttressed Colosseum. Mrs. Browning is similarly posed and dressed, but the Colosseum is less dramatically related to the figure. The Brownings were great admirers of Page and shared his spiritualist interests. Besides Flexner, see Julia Markus, "William Page: The American Titian," *Horizon* 22, no. 3 (March 1979):19–23, and Joshua C. Taylor, *William Page: The American Titian* (Chicago: University of Chicago Press, 1957).

33. Theodore S. Fay, *Norman Leslie* (New York: Harper, 1835). The version of 1869 (New York: G. P. Putnam & Son) transfers the scene to the Corso during Carnival, where Rosalie's behavior seems less remarkable, and where the villain is simply shot.

34. Washington Allston, *Monaldi* (Boston: Charles C. Little and James Brown, 1841), 65.

35. *Childe Harold's Pilgrimage,* canto 4: 96.

36. *Collected Works of Edgar Allan Poe,* ed. Thomas Ollive Mabbott, 3 vols. (Cambridge: Harvard University Press, 1969), 1:228–30.

37. Nathaniel Hawthorne, *The Marble Faun,* Centenary ed. (Columbus: Ohio State University Press, 1968), 153–58.

38. *The Complete Tales of Henry James,* ed. Leon Edel, 12 vols (Philadelphia: J. B. Lippincott, 1962–64), 3:229.

39. Henry James, *Roderick Hudson,* New York ed. (New York: Charles Scribner's Sons, 1907), 257–70 (chap. 13).

40. Henry James, *Daisy Miller,* New York ed. (New York: Charles Scribner's

Sons, 1909), 84–93. I have partially quoted from the original 1879 text, which differs slightly.

41. There is an excellent survey of the scholarship on the subject by Meyer Reinhold in John W. Eadie, ed., *Classical Traditions in Early America* (Ann Arbor: University of Michigan Press, 1976). I am indebted in addition to the essays in this book by A. Owen Aldridge, John E. Cowley, and George Kennedy.

42. Quoted by Aldridge in ibid., p. 115.

43. Timothy Dwight, *Greenfield Hill: A Poem* (1794; facsimile reprint, New York: AMS Press, 1970), pt. 8 (The Vision), lines 251–78.

44. Alexis de Tocqueville, *Democracy in America,* 2 vols., trans. Henry Reeve, ed. Phillips Bradley (New York: Alfred A. Knopf, 1945), 2:195.

45. See Edwin A. Miles, "The Young American Nation and the Classical World," *Journal of the History of Ideas* 35, no. 2 (April–June 1974): 259–74, especially 272–73, and n62.

46. William Dean Howells, *Italian Journeys* (Boston: James R. Osgood & Co., 1877), 173. The characterization of imperial Rome is in *Roman Holidays and Others* (New York: Harper and Brothers, 1908), 92–95. Howells looks with dull indifference at the Colosseum and concludes: "Rome, either republican or imperial, was a state for which we can have no genuine reverence, and . . . mostly the ruins of her past stir in us no finer emotion than wonder" (p. 95).

47. Henry Adams, *Education,* 367, 499.

48. According to Jordy, *American Buildings,* 333 and 370, the Colosseum was claimed as a direct inspiration by Charles F. McKim for the arcuation on the facade and in the courtyard of the Boston Public Library (1888–95). He further cites Bernard Maybeck's terrace in the Palace of Fine Arts, San Francisco (1915) as a conscious derivation from the Colosseum of Gérôme's *Pollice Verso,* 391–92, n6. Other aspects of the building connect it with the Pantheon and the Arch of Constantine, and—most interestingly—with Piranesi's ruins, so that the future condition is implied in the present grandeur (see 292–98 and 392, n17).

49. Philip Freneau, "Expedition of Timothy Taurus, Astrologer," quoted by Aldridge in Eadie, *Classical Tradition in Early America,* p. 109.

50. Henry Wadsworth Longfellow, *The Complete Poetical Works,* Cambridge Ed. (Boston: Houghton Mifflin Co., 1893), 575–76.

51. Hawthorne, *Marble Faun,* 159–63 (chaps. 17–18).

Elizabeth Block

The Rome of Henry James

Wandering in Florence, Henry James found himself drawn to those ecclesiastical monuments that "reminded me so poignantly of Rome. Such is the City properly styled eternal—since it is eternal, at least, as regards the consciousness of the individual. One loves its corruptions better than the integrities of other places."[1] In this somewhat offhand remark, embedded in a mosaic of Florentine images, lies a clue to James's view, or views, of Rome, and the fictional uses to which he put his impressions. James's Rome is an eternal city, not simply in the length of its actual history, but in the sense that it endures, despite or even because of change, as a physical monument to the historical imagination. Rome represents for James an atmosphere in which individual experience seems to acquire an element of universality. James shares with his contemporaries and his predecessors a transhistorical vision of a Rome that is at once alluring and dangerous, enlightening and corrupting; permanent and decaying; in which the city is measured against the surrounding countryside; and the life of the individual is, finally, measured against these powerful ideas. Yet with all of its strong contrasts, the city and its rural surroundings appear only as a setting, an atmosphere, a mass of impressions—the quality of the light, the breath of moldering ruins, views and familiar walks—rather than in specific images, detailed descriptions, still less historical facts. Rome, an amalgam of recurring impressions on the physical, emotional, and even stylistic level, becomes the context in which James defines an antithesis integral to his perspective: the beautiful, old, decaying world of Europe set against the new, raw, philistine, vital world of America. While other cities contain such contrasts, and other settings awaken James's impressionistic and pictorial sense, Rome seems by its very existence to epitomize the ambiguities that most strongly engaged his imagination.

Towards the end of this essay I shall argue that James's vision of Rome and the past, despite his more immediate debts to Hawthorne, and to the authors of "novels in three volumes,"[2] derives from his exposure to the experience of what is broadly defined as a classical education. It can be shown that James's education included just enough access to Roman literature—especially Augustan literature—to account for his attitude towards Rome. The traces of classical Rome found in James are not allusions in any technical sense; rather, they are the imaginative distillation of a culture only vaguely grasped and recalled with deliberate vagueness. In *Italian Hours* James suggests the process through which individual consciousness merges with the past. "The whole backward past, the mild confused romance of the Rome one had loved,"[3] is present in his fiction in an essentially subjective form—the memory of an education and of the feelings that education had evoked.

In the Roman "sketches" and in early stories such as "The Sweetheart of M. Briseux," "Adina," and "The Last of the Valerii," and in the early novels *Watch and Ward,* and *Roderick Hudson,* Rome's several facets and conflicting forces play their own part, almost without disguise. As James's style matured in works such as "Daisy Miller," and *The Portrait of a Lady,* his view of Rome, while essentially unchanged, became more oblique, until the city sank almost beneath the surface of the prose, as in *The Golden Bowl.*[4] Whether it is openly exploited or covertly suggested, however, the image of Rome supplies a context for the absorbing events that define the individual life.

At the simplest level the Roman duality is physical. In "A Roman Holiday," James writes of how one may dodge the "unsavory" aspects of the city by contemplating its art treasures, but "the squalor of Rome is certainly a stubborn fact, and there is no denying it is a dirty place. . . . The nameless uncleanness with which all Roman things are oversmeared seems to one at first a damning token of moral vileness" (p. 127). A friend of James's goes on in this sketch to complain that the dirt of Rome conveys a "shameless degradation," to those who yearn for the veneer of civilization, but the fact is that this decay defines the Roman appeal; the inertia that keeps the city's citizens in rags, also binds the enthusiast to it. The love of Rome, James imagines writing to his friend, "is, in its last analysis, simply that perfectly honorable and legitimate instinct, the love of the *status quo*. . . . 'What you call dirt,' an excellent authority has affirmed, 'I call color'" (p. 129).

In James's fiction, an element of moral decay infects the physical decay made "picturesque" by appreciation for the status quo. The concrete and the symbolic become in effect inseparable. "A passive life in Rome," says Rowland Mallet at the beginning of *Roderick Hudson*, "thanks to the number and quality of one's impressions, takes on a very respectable likeness to activity. . . . It's all very well, but I have a distinct prevision of this—that if Roman life doesn't do something substantial to make you happier, it increases tenfold your liability to moral misery. It seems to me a rash thing for a sensitive soul deliberately to cultivate its sensibilities by rambling too often among the ruins of the Palatine or riding too often in the shadow of the crumbling aqueducts."[5] The forces upon which depend Rome's ability to educate the soul may also prove ruinous. The crumbling monuments of the city constitute at once its beauty, its power, and its malevolence, by suggesting that relentless continuity that renders insignificant any individual effort. At the end of *Roderick Hudson*, Rowland's sense proves accurate: while Roderick lackadaisically contemplates leaving Rome, his mother laments that "it's this dreadful place that has made us so unhappy. Roderick's so fearfully relaxed!" (chap. 21:292).

This effect, exposing in a passive, oblique way, elements of one's character that might better be disguised by the modern "march of mind,"[6] is for James irresistibly seductive: "one parts half willingly with one's hopes in Rome and misses them only under some very exceptional stress of circumstance. For this reason it may perhaps be said that there is no other place in which one's daily temper has such a mellow serenity, and none at the same time in which acute attacks of depression are more intolerable."[7]

The combined polarities of moral education and moral decline surface briefly in *Watch and Ward*, an early novelette that, although uncollected in the New York Edition, deserves attention not least because of its anticipation of major Jamesian themes. The orphan Nora Lambert, sent to Rome to be "brought out," writes rapturously to her guardian and secret lover about the beggars and models on the steps of the Piazza di Spagna: "Some of them are so handsome, sunning themselves there in their picturesqueness."[8] Nora sees charm precisely where James's own fictional friend, in *A Roman Holiday*, saw utter rottenness: "I could strangle every one of those filthy models that loaf there in their shameless degradation. . . . Isn't it an abomination that our enjoyment here directly implies their wretchedness; their knowing neither how to read nor to write, their draping themselves in mouldy rags . . . ? So they're kept, that Rome may be picturesque" (p. 128). Nora mentions too her fascination with the story of a German girl, jilted by her lover, who immured herself in the convent of the Sepolte Vive. She enjoys making up a weekly bouquet for this invisible victim: "It is a dismal amusement, but I confess it interests me" (p. 102). This little romance prefigures the story of Pansy Osmond in *The Portrait of a Lady*. In her pathetic history any sense of an "interesting situation" is quite overshadowed by the harsh contrast between the helpless girl and her entrapment. Pansy lives with her father and Isabel "in a high house in the very heart of Rome; a dark and massive structure overlooking a sunny piazzetta in the neighborhood of the Farnese Palace." To Pansy's lover, the Palazzo Roccanera seemed "a kind of domestic fortress, a pile which bore a stern old Roman name, which smelt of historic deeds, of crime and craft and violence, which was mentioned in 'Murray' and visited by tourists who looked, on a vague survey, disappointed and depressed."[9] This house is the secular representative of the convent Pansy will eventually enter. Papal rather than imperial Rome destroys Pansy, but this might be called mere fictional chance. Her story is but a microcosm of her stepmother's, for Isabel too is buried alive in a psychological prison.

In the much-discussed meditative scene at the center of the *Portrait* Isabel contemplates "the incredulous terror with which she had taken the measure of her dwelling. Between those four walls she had lived ever since; they were to surround her for the rest of her life. It was the house of darkness, the house of dumbness, the house of suffocation. Osmond's beautiful mind gave it neither light nor air; Osmond's beautiful mind indeed seemed to peep down from a small high window and mock at her" (chap. 42, 2:196). Isabel realizes that she has constructed this house out of her own romantic notions about Osmond and his aesthetic sensibility. At her first heady encounter with Rome, she had seemed to see the heavy human past inspired and informed by her own future. In an indefinable way, she has discovered both more and less than the city "really" holds. "Rome, as Ralph said, confessed to the psychological moment" (chap. 27, 1:414). As she recognizes what she has done, Isabel realizes that it is neither her surroundings nor her husband that have changed, but her own perceptions. Her desire to link her life to the aesthetic pleasures of the city brings her into the power of a sinister passivity inherent in the love of the Roman past.

Isabel, whose appreciation of Rome's past and present leads her not into a momentary misjudgment, but into a permanent prison whose walls are her own idealism, is a thoroughly developed version of Nora Lambert. Nora, even after her brief experience, realizes that "nothing can ever be the same after a winter in Rome" (p. 104). Having "bloomed into ripeness in the sunshine of a great contentment" (p. 114), she wanders from the ways of wisdom. She soon returns, but not before she has shown how the idealistic weakness of her character, her desire to romanticize what is ugly, to ignore what is horrible, blossom too in the Roman winter. In other stories of this early period James develops the recurring motif, hinted at in *Watch and Ward*, that defines the city: the contrast between what is aesthetically intoxicating and what is morally corrupting. This contrast often takes the form of a dualistic vision of the Roman past as at once seductive and destructive.

The central character in "Adina" is an imperial topaz intaglio, which the Campagna, "full of treasures yet" (p. 216), yields up to a young Italian peasant, Angelo Beati.[10] Beati ingenuously sells his as yet unidentified gem to the ugly, harsh American, Sam Scrope, for eleven *scudi*. Beati, "a puzzling mixture of simplicity and sense" (p. 218), represents at first the rustic innocent, the happy man in the old Roman sense: he who is truly *beatus* is rich beyond wealth or possessions—in fact, he is happier without them. Beati feels immediately, however, the wrong done to him by Scrope's duplicity. In answer to the American's question, "Are you satisfied?" Angelo asks, "Have *you* a good conscience?" (p. 219). Scrope, "a competent classicist" (p. 213), is utterly smitten with the intaglio, which he identifies as the priceless seal of the Emperor Tiberius Caesar, *totius orbis imperator,* but the stone "seemed to have corrupted him" (pp. 221–23). Thus the happy innocent appears to have been exploited by American greed and unscrupulousness. This story, however, presents more than a simple antithesis between good and evil. Angelo, no longer satisfied with his lot or the meagre wealth of the *scudi,* regrets bitterly not the innocence he lost, but the money.

When the narrator encounters him in the Colosseum a few weeks later, "he looked three years older. . . . His simple-souled smile was gone. . . . He looked graver, manlier, and very much less rustic" (p. 229). Beati's need for revenge becomes part of his life, and when he meets Scrope and his newly affianced lover in the Villa Borghese, the wheels are set in motion. Wordlessly, inexorably, Beati woos the girl Adina from afar, until at last she disappears with him, leaving only a note: "'Only forget me and believe that I am happy, happy, happy!' Adina Beati" (p. 253). A few weeks later Scrope pauses on the bridge of St. Angelo and tosses into the Tiber "the beautiful, the imperial, the baleful topaz. . . . It had been a curse, the golden gem, with its cruel emblems; let it return to the moldering underworld of the Roman past!" (p. 257).

The disinterment of the past does no one any good, for although Beati gets the girl, he unmistakably loses his innocence, and even when he wins Adina, he cannot forget the topaz. He is not ruined, but corrupted. In "Adina" the desire to possess the material aspects of the past controls the characters and changes their lives. The past has a vitality of its own that goes beyond mere aesthetic charm; it has an irresistible allure through which its physical artifacts can quickly become literally enthralling.

In "The Last of the Valerii," the characters long to appropriate the treasures of Rome, but find, as in "Adina," that the direction of this possession may quickly reverse itself. A young American girl, Martha, has fallen in love with an Italian count. The count, like Angelo Beati, seems perhaps a little slow, but he looks like a bust of the Emperor Caracalla, "with the same dense sculptural crop of curls . . . it was such hair as the old Romans must have had" (p. 90). He looks, indeed, quite like Beati, and even perhaps like the "low-browed" figure on the intaglio. Martha loves the count, but she also loves his Roman villa: "next after that slow-coming, slow-going smile of her lover, it was the rusty complexion of his patrimonial marbles that she most prized" (p. 91). She sets out to rescue the Villa Valerio from its "antique decay," and in the process discovers a fabulous ancient Juno, by which the count becomes mesmerized. This goddess represents a primitive female force. Roderick Hudson first sees Christina Light as he is sketching "a memento of the great Juno" that belongs to the Villa Ludovisi. He finds in the girl's face the "subject" that brings to life the statue's blank eyes."[11] Conte Valerio too falls in love with the female of the statue and is transported back to his pagan Roman ancestry.

After the narrator discovers him one day in the Pantheon, where the count expresses an impassioned desire to rediscover the old gods, the only solution to the malevolent force of the past is to rebury it. Camillo Valerio, released from the influence of the Juno, returns to the adoration of his wife. The count retains, from his experience, only the marble hand of the Juno, tangible evidence of the physical hold the past maintains, and of his encounter with it. "The Last of the Valerii" is expressly not a religious parable; it is neither pro-Christian, nor anti-pagan. It is a chronicle of the vitality of the past, and of the manner in which it can overwhelm the present.

In each of these stories ancient Rome exerts, through its concrete images, a force that transcends the concrete. In each situation, furthermore, the tension is not simply between the old and the new, the innocent and the civilized. Both the children of the Italian past and their admirers are caught in the fascination, and are transformed by it; and in each case the hold of the past is eluded, not dissolved. As Martha drops the first handful of dirt on the Juno she exclaims: "May it lie lightly, but forever." Similarly the intaglio lies in the river: "Some day, I suppose, they will dredge the Tiber for treasures, and, possibly, disinter our topaz."[12]

James in these stories suggests that Rome's past comprises both her appeal and her malignancy, that a love of the past is itself malign.

At the same time, this corrosive force is linked to a crumbling beauty and a sensuous decay. The Roman past invites its admirer to succumb to the sheer pleasure of observation, but it is difficult to maintain a detached involvement, to avoid the pitfalls of a Roderick Hudson, of a Sam Scrope, of a Conte Valerio.

The intensity of the Roman past is tempered, or complemented, by the distant, vague vistas with which James defines the city. These images, in their ability to link the observed moment to a sensuous continuity, reinforce by their very lack of specificity the survival of the general and shared past in the present. The countryside surrounding Rome offers a physical embodiment of this perspective.

As the observer gazes from St. John Lateran through the gates of Rome, his eye rests upon "the long gaunt file of arches of the Claudian aqueduct, their jagged ridge stretching away like the vertebral column of some monstrous, mouldering skeleton, and upon the blooming brown and purple flats and dells of the Campagna and the glowing blue of the Alban mountains"[13] The Campagna seems most insistently to preserve, in its silence and forlornness, the sense of the past as eternal both within the consciousness of the individual, and despite him. Its light is "full of that mellow purple glow, that tempered intensity, which haunts the after-vision of those who have known Rome like the memory of some supremely irresponsible pleasure" (*TS*, p. 136). From the Campagna, Rome seems somehow smaller, less important. James and his characters retreat into the country to immerse themselves in the silences that the immortal past produces, to escape the more insistent impressions and presences of Rome and to regain, or discover, the perspective that the unchanging light and shadow of the Campagna offers on the life and struggle of the city itself.

When the Roman spring arrives, with its unhealthful sirocco and troubling shifts in Adina's affections, Adina and her stepmother depart from the city to take refuge in a little country town where the windows of the inn offer a view of the "great misty sea-like level of the Campagna" (p. 241). When Isabel Archer at last understands her position, she drives alone into the Campagna: it had become her habit to drop "her secret sadness into the silence of lonely places. . . .

She could almost smile at it, and think of its smallness. Small it was, in the large Roman record" (chap. 49, 2:237). The pastoral landscape, the "picturesque neighborhood of strange old mountain towns" (*Adina,* p. 241), offers a soothing counterforce to Rome, the "natural home of spirits with a deep relish for the artificial element in life and the infinite superpositions of history" (*Roderick Hudson,* chap. 5, p. 79). The countryside of Rome is "so bright and yet so sad, so still and yet so charged, to the supersensuous ear, with the murmur of an extinguished life" (*TS,* p. 137). The Campagna gives one a sense of "boundless space," especially potent at the first stirrings of the Roman spring, soon to "come wandering into the heart of the city and throbbing through the close, dark streets." Yet these charms are but "so many notes in the scale of melancholy" (*TS,* pp. 148-50).

The sometimes sinister aspects of the city produce in the country a numinous sadness; stripped of its human leavening, the weight of the past is not threatening, but forlorn. These two aspects coalesce in James's descriptions of Roman cemeteries, where "the ancient and the modern world are most impressively contrasted." Here "you seem to see a cluster of modern ashes held tenderly in the rugged hand of the Past;" "the weight of a tremendous past appears to press upon the flowery sod."[14]

Rome, then, embodies contrast: beauty and squalor, the past and the present, urban life and country solitude, delight and melancholy. With all this force of emotion, however, Rome remains for James essentially a source of "impressions." Here one may gather "impressions as thickly clustered as the purple bunches of a vintage."[15] But these impressions are vague, indefinable, and repetitive, concentrating on atmosphere, light, views, rather than archaeological detail. Rome is overwhelmingly present, its distinctive character is its resistance to analysis: "who can analyze even the simplest Roman impression? It is compounded of so many things, it says so much, it suggests so much, it so quickens the intellect and so flatters the heart, that before we are fairly conscious of it the imagination has marked it for her own."[16] A few ancient monuments and familiar images loom out of these impressions: the Forum, the Ara Caeli, the Palatine and

Capitol and the "ponderously sad" Rome of the Caesars. In the country James observes the "kind of joyless beauty" of the Alban Lake, the ilex walks, Soracte.[17]

His characters, too, are observers, gatherers of impressions. In "The Last of the Valerii," the narrator is himself a painter, lurking throughout the story in the avenues and gardens of the villa, sketching and watching. Men's lives unfold in the foreground, while Rome and its memories stretch into a sort of pictorial distance. Often James chooses galleries and vistas of Rome against which to throw his characters into relief. The sights of the city awe and overwhelm Mary Garland in *Roderick Hudson*. She feels the weight of the past in St. Peter's, in the streets and squares; but James is far more interested in her sensibility than in what she sees, and in her awareness that the Roman past demands of her a new kind of commitment. Daisy Miller, on the other hand, is pertly uninterested: "I foresaw we should be going round all the time with one of those dreadful old men who explain about the pictures and things."[18]

The pictorial view often frames the actions of the characters, at once rendering them concentrated, and somehow impersonal. Winterbourne's friend relates how, contemplating a "great portrait of Innocent X," he saw Daisy and Giovanelli "in the secluded nook in which the papal presence is enshrined" (p. 79). The scene in which Winterbourne sees Daisy and Giovanelli in the Pincian Gardens uses the same visual device to reveal the couple's intimacy:

> They evidently saw no one; they were too deeply occupied with each other. When they reached the low garden-wall they remained a little looking off at the great flat-topped pine-clusters of Villa Borghese; then the girl's attendant admirer seated himself familiarly on the broad ledge of the wall. The western sun in the opposite sky sent out a brilliant shaft through a couple of cloud-bars; whereupon the gallant Giovanelli took her parasol out of her hands and opened it. She came a little nearer and he held the parasol over her; then, still holding it, he let it so rest on her shoulder that both of their heads were hidden from Winterbourne.

Here the Roman view, seen from afar, vague but suggestive, frames for Winterbourne's and the reader's vision the small, momentous movements of Daisy and her Italian lover. The crowded gardens recede as the couple comes into focus for the observer, yet their intimacy seems finer, more portentous, because of the way it closes them off amidst the "slow-moving, idly-gazing Roman crowd" (p. 54).

The powerful atmosphere of the antique looms over the lives of James's characters, but in antiquity itself, as documented in texts or monuments, they are uninterested: "here was history in the stones of the street and the atoms of the sunshine" (*Portrait,* chap. 27, 1:413). To this atmosphere the guidebook is antithetical. Indeed, Mary Garland's reliance on guides is rightly taken by Mallet as an inability to break freely into the sensuous richness of Rome; and in "The Sweetheart of M. Briseux," the girl, at first charmed by her lover's attention to "facts," soon recognizes his humorless interest in aqueducts (the scene of his proposal), as a complete lack of imagination and passion.

Along with this romantic antipathy to "facts," James's "impressions" often repeat themselves, suggesting a typology of images. Perhaps James's favorite Roman impression is that of the Colosseum. The great empty space is alive with the past, at once evocative and deadly, as is the city itself. James liked the perspectives of the looming ruin, so easily adaptable from the physical to the spiritual: "The upper portions of the side toward the Esquiline seem as remote and lonely as an Alpine ridge, and you look up at their rugged sky-line, drinking in the sun and silvered by the blue air, with much the same feeling with which you would look at a gray cliff on which an eagle might lodge. This roughly mountainous quality of the great ruin is its chief interest; beauty of detail has pretty well vanished, especially since the high-growing wild-flowers have been plucked away" (*TS,* p. 121).

Here, Daisy Miller contracts her famous, fatal Roman fever. Here too, amongst "the winding shafts where the eager Roman crowds had billowed and trampled," Roderick Hudson, in his aborted attempt to snatch one of those same high-growing flowers, exposes to the reader, Rowland, and Christina Light, both his reckless love and his feckless weakness. The Colosseum, empty on Christmas Day, frames Angelo Beati's lonely and vengeful brooding. The cross at its center suffices to define its starkly powerful atmosphere, and the ominous monomania of Beati's need for revenge. In Isabel Archer's story, too, the Colosseum provides the background for one of the central scenes. Again James emphasizes "the far skyline," "the immense ruin." Isabel is already familiar with the site, and with its ever-present past: "She had often ascended to those desolate ledges from which the Roman crowd used to bellow applause and where now the wild flowers (when they are allowed) bloom in the deep crevices" (chap. 50, 2:340). Here she learns that Rosier has sold his prized bibelots in a vain attempt to earn Mr. Osmond's approval of his suit for Pansy's hand. This poignant episode illuminates Isabel's own situation, for she too has become merely a bibelot sold to satisfy a hopeless infatuation. In sketching the atmosphere of this passage, James once more evokes a vague but strong flavor of the distant Roman past, its moldering persistence, its haunting beauty of light and color, its way of intruding into and shaping the present. Isabel's experience is both dwarfed by comparison to the Colosseum as a vehicle of meaning, and at the same time deepened, both for herself and the reader. It is this power of the Roman past that most interests James.

As a result, while the Roman past provides a canvas on which to depict individual consciousness, the canvas at the same time is the picture, the characters only a shifting element in the continuity that Rome embodies. The individual impression is a moment of stopped time that immediately becomes itself an image of the past. The effect is of a sense of reflections of the physical past in which the observer rather than the object observed moves continuously through time. In the passage that follows the sinuous shapes of the aqueducts define this individual and universal movement: "It is partly, doubtless, because their mighty outlines are still unsoftened that the aqueducts are so impressive. They seem the very source of the solitude in which they stand; they look like architectural spectres, and loom through the light mists of their grassy desert, as you recede along the line, with the same insubstantial vastness as if they rose out of Egyptian sands. It is a great neighborhood of ruins, many of which, it must be confessed, you have applauded in many an album" (*TS*, p. 147). The observer, framed against the ruins is himself absorbed, or as James puts it, "recedes along the line" of vision into the sketches of innumerable albums in the hands of other observers. Rome presents to the Jamesian observer a "sketch," an "impression," a source of "predestined memories" (*TS*, p. 201). As the present slips into the stream of the past, it takes on a flavor of subdued nostalgia, so that although the Roman past is decayed and malign, the present is never quite as good. The statue of Marcus Aurelius, for example, represents an "irrecoverable simplicity . . . that the sculptors of the last three hundred years have been laboriously trying to reproduce" (*TS*, p. 117). Resignation to this inevitability produces an "aesthetic luxury," and the lure of an ennui with a "throbbing soul" (*TS*, p. 199). Time and change seem to dominate Rome, and to become timeless and changeless. "Life on just these terms seems so easy, so monotonously sweet, that you feel as if it would be unwise, really unsafe, to change" (*TS*, p. 199). But this state is like the calm at the center of a whirlpool: contemplation of a monument of papal Rome makes James "linger there in a pensive posture and marvel at the march of history" (*TS*, pp. 156–57). The Capitol offers vivid proof of this march, standing in an atmosphere of "conscious, irremediable incompleteness." The observer's eye measures "the long plumb-line which drops from the inhabited windows of the palace, with their little overpeeping balconies, their muslin curtains, and their bird-cages, down to the rugged handiwork of the Republic" (*TS*, pp. 117–18). As the observer is absorbed into this immortal movement, "the city of his first unpremeditated rapture shines to memory. . . . In the manner of a lost paradise the rustle of whose garden is still just audible enough in the air to make him wonder if some sudden turn, some recovered vista, mayn't lead him back to the thing itself."[19]

Carl Maves traces James's response to Rome in part to an "oddly persistent Anglo-Saxon conception of it, dating at least from the Renaissance," which sees Italy as "a venerable relic of the Roman Empire," and also as "the sink of elegant vice and luxurious corruption."[20] Rome seems to carry with it its own symbolic force, so that its very history, rather than any specific event or building, defines it. The "oddly persistent" quality that marks the continuities of James's

Rome results from the repetition of broad central ideas, and from the pictorial, observational, sensuous manner in which James presents these ideas. These concepts, and even the style in which they emerge, whether as "sketch" or fiction, themselves derive from a complex literary tradition; I would also suggest that it persists most strongly through the nineteenth century as a result of the continuity of an educational ideal based on the literature of classical Rome.

It has proved difficult to define with any scholarly exactitude the direct influence of the classics on early American art, letters, or political theory. Although determined attempts have been made to document references and allusions, the picture is complicated by the practice of decorating discourse with classical, especially Latin, tags and commonplaces (a practice, it should be noted, that itself has classical origins).[21] On the other hand, this practice attests to a widespread familiarity with certain general notions of the classical. Reference to such notions ought not to be taken as allusion in any contemporary sense: when James writes of a "bourgeoise Egeria," or a "taste of Cornelius Nepos," he hardly expects his reader to think of more than a shadowy idea of feminine inspiration or history. But he does expect his reader to think of these. James's own education did not follow any traditional curriculum, but he does admit that as a child he "worried out Virgil and Tite-Live."[22] Indeed, when Henry James Sr.'s experiments in a broader practical education faltered, the adolescent son, released from engineering and mathematics courses, fell back on "German, French, and Latin."[23] The real extent of his exposure to Latin is hinted at by his lifelong friend Thomas Sergeant Perry: "H.J. in his books speaks without enthusiasm of his school studies, but he and I read at Mr. Leverett's school a very fair amount of Latin literature. Like Shakespeare he had less Greek."[24] Furthermore, even if Henry Sr. was reluctant to send his sons to college, he could not have been unaware that during the years of their schooling, Harvard College required for admission examination the following: the whole of Vergil, the whole of Caesar's commentaries, Cicero's select orations, plus grammar, prosody, and composition. In Greek the requirements were: Felton's Greek Reader, plus grammar and prosody, and "writing Greek with the Accents" (no mean task). The

College also assigned readings in history, adding that "the *Ancient History* is the part of this book which is *required*. Equivalents for the prescribed textbooks, if *real* equivalents, are accepted." The actual course of study during the first years at Harvard concentrated, in Latin, on Horace, Livy, Cicero, and Latin Composition.[25] This conservative program was remarkably unchanged since the time of the Roman Empire. Quintilian recommends that a young man's education commence with Homer and Virgil, that he emulate Cicero and Livy, but that erotic elegy be banned, and comedy be introduced carefully. This canon conveys a vision of Rome that persists in James's treatment of the city.

The contrasts that underlie James's impressions of Rome originate in the classical writers apparently covered even in James's iconoclastic education. While it is neither wise nor necessary to seek recondite references or specific echoes, it is possible to show that Roman writers themselves focused, broadly, on the Roman contrasts found in James's writings, and that they evoked an impression of their own city more as background than as an object of interest in itself. I have deliberately chosen as examples of this continuity the most familiar and "classic" of the classical writers and their production, for I am claiming not that James referred to such writers and their ideas, but that he could not escape them.

In a famous passage at *Aeneid* 8.377 and following, Vergil describes his hero at the site of future Rome. As Aeneas's host conducts him on a tour of his humble, but just and happy, kingdom, the narrator reminds his audience that here, where Aeneas sees straw stables and mud huts, will be the golden Capitol, the Forum, the Carmental Gate. The scene describes both continuity and contrast. Vergil's audience looks backward to its own past in Aeneas's future; Jupiter's promised *imperium sine fine* (*Aeneid* 1.279) is at the same time part of the *mos maiorum*, the defining historical context of Roman life. Like Aeneas, the individual is at the center of this temporal perspective, but at the same time is merely part of the flow of history. Vergil wants his reader to think on the virtues of Rome's rustic beginnings, of the simple life and its morality, but at the same time to recognize the greatness the city has attained, its progress and achievement. He suggests that Rome is based on its past, that the past lives in the present, and that the present outshines the past. For the Roman of Augustus's new Golden Age, this relationship was problematic. Hope and political expediency urged one to believe that the present held unprecedented possibilities (if also unprecedented threats): "There is nothing the Claudian line, which Jupiter guards with loving grace, cannot accomplish; their wise attention guides through the hardships of war." On the other hand, Horace, who wrote these optimistic lines, also attacked the corruption that had taken hold in Rome:

> They were a tough race of rustic soldiers. They knew how to turn the Sabine fields with the hoe, and to carry hewn wood at the orders of a stern mother, when the sun shifted the mountain shadows, and released the tired oxen from the yoke, bringing relief as he rode his chariot down the sky. What does corrupting time not weaken? Our parents' age brought worse than its ancestors', and ours is worse yet, and our children soon will produce even more degenerate progeny.

For Horace (at least sometimes) change and progress mean degeneration:

> Soon rich buildings will leave few acres for the plow, everywhere ponds stretching further than Lake Lucrinus; bachelor plane trees will root out elms, violets and myrtle and sweet-smelling trees will breathe their odors where the fertile olive once nourished its master.[26]

The city's grandeur has as its price the loss of the past upon which it is built; its glories imply decay.

The preface to Livy's history of Rome, written over a span of perhaps forty years in the earliest period of the empire, summarizes this dualistic attitude toward the past and the present:

> I invite the reader's attention to the much more serious consideration of the kind of lives our ancestors lived, of who were the men, and what the means both in politics and war by which Rome's power was first acquired and subsequently expanded; I would then have him trace the progress of our moral decline. . . . and the dark dawning of our modern day when we can neither endure our vices nor force the remedies needed to cure them. . . . I hope my passion for Rome's past has not impaired my judgment; for I do honestly believe that no country has ever been greater or purer than ours or richer in

good citizens and noble deeds; none has been free for so many generations from the vices of avarice and luxury, nowhere have thrift and plain living been for so long held in such esteem.[27]

While this simultaneous and antithetical glorification of the past and the present poses a number of interpretive difficulties for the classicist, the finer problems are hardly relevant to an understanding of James's Rome. It is sufficient to note that as the city's image developed in its literature, it emerged as dualistic, self-contradictory, and seductively both good and evil.

As counterpoint to the city's multifaceted lure, the Roman countryside was seen as offering both a contrast and an escape. The pastoral life offered the virtues of ancient morality and the pleasures of leisure, health, and home, uncorrupted by the profligate life of the city. On his Sabine hill farm, says Horace in Satire 2.6, there are "no corrupting forces, and no winds of the sirocco to make the gloomy funeral goddess wealthy." Like the tourist in James's Rome, Horace leaves the city to escape its fatal influences, and its dangers to body and soul. Horace's parable of the city mouse and the country mouse, contained in this same satire, dramatizes the contrast: the city offers luxury, pleasure, sensual delight, and terrifying danger: the country offers plain food, plain living, rustic hospitality; the appeal of each, however, is predicated on the defining contrast of the other.

The beauty and richness—and even the melancholy—of the Roman countryside suffuse Vergil's *Georgics,* in which the hard-won productivity of the land is at root a metaphor for Rome's success. In like manner caught images of untamed beauty offer moral comment: the distant cold of snowy Soracte reminds Horace to look for pleasure to the warm dark corners of the city; the advent of spring, sparsely evoked in a phrase or two about the west winds and the relaxation of winter's grip, reminds him of the briefness of life. The awareness of continuity in nature defines the scope of individual life, and fleeting impressions of passing time crystallize, as they minimize, the importance of the human perspective. The country is a place to be, or to imagine oneself, in order to acquire the perspective on Rome that enriches rather than weakens its immediacy, that redefines one's obsessions (as for Isabel Archer), and makes them part of a greater picture.

From the beginning, Rome conveyed a vitality that made specific description irrelevant. Although Horace and Vergil speak of the Forum, the Capitol, the elegant residential neighborhoods, they are less interested in the concrete features of such monuments than in their atmosphere, their fictional image. In Satire 1.9, Horace describes himself taking a walk on the Sacred Way. Overtaken by a pesky acquaintance, he tries desperately to escape, alleging as an excuse a necessary trip to Caesar's Gardens, but the man sticks to him past Vesta's temple, until fortune at last intervenes, and amidst shouting and confusion, the bore is hauled off to court. The walk takes several hours, the way is through the crowded streets of the city, there are even indications that a quite specific route is marked out, by allusions to a variety of sites, but these landmarks barely rise above the cloud of words and worries that beset Horace. Similarly, the lovers of Augustan Rome wander through the streets, linger importunately outside houses, visit the theater or the Forum in search of amusement, but almost never do they describe a building or explain a route. The Roman poets are far less interested in the city itself than in the spirit, the noise, the crowds, and the individual life within it. Intense individual experience of the concrete and visual, suggesting rather than pinpointing the realities of daily life, evokes the physical as a context, and transforms it into an emotional representation. One result of this technique is a pictorial and impressionistic style that epitomizes and produces the shifting perspectives of characters, narrator, and therefore audience.

James's descriptions of his oblique, impressionistic stance, his pictorial approach to experience, and his fascination with the possibilities of exposing individual consciousness through refracted observation constitute, it has been claimed, "a veritable cornerstone of modern fictional theory."[28] But the precepts on which this theory is grounded have themselves roots in classical rhetorical theory and literary practice. In one sense this is only a general truth about Western literature; at the same time, there are points at which it seems clear that James has so thoroughly absorbed his classical predecessors that their literary values shapes his style. James would agree with the classical theorists that one of the cardinal sins of literary production is the exposure of art and the violation of illusion. While he writes somewhat deprecatingly about readers who think that art should be either amusing or instinctive (what Horace calls *dulce et utile*), he can only add the stricture that it be "interesting": not far from the classical requirement that literary art have the power to please, to move, and to instruct its audience. To this end, James strives for the vivid impression, the encapsulization of experience in the vision of the "author."

As a result, James is in agreement with the ancient critics in suggesting that the art of literature and the art of painting are the closest of kin. James sees the "air of reality (solidity of specification)" as "the supreme virtue of a novel." It is here, according to James, that the novelist "competes with life; it is here that he competes with his brother the painter in *his* attempt to render the look of things, the look that conveys their meaning, to catch the color, the relief, the expression, the surface, the substance of the human spectacle."[29] Horace begins the *Ars Poetica* with a comparison of the unity demanded of painting and poetry; later he adds: "Poems are like pictures; the closer you stand to one, the better it holds you; another gains as you withdraw. This one loves shadow, this likes being seen in light."[30]

The infusion of classical attitudes affects both James's practice, and his critical pronouncements. His treatment of Rome, and his apprehension of the city as a mixture of allure and degeneration, beauty and ugliness, originate in the literature of the Augustan age. The juxtaposition of city and country, and of the past and the present, became, long before James, integral to the idea of Rome. These antitheses shifted, of course, as the city successively provided a setting for the shifting events of history—the emergence of Christianity, the evils of papal Rome, the beauty and corruption of the Renaissance—but their basic structure had become canonical. For James this structure of general ideas acquired the status of universality, a paradigm of the shared elements in the consciousness of individuals. At its most fundamental, Henry James's Rome is the sum of innumerable impressions, whose similarity over time constitutes the "classical" idea of Rome. This impressionistic historicity, this subjective grasp of the object, is, of course, James's conception of his fictional endeavor; and it would be hard to find a better statement of his aesthetic, finally, than this passage from the *Italian Hours:*

> The great and subtle thing, if you are not a strenuous specialist, in places of a heavily charged historic consciousness, is to profit by the sense of that consciousness—or in other words to cultivate a relation with the oracle—after the fashion that suits yourself; so that if the general after-taste of experience, experience at large, the fine distilled essence of the matter, seems to breathe, in such a case, from the very stones and to make a thick strong liquor of the very air, you may thus gather as you pass what is most to your purpose; which is more the indestructible mixture of lived things, with its concentrated lingering odour, than any interminable list of numbered chapters and verses.[31]

NOTES

1. *Transatlantic Sketches* (Boston: Houghton Mifflin Co., 1875, 1903), 310; hereafter referred to in the text as *TS.* This edition includes the Roman sketches: "A Roman Holiday"; "Roman Rides"; "Roman Neighborhoods"; "The After-Season in Rome"; "From a Roman Notebook."

2. *A Small Boy and Others* (New York: Charles Scribner's Sons, 1913), 413.

3. *Italian Hours* (Boston: Houghton Mifflin Co., 1909), 317. This later edition includes the Roman sketch entitled "A Few Other Roman Neighborhoods," as well as the other Roman sketches.

4. Cf. John Lucas, "Manliest of Cities: The Image of Rome in Henry James," *Studi Americani* 11 (1965):117–36, esp. 122f.

5. *Roderick Hudson,* chap. 1:27. I have used the first revised text of 1878, available in Penguin paperback (New York: Penguin Books, 1969, 1981).

6. *Transatlantic Sketches,* 128.

7. *Roderick Hudson,* chap. 9:128. Quentin Anderson, *The American Henry James* (New Brunswick, N.J.: Rutgers University Press, 1957), discusses the appeal for James of the role of passive receptivity to experience offered by Italy; cf. esp. 135–36.

8. *Watch and Ward* (London: Macmillan and Co., 1923), 101.

9. *The Portrait of a Lady* (New York: Charles Scribner's Sons, 1908), chap. 36, 2:100.

10. All quotations of "Adina" and "The Last of the Valerii" are from *The Complete Tales of Henry James,* ed. Leon Edel (Philadelphia: J. P. Lippincott Co., 1962), vol. 3.

11. *Roderick Hudson,* chap. 5:80, 82, 74; see also *Transatlantic Sketches,* 207. On the Juno as a symbol of the female in James, see Charles R. Anderson, *Person, Place, and Thing in Henry James's Novels* (Durham, N.C.: Duke University Press, 1977), 17 ff.

12. "The Last of the Valerii," 121; "Adina," 257. Edel oversimplifies when he suggests, in the introduction to the tales, that these stories represent the conquest of "ancient evil" by American vitality (p. 9).

13. *Transatlantic Sketches,* 123–24; see also *The Portrait of a Lady,* chap. 49: 2:328. In Rome, the country seems part of the background; in the country, even St. Peter's seems merely "a small mountain on the horizon"; the Campagna mediates between them, "swimming mistily in a thousand ambiguous lights and shadows in the interval" (*Transatlantic Sketches,* 156). See also Anderson (n. 7), 152: the Campagna "becomes a kind of shorthand symbol for an equivocal and complex response to Europe."

14. The first two quotations are from *Transatlantic Sketches,* 185; the last from 191.

15. *Roderick Hudson,* chap. 17:224. For discussion of James's impressionistic technique, see Anderson (n. 11), 277–84). See also Henry James, *The Painter's Eye,* ed. John L. Sweeney (Cambridge: Harvard University Press, 1956).

16. *Transatlantic Sketches,* 182–83. Alan Holder, *Three Voyagers in Search of Europe* (Philadelphia: University of Pennsylvania Press, 1966), 197, rightly points out that for James the past was essentially "a glamorous lump of eventfulness."

17. *Roderick Hudson,* chap. 18:238; *Transatlantic Sketches,* 166.

18. "Daisy Miller" (New York: Charles Scribner's Sons, 1909), 55.

19. *Italian Hours,* 304. For further expression of James's nostalgia for his own past see R. C. Harrier, "'Very Modern Rome'—An Unpublished Essay of Henry James," *Harvard Library Bulletin* 8 (1954):125–40.

20. Carl E. Maves, *Sensuous Pessimism: Italy in the Work of Henry James* (Bloomington: Indiana University Press, 1973), 5.

21. For bibliography see John W. Eadie, ed., *Classical Traditions in Early America* (Ann Arbor: University of Michigan Press, 1976).

22. *Notes of a Son and Brother* (New York: Charles Scribner's Sons, 1914), 8.

23. Robert C. LeClair, *Young Henry James* (New York: Bookman Associates, 1955), 303.

24. Ibid., 282.

25. Bulletin of Harvard College, 1850–1865.

26. Horace, *Odes* 4.4.73–6; 3.6.37–48; 2.15.1–8. James's last Italian reminiscences capture precisely this nostalgia for the "uncomplicated," simple past of his *own* Rome.

27. Livy, 1.1; trans. Aubrey De Sélincourt, *Livy: The Early History of Rome* (Baltimore: Penguin Books, 1960).

28. Henry James, *The Future of the Novel,* ed. Leon Edel (New York: Random House, 1956), 43 (the phrase is Edel's).

29. Op. cit., "The Art of Fiction," 14.

30. *Ars poetica* 1ff., 361ff. For an even older version of the same idea, see Simonides "quoted" in Plutarch, *Moralia* 346ff.: "Simonides calls painting 'silent poetry' and poetry 'talking painting.' For literature relates and sets down as having happened the same events that painters represent as happening."

31. *Italian Hours,* 367.

Annabel Patterson

Vergil's *Eclogues:*
Images of Change

In one of his more legislative moments, C. S. Lewis pronounced Sir Philip Sidney's *Arcadia* a "touchstone." "What a man thinks of it," he declared, "tests the depth of his sympathy with the sixteenth century."[1] If one believes in the efficacy of such pronouncements, one might risk an even more sweeping one about the core text from which Sidney's *Arcadia* derived much of its authority—namely, Vergil's *Eclogues.* I shall argue here that what people think of Vergil's *Eclogues* is a key to their own cultural assumptions, especially as those are organized by the concept of the artist/intellectual. What every generation has felt (and this includes their disagreements) about the role of the artist/intellectual in society (or outside it) can usually be determined by a careful scrutiny of how the *Eclogues* have been read at that time. As Vergil himself saw, the *Eclogues* required the interpretive frame of a theory of pastoral, which in turn required a theory of literature—its relation to history, ideality, ideology, the expressive needs of the individual, and the hegemonic needs of the holders of power. As each new set of readers has struggled, ever since, to meet the demands made on them by this subtle text, their own aesthetic or societal premises have been strikingly manifest.

The *Eclogues* are, surely, an ideal text by which to document cultural history. The great Vergil collections of the British Library, Princeton University Library, and the Library of Congress suggest that few texts can have been so frequently edited, annotated, translated, imitated, and *illustrated.* The list of big names is itself provocative raw material for a reception history: among early editors and scholarly commentators, Badius Ascensius (Josse Bade), Peter Ramus, Christopher Landino, Ludovico (Juan Luis) Vives; among translators, Bernardo Pulci, Clement Marot, John Dryden, Paul Valéry; among imitators, Petrarch, Ronsard, Spenser, Milton, Pope, Wordsworth; among illustrators, Sebastian Brandt, Francis Cleyn, Wenceslaus

Hollar, Gérard, Girodet, Blake, Palmer, Aristide Maillol, Jacques
Villon. But the point of such a list is not who was involved in the
constant reinterpretation of the *Eclogues,* but why; and the point is
also that the different forms of interpretation control and elucidate
each other. A classical text in translation, obviously, is a precise lexi-
cal instrument by which to measure interpretive choice; prefaces to
editions reveal larger hermeneutic principles; annotations show which
details were thought of as salient to a particular reading; illustrations
not only interact with the text to form another kind of gloss, another
mechanism of foregrounding, but also, in their changing styles and
iconography, make available for use (and testing) the findings of art
historians.

It is true, of course, that a great deal of this interpretive energy
was directed to Vergil's work as a whole. But the *Eclogues* seem to
have had, from the earliest stages of the Renaissance in Europe, a
special role as cultural catalyst and emblem. Obviously, they came
first in editions of Vergil; their brevity made them a natural exercise
for elementary education in the classics, so that they entered the
European consciousness at a formative stage; and, for reasons that
will shortly become apparent, they tended to invite reinterpretation
more cordially, more urgently, than the *Georgics* or the *Aeneid,* to
present themselves as a continual challenge to intellectuals everywhere.

Let us consider, as a preliminary test of these statements, the
illuminated frontispiece to Petrarch's own manuscript of Vergil (fig.
1).[2] The artist was the Siennese painter Simone de Martini. On the
right sits Vergil, pen in hand, under a tree. Below him sheep (or
goats?) are being milked and trees pruned. Beside him stand two
figures, the one with the spear completing the triple allusion to the
Eclogues, Georgics, Aeneid. Yet the ambience of the painting is pre-
dominantly pastoral, Virgil's own pose reflecting the rural leisure
that makes writing possible. Even more telling is the portrayal of
the other standing figure, not onlooker but interpreter, who draws
away the veil (actually a neat muslin curtain, rings and all), behind
which, without his mediation, Vergil would have remained partially
obscure. Two Latin epigrams complete the story:

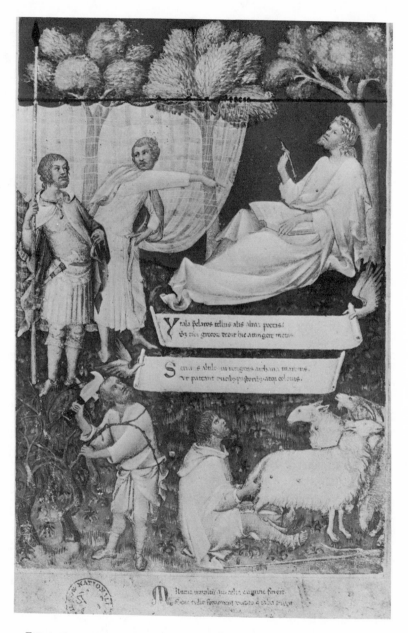

FIG. 1. Simone de Martini, frontispiece to Petrarch's manuscript of Vergil.

Ytala perclaros tellus alis alma poetas!
Sic tibi grecos dedit hic attingere metas.

Servius altiloqui redegens archana maronis
ut pateant ducibus pastoribus atque colonis.

[Italy, kind country, you feed famous poets. So this one, (Vergil), allowed
you to attain the Grecian goals. (Here is) Servius, recovering the mysteries of
high-spoken Vergil, so that they are revealed in generals, shepherds and farmers.]

As the painting represents a hermeneutic on two levels, so the epigrams explain the process of cultural transmission as a two-stage
translatio studii. In the first, Vergil passes on the Greek heritage to
Italy; in the second, Servius, teacher of rhetoric in the fourth century,
reveals to a fourteenth-century Italian the high significance in all of
Vergil's major works. Inside Petrarch's precious manuscript, the commentary of Servius embraces the text of Vergil on every page, inspiring the Italian poet to add his own interpretive glosses, especially to
the *Eclogues.*

In his brilliant essay "Petrarch and the Humanist Hermeneutic,"
Thomas Greene has described the birth of cultural self-consciousness
in Petrarch, stimulated equally by the ruins of Rome and the ancient
texts for whose fragments he also used the term *ruinae;* and Greene
has eloquently described what he calls Petrarch's "sub-reading" or
"archeological scrutiny" of both the physical and the intellectual
ruins of ancient Rome.[3] Sub-reading, an essentially historicist, humanist activity, is to be distinguished from and preferred to Petrarch's
other, and in Greene's view, faulty hermeneutic, the "Alexandrian
method that presumed a poetic truth concealed by an allegorical
veil."[4] It is that veil, of course, that is represented on the frontispiece
of Petrarch's *Vergil;* yet it seems to me that Greene draws an unneces-
sarily sharp distinction between the two kinds of interpretation, as
he is perhaps unduly dismissive of Petrarch's allegorizing notes to the
Eclogues, as well as of his allegorical practice in his own *Bucolicum
Carmen.* The message of Simone di Martini's painting, when explained
by the Latin epigrams, is that interpretation, the drawing of the veil,
is an ongoing historical process.

In fact, Servius had himself been opposed to the excessive and arbitrary allegorization of the commentators who preceded him,[5] and the kind of reading that he instituted was arguably a form of historicism. Servius established the tradition that the first and ninth eclogues referred to actual historical incidents—the confiscation of farm lands by Octavian after the battle of Philippi in 42 B.C. and Vergil's recovery of his own estate through the intervention of Maecenas. Similarly, the fifth eclogue was read in the Servian tradition as a lament for Julius Caesar, whose apotheosis, naturally, reflected well on his heir. The *Eclogues,* then, in Servian commentary, were unintelligible without a grasp of the historical Roman context; the prophecies of the fourth eclogue, the promised return of the Golden Age, referred to the future of Augustan Rome, not, as the medieval Church Fathers had proposed, to the messianic prophecies of Isaiah. Not only were the Servian readings historically plausible and potentially compatible with a theory of authorial intention, as those of Augustine and Eusebius were not; but whenever Servius glossed a passage as capable of being read "*simpliciter*" rather than "*allegorice*" he prompted, one must suppose, a form of interpretive self-consciousness.

The other primary contribution of Servius, and the one that led most directly to the placing of the *Eclogues* at the heart of cultural self-consciousness, was the tradition that Tityrus, relaxing in the shade of a beech tree at the opening of the first epilogue, stood, in some problematical way, for Vergil himself; problematic not because of the naïve disparity between Vergil's real age in 42 B.C. and the old age of Tityrus, but because of the irony that accrues to the *fortunatus senex,* the happy old man, in his dialogue with Meliboeus, his much less fortunate neighbour. Tityrus is represented as the man who has, thanks to a powerful, godlike patron, gotten back his patrimony, and hence the idyllic posture, at ease in the shade [*lentus in umbra*] that both enables and symbolizes the intellectual life. The kind of poetry he is described as creating is simple Theocritan love-lyric ("making the woods resound with the name of Amaryllis"). In contrast to Meliboeus, who having lost his farm irretrievably must head into exile and out of poetry [*carmina nulla canam*], the idyll of Tityrus comes to seem naïve and insensitive. Yet Vergil, of course, expressed himself through both figures, as under Simone di Martini's tree, still in the posture of Tityrus, he wrote his whole problematical, arcane, multivalent work. The effect of this tradition was incalculably broad. The *Eclogues* were revealed, in effect, as a dialectical poetics, their subject the proper subject of poetry, the rightful conduct of poets. On one side of the dialectic was idyll, nostalgic for Theocritus, concerned with the love songs and song-contests of shepherds, lyric as its own subject; on the other a form of realism, concerned with the historical Roman moment, the consequences of civil war, problems of landownership and the relationship of writers to rulers. The two sides of the dialectic matched the two ways of reading the *Eclogues, simpliciter* and *allegorice;* but together they formed a metaphorical system by which later writers could allude to the power structures of their own society, describe their own poetics, determine their own cultural stance.

Let us now move on to Renaissance readings of the *Eclogues.* I have chosen as my first exhibit a mid-sixteenth-century (1537) commentary by the Spanish humanist Ludovico Vives.[6] Fortunately for this occasion, the important theoretical preface to this work was translated for an English audience in 1628 by a minor academic called William L'Isle. Vives had written the preface partly in order to reconcile his reputation as a serious scholar with his interest in the *Eclogues;* it was in this context that he defined his own Vergilian hermeneutics. Vergil, he pointed out, had taken three whole years to write the *Eclogues* and had addressed them to "the greatest wits of Rome," Gallus, Pollio, "yea the Prince himselfe Augustus," men who would never have concerned themselves "with such kindes of light matter as Pastoralls, had they not afforded some hidden meaning and sense of a higher nature." "This worke doth plainly witnesse . . . that it is not simply, but figuratively spoken, under a shadow (*sub umbra*)."[7] The pastoral shade under which Vergil, as Tityrus, figured himself, *"lentus in umbra,"* becomes recognized here as a pun. *Umbra* equally connotes natural shade and image, figure. Vives's intention as commentator was, therefore, to "restore":

the Poet to the true scope and aime of his meaning, and show, that his purpose was not to consume so much precious time, and exquisite verses in triviall
light matters of no moment; and that those things which Theocritus in a
ruder barbarous age, did sing in a Pastorall plaine sense, Virgil here doth apply
to the Romans, making them his owne, under a mysticall understanding,
worthy the eares of the most learned: notwithstanding I make no doubt but I
have fitted some of his verses with such an allegory and explication, as the
Author himselfe never dreamed of. (Pp. 11–12)

"Making them his owne": in one deft phrase Vives explained the
whole process of historical transmission and reinterpretation to which
he was now adding another stage. As Vergil had adapted Theocritus
to the Roman context, so Vives adapted Vergil to the expectations
of a Christian culture, seeing no problem in a mixed hermeneutic,
historicist restoration blending calmly with christic allegorization,
learning with belief.

Half a century after Vives wrote his preface for European scholars,
a minor English critic, George Puttenham, published an *Arte of English Poesie* (1589). In the course of a survey of the classical genres,
Puttenham produced a definition of pastoral that, though often cited,
has seldom been carefully scrutinized. According to Puttenham,

the poet devised the Eglogue . . . not of purpose to counterfait or represent
the rusticall manner of loves and communication, but under the vaile of
homely persons, and in rude speeches to insinuate and glaunce at greater
matters, and such as perchance had not bene safe to have disclosed in any
other sort, which may be perceived in the Eglogues of Virgill, in which are
treated, by figure, matters of greater importance then the loves of Titirus and
Corydon.[8]

The references to the "vaile" of pastoral metaphor, "under" which
"matters of greater importance" are presented derive obviously from
the tradition of Servian commentary, as mediated to the Renaissance.
Puttenham implies that he shares with Vives the sense that the Theocritean roots of the *Eclogues,* "the loves of Titirus and Corydon,"
are the least valuable and interesting of Vergil's components. But the
sense of hidden danger in this passage, the "greater matters . . . such
as perchance had not been safe to have disclosed in any other sort,"
provides a different emphasis.[9] Hermeneutical subtlety in the *Eclogues*

is still a reason to take them seriously; but Puttenham reads the text, not, like Vives, as an infinitely broad and flexible vehicle of cultural revisionism, but as a necessary political tool. If Servian commentary implied that Vergil addressed Augustus "by figure" about the harshness of his resettlement policies, for example, then the pastoral tradition, the *Roman* tradition, was from the start encoded ideology. As a vehicle of oblique sociopolitical commentary, the eclogue allowed, up to a point, immunity to the intellectual (the privileged stance of Tityrus), provided that the ruler he addressed perceived and valued the subtlety of the code.

Puttenham's version of Vergil's intentions was, however, certainly influenced by the special conditions of Elizabethan culture. In the 1580s, pastoral was a privileged discourse under two different (but not separate) dispensations. On the one hand, it was the language of Elizabethan courtiership at its most affirmative, if subservient; on the other, due to the intensified political censorship of the early 1580s, it became the vehicle also of the analysis, even criticism, of Elizabeth's policies.[10] Spenser's *Shepheardes Calender* could invoke her as "the Queene of Shepheardes all," in the "Aprill" eclogue while reflecting darkly in others on her handling of church polity and her plans, in 1579, to marry a French prince.[11] His twelve eclogues were framed in a pseudo-Servian commentary by E.K., full of hints that there are secrets or enigmas in the text beyond the commentator's reach.[12] The *Calendar* was dedicated to Sir Philip Sidney, whose *Arcadia*, written and revised 1580–85, located its five sets of eclogues in a complicated ethical and political narrative, which becomes a form of commentary upon them, as they upon it. The role of Tityrus, as the poet's own persona, is here taken by the mysterious figure of Philisides, who is certainly not, however, happy, privileged, or complacent; and the entire text, including its unfinished state, can be read as a critique of English arcadianism, in both life and art.

Sidney's *Apology for Poetry*, published in 1595 but written in the 1580s, made essentially the same point as Puttenham's *Arte* in explaining Arcadia's Roman origins:

> Is the poor pipe disdained, which sometimes out of Meliboeus' mouth can
> show the misery of people *under* hard lords or ravening soldiers? And again,
> by Tityrus, what blessedness is derived to *them that lie lowest* from the good-
> ness of *them that sit highest;* sometimes, *under* the pretty tales of wolves and
> sheep, can include the whole consideration of wrongdoing and patience.[13]
> [Italics added]

In an apparently innocent syntax, Sidney articulated a set of causal
relationships between genre and sociopolitical experience: humility,
repression, suppression, and covert discourse—lying low in more
senses than one.[14]

The two voices of Elizabethan pastoral—the one idyllic, myth-
making, or myth-supporting, the other ambiguous and sceptical—
would seem to continue the essential argument that Vergil had with
himself and posed for his contemporaries. Really strong writers and
thinkers would continue, as both Spenser and Sidney clearly did, to
build both voices into their work. We are sadly missing the point if
we see them, from a modernist perspective, as contributing to "the
Renaissance Perversion of Pastoral"[15] by denying the reader the
psychic satisfactions of "pure pastoral." And it is equally erroneous
to assume that this version of pastoral was specific to the Renaissance.
In the seventeenth century, when English imagination was to make its
fullest and closest identification with Roman history and literature,
we find one of the most striking examples of a writer making Vergil
his own for political purposes, while at the same time giving full credence to the meaning and value (the seventeenth-century meaning
and value) of idyll.

During the revolution, drawing analogies between the Roman civil
war and the English one became a national habit; and in 1649, the
year of Charles I's execution, a Royalist named John Ogilby published
a translation of all of Vergil's works designed to exploit the habit. In
his version of the first eclogue, for example, Ogilby's Meliboeus makes
an unmistakably topical comment on Tityrus's good fortune:

> I envy not, but wonder thou art so blessed
> Since all by sequestrations are oppressed.[16]

The term *sequestration* was that formally used by the Long Parliament during the 1640s to describe its confiscations of royalist estates. The first eclogue therefore becomes a question peculiarly relevant to Royalist writers considering what posture to adopt, now that their side had lost the war. Should they head out into exile as writers like Richard Fanshawe, Abraham Cowley, William Davenant chose or were forced to do; or should they accommodate themselves, at least temporarily, to those now in power, take the Engagement, retain the privileges of Tityrus? After 1650, when Charles II was decisively defeated at the Battle of Worcester, the value of expedient passivity as compared to active confrontation was perceived by Charles himself and his chief advisors in France;[17] and in 1654 John Ogilby reissued his translation, in a new format, one that made its contribution to this new policy almost, but not quite manifest. The 1654 edition was a large folio, complete with marginal commentary in the Servian tradition, and adorned with magnificent plates designed by Frances Cleyn, and executed by Hollar, Lombart and others. The illustration for the first eclogue (fig. 2) clearly shows Tityrus as passive and Meliboeus as the more vital, sympathetic figure. In the background is a scene of violence, showing the farmers being driven from their lands; and in the marginal commentary a specious little note draws attention to the peculiar word "*sequestration,*" arguing that on reflection the term is an acceptable translation of the original "*turbatur agris.*" Ogilby's phrase for the kind of reflection required is "by rational consequence," a phrase that encapsulates the process by which Vergil was to speak to a certain English audience in 1654. We have some sense, also, of just how well defined that audience was. Not only was the volume extremely expensive—a book for the elite, either financial or intellectual. Anthony à Wood noted that "it was the fairest Edition that till then the English Press ever produced" and that it was "reserved for libraries and the Nobility."[18] In addition, each of the engraved plates was dedicated to a member of the aristocracy. In fact, the first six plates were all dedicated to members of the great Seymour family, the leaders of the Western Association, Charles's chief resistance movement in England until the Battle of Worcester, when the movement was crushed, and the family's head, Henry, Lord Beauchamp, imprisoned.[19]

Daphnis ego in Silvis,   hinc usq, ad Sydera notus
  Formosi pecoris custos,   formosior ipse. Eclog: 5

Honoratissimo Dñ. Domino,   Henrico Baroñi Beuchampe
      Tabula merito   Votiua.

FIG. 2. William Hollar and Francis Cleyn, Eclogue 1, from *The Works of Publius Virgilius Maro*, trans. John Ogilby (London, 1654).

This fact lends both poignancy and additional complexity to Ogilby's fifth eclogue (fig. 3), which was dedicated to Beauchamp. In his marginal commentary to the elegy, Ogilby reminded his audience that there were different traditions for identifying Daphnis, including Christ and Julius Caesar. Yet his plate clearly selects the preferred, Roman, historical interpretation. It does more. It suggests, by its composition, that that meaning is superior, literally over the heads of the shepherds whose songs give rise to it, accessible only to learned men. In a brief verse "argument" added to the poem as a preliminary gloss, Ogilby made this point explicit and added yet another level of significance:

> Since Kings as common Fathers cherish all,
> Subjects like children should lament their fall;
> But learned men of grief should have more sense
> When violent death seizes a gracious Prince. (1654; p. 23)

Given the recent English experience of a monarch's death by violence, the "more sense" that Ogilby's version was designed to promote was, above all, a sense of history. Englishmen, Royalists, intellectuals, were encouraged to understand the regicide in the light of its Roman analogue; and, rather than submit to useless grief or self-destructive provocation of Cromwell, to await, sensibly, the advent of a Stuart Augustus.

In the early eighteenth century, the Vergilian dialectic was still potent, still capable of cultural adaptation and relevance. It is sometimes forgotten that Pope's later demotion and mockery of pastoral was the product of a serious rivalry between himself and Ambrose Philips, a quarrel that disrupted literary relationships in England for the better part of a decade. The origins of this quarrel can be traced to a major disagreement about pastoral, its appropriate tone, subject matter, and, above all, cultural function. Pope's *Pastorals* were published in 1709 in *Tonson's Miscellany,* in last place, as Philips's were the first item in that collection. Philips's *Pastorals* were, moreover, publicly recommended by Addison. In the *Spectator* of 1712, Addison declared that Philips had given pastoral "a new life, and a more natural beauty . . . by substituting, in the place of . . . antiquated

FIG. 3. William Hollar and Francis Cleyn, Eclogue 5, from *The Works of Publius Virgilius Maro*, trans. John Ogilby (London, 1654).

fables, the superstitious mythology which prevails among the shepherds of our own country." The overt contrast was with Pope's consciously "neoclassical" mood poems, elegant tissues of verbal allusions to Vergil's *Eclogues,* but with all of the Roman context, the "realism," smoothed away. The idea that Philips had discovered a realistic, native version of the eclogue was further developed by an anonymous *Guardian* critic in 1713.[20]

There is very good reason to believe, however, that what Addison and his circle praised as native and realistic went far beyond the merely literary. Addison and his friends belonged, in 1712, to the Hanoverian Club, dedicated to ensuring that a member of the Protestant House of Hanover, not a Stuart, should succeed Queen Anne. Philips was, in 1712, secretary of that club.[21] But even in 1709 he had built into his *Pastorals* a Hanoverian position, for those who cared to look. They are dedicated to Lionel Cranfield, Duke of Dorset, who had in 1706 accompanied the Earl of Halifax on his mission to inform the Elector of Hanover of the Regency Act. Addison had himself accompanied Halifax in 1707 to invest the Elector with the Order of the Garter; and he appears as the mysterious patron of Philips's second pastoral. The third is the elegy for Anne's young son, George, who died in 1700, an event that, obviously, exacerbated the problem of succession. In the sixth pastoral, Philips introduced a series of speakers recalled from Spenser's *Shepheardes Calender* and Sidney's *Arcadia;* including "Lanquet," or Sidney's Huguenot mentor and friend, Hubert Languet;[22] these speakers explain the cultural analogy between Elizabeth and Anne, while implying another, between Eliza's "Maiden Rule" and Anne's now childless state. Pope, on the other hand, had inserted into his first pastoral two riddles that reminded his audience of Anne's Stuart heritage. The quarrel over the two sets of *Pastorals* was, therefore, surely motivated by more than stylistic preferences, or by the preference for native realism over neoclassical pastiche.

In fact, Philips's *Pastorals* were quite as neoclassical, just as Vergilian, as Pope's, although in a very different and far more "original" way. This apparent contradiction can best be understood with the help of an extraordinary document, a schoolboy edition of Vergil

edited by Dr. Robert Thornton in 1821. For this, the third edition
of his textbook, Thornton conceived the plan of interpreting Vergil's
text for his juvenile audience by giving each eclogue the largest possible context: learned commentary, visual illustration, and, by way
of cultural explanation, poetic analogues and imitations of individual
eclogues. Philips's second pastoral appears, therefore, as an analogue
to Vergil's first eclogue; and Thornton left his readers in no doubt as
to the relationship between the two poems:

> Philips, an admirable poet, has ably imitated the first Pastoral of Vergil, and
> designates himself under the character of a shepherd, in order that he might
> publicly declare his gratitude to his patron; for he had come up a lad from
> Scotland to England with very scanty means, was attacked in his writings
> by ill-natured critics, and envious poets; but found at length a [Maecenas]
> ... who stood forward as his friend. [23]

Given this basic perception, the reader could easily see that Philips's
poem was not just a naive imitation, but an ideological revision of its
model. It, too, is a debate between a happy shepherd and a sad one;
but now the poet himself is represented by the sad one, the young
and melancholy Colinet, alien and wanderer. The effect of this move
was, surely, to create a powerful imbalance in the Vergilian system;
and by making Meliboeus, the outsider, the figure of the intellectual,
Philips, remarkably, predicted Romanticism. One has only to look at
what he did to the pastoral shade-tree, the protecting *umbra,* to grasp
the force of the change. Colinet speaks:

> My piteous Plight, in yonder naked Tree,
> That bears the Thunder Scar, too well I see.
> Quite destitute it stands of shelter kind,
> The Mark of Storms and Sport of ev'ry Wind:
> . . . .
> No more beneath thy Shade shall Shepherds throng
> With merry Tale, or Pipe, or pleasing Song.
> Unhappy Tree! and more unhappy I.
> From thee, from me, alike the Shepherds fly. [24]

The tree still needs to be read figuratively; but the act of figuration
has now been recovered from the reader, the commentator, the
learned gloss, and reabsorbed into the poem, into the consciousness

of the poet/protagonist, who reads the tree by the light of his visionary imagination. Colinet thus points forward to Wordsworth's aliens
and wanderers, to the Wordsworthian landscape of twisted trees and
wrecked lives, and to Wordsworth's explicit rejection of idyllic pastoral, "the perpetual warbling," as he put it in *The Excursion*, "that
prevails/In Arcady, beneath unaltered skies."[25]

It would be fascinating to know whether Dr. Robert Thornton
knew what he was doing when he commissioned William Blake to
illustrate, not Vergil, but Ambrose Philips's second pastoral. Blake's
woodcuts, as in this series (fig. 4), are an extraordinary interpretation
of a new interpretation of Vergil, in which we can almost see how
the change of imaginative focus occurred, how the shepherds changed
roles, how the tree became blasted. But it is important to remember
that Blake's reading of Philips was itself cultural revision, his own role
as an artist/outsider sensitizing him to the tone of Philips, but not to
the problems of a Hanoverian Scot trying to make his way in London
more than a century earlier!

It is also important to realize that, as Philips initiated one kind of
imbalance in the Virgilian dialectic (that would have, through Blake,
a profound influence), so Pope aligned himself with its polar opposite,
with equally lasting consequences. Pope's Golden Age concept of
pastoral (before he abandoned the genre to parody) was totally idyllic,
totally committed to the stance of Tityrus. It was also, as is well
known, derived eclectically from French theorists, particularly René
Rapin, whose relation to the dialectic we have been following is un-
usually interesting. In 1659 Rapin had felt impelled to challenge
directly the pastoral theory of Vives, whose treatise he had obviously
read with some care. "Great things," he asserted, "cannot in the least
be comprehended within the subject matter of Pastorals":

> no, it must be low and humble . . . the affairs of Shepherds, especially their
> loves . . . Sports, Jests, Gifts, and Presents, . . . every part must be full of the
> simplicity of the Golden Age.[26]

Rapin actually quoted Vives, or rather misquoted him, producing a
brilliantly deformed justification of pastoral consistent with the
tenets of French neoclassicism:

COLINET.

THENOT.

COLINET AND THENOT.

COLINET.

FIG. 4. William Blake, Ambrose Philips's Eclogue 2, from *The Pastorals of Virgil*, ed. Robert J. Thornton (London, 1821).

'tis not probable that Asinius Pollio, Cinna, Varius, Cornelius Gallus, men of
the neatest Wits, and that lived in the most polite Age, or that Augustus
Caesar the prince of the Roman elegance, as well as of the Common Wealth,
should be so extremely taken with Virgil's Bucoliks . . . unless [they] had
known that there is somewhat more than ordinary Elegance in those sorts of
Composures, which the wise perceive, tho far above the understanding of the
Crowd. (p. 6)

"*Neatest* Wits"; "the most *polite* age"; Augustus, Caesar, "the *prince
of the Roman elegance, as well as of the Common Wealth*"; How
cleverly has Vives's text been reworked to create a formalist account
of Vergilian pastoral, a gentleman's account, one in which, as Fontenelle was to put it more directly, "Laziness and Love" are the only
permissible subjects,[27] while the cultural elite suppresses all thoughts
of a dialectical nature, such as the sociopolitical supports for gentle-
men of letters. It was no coincidence that Pope's position, formally
articulated in his 1717 *Discourse on Pastoral Poetry*, was both
francophilic and Tory; nor that Philips, who, as Addison had observed, addressed himself to "the shepherds of our own country,"
was a Whig.

Pope's position on pastoral was, therefore, really a metaphor for
the role of the man of letters, idealist, apolitical, serenely oblivious
to the pressures and conflicts of society. Nothing could less resemble
the actual shape of his own career. Yet the position that he natural-
ized survived, despite Crabbe's indignation in *The Village*,[28] despite
the more profound challenges of Wordsworth; and, fueled perhaps by
post-Romantic theories of subjectivity, perhaps by two world wars,
emerged as the dominant, almost exclusive theory of pastoral in the
twentieth century. This has been one period of cultural history in
Europe in which, under the psychic pressure of phrases like "the green
world" and "the country of the mind" the Vergilian dialectic has
almost disappeared.[29] It is impossible not to wonder what is at stake.
What is the connection between an idyllic definition of the *Eclogues*,
of all pastoral, of pastoral as a metaphor for all intellectual activity,
and the institutionalization of the country of the mind in the universities of the present, with all their institutional privileges and
protections?

I will leave this incomplete polemic with two examples of what happened to Vergil's *Eclogues* in the modernist phase. The first is a fine art edition issued by the Cranach Press in 1927, with woodcuts by Aristide Maillol, attached to separate translations of the text in English, French, and German; in French by Marc Lafargue, in German by Thomas Achelis and Alfred Koerte, in English by J. H. Mason. It was the Maillol woodcuts, however, that gave these editions their significance; and culturally significant they clearly are. Almost all representation, let alone hidden meaning, has been removed, so that one can barely tell which picture belongs to which poem. The example here (fig. 5), from *Eclogue* 6, the "Silenus," is more recognizable than most, but no more erotic. "Laziness and Love," as Fontenelle had directed, are certainly the only discernible subjects of these *Eclogues,* naked figures not in intellectual but in sexual repose; and the influence of formalism is clearly apparent in the minimalism of the design, the reduction of significance to a pattern of lines.

The other example is more compex: Paul Valéry's *Variations sur les Bucoliques,* written between 1942 and 1944 and published posthumously in Paris in 1953, with illustrations by Jacques Villon. As there is a striking contrast between Valéry's very public career and his claim to have originated the creed of "poésie pure," so there is an inherent contradiction between the *form* of this fine art edition, possessible only by the privileged few, and its contents. For what it contains, along with the translation and the illustrations, is an essay by Valéry on the significance of the *Eclogues,* a meditation on the "relations de la Poésie avec les regimes ou gourvernements divers," which I shall translate at some length, letting it serve as my peroration:

> This problem admits of as many solutions as individual temperament and circumstances propose. There are economic solutions, for one must live. Others are solutions of a moral order, and others, purely emotional. One regime seduces by its exterior perfections, or by its brilliance, its triumphs, one masters by its genius, another by its generosity, sometimes by a simple smile. In other cases, there are reactions of opposition, excited by the political state of affairs: the man of spirit rebels more or less openly, or shuts himself away in his work, which stealthily surrounds his sensibility with a sort of

FIG. 5. Aristide Maillol, Eclogue 6, from *Les eglogues de Virgile*, trans. Marc Lafargue (Weimar, 1926).

intellectual isolation. . . . Personal interest speaks with a powerful voice. One must never forget that every individual who distinguishes himself by his talents places himself, in his heart, in a certain aristocracy. . . . He observes that an egalitarian democracy is incapable of giving a poet a pension. Judging men in power and men dominated by them, he despises them, but feels the temptation himself to make a political figure, to participate in the conduct of affairs. This temptation is not rare among lyric poets. It is remarkable how that purest of all human occupations, which is, like Orpheus, to tame and uplift creatures with song, is so often accompanied by the most impure desire of all.[30]

At the end of his career, Valéry rediscovered the Vergilian dialectic, felt, in its original Roman context, a transhistorical force that merged

MELIBOEUS – TITYRUS

MELIBOEUS

Tityre, tu patulae recubans sub tegmine fagi
Silvestrem tenui musam meditaris avena :
Nos patriae fines et dulcia linquimus arva :
Nos patriam fugimus ; tu, Tityre, lentus in umbra
Formosam resonare doces Amaryllida silvas.

MÉLIBÉE – TITYRE

MÉLIBÉE

O Tityre, tandis qu'à l'aise sous le hêtre,
Tu cherches sur ta flûte un petit air champêtre,
Nous, nous abandonnons le doux terroir natal,
Nous fuyons la patrie, et toi, tranquille à l'ombre,
Tu fais chanter au bois le nom d'Amaryllis.

3

FIG. 6. Jacques Villon, Eclogue 1, from Paul Valéry, *Variations sur Les Bucoliques* (Paris, 1953).

with, and modified, his modernist creed. Similarly, Villon's illustrations, as here (fig. 6) for the first eclogue, combine the techniques of cubism and other modes of abstraction with a kind of realism that has both psychological and historical force, strangely recalling both Ogilby and Blake. The *Variations* look both backwards and forwards. Imperfect Latinist as he was when he began the translation, Valéry felt the fragments *"du language de Rome"* (p. xvii) that had survived in his memory from his schooldays to be *"infiniment precieuse,"* a humanist emotion that connects him also to Petrarch. But his preface, above all, acknowledges the perpetual relevance of the *Eclogues* for cultural theory, their permanent challenge to the artist/intellectual to declare himself, and to recognize the historical forces that have brought him to where he stands.

NOTES

1. C. S. Lewis, *English Literature in the Sixteenth Century, Excluding Drama* (Oxford: Clarendon Press, 1954), p. 339.

2. Bibliotheca Ambrosiana, Milan, codex A.49.inf.; reproduced in facsimile (Mediolanus, 1930). I am indebted to Cornell University Library for permission to reproduce the frontispiece from their copy.

3. Thomas M. Greene, *The Light in Troy: Imitation and Discovery in Renaissance Poetry* (New Haven: Yale University Press, 1982), pp. 81-103.

4. Ibid., pp. 35, 94. This attitude to Petrarch's hermeneutics was established by Pierre de Nolhac, *Petrarque et L'Humanisme,* 2 vols. (Paris: Champion, 1807), 1:145-48.

5. Servian commentary exists in two versions: one that appears in medieval manuscripts and early Renaissance editions of Vergil, and a longer version (Servius Danielis) first printed by Peter Daniel in 1600, which incorporates an earlier commentary. For the complex textual history, see Georg Thilo and Hermann Hagen, eds., *Servii Grammatici qui feruntur in Vergilii carmina commentarii,* 3 vols. (Leipzig: B. G. Teubner, 1878). For Servius versus earlier allegorizers, see Emile Thomas, *Servius et son commentaire sur Virgile* (Paris: Ernest Thorin, 1880), pp. 48-49, 242-45.

6. G. L. Vives, *In allegorias Bucolicorum Vergilii Praefatio,* first published in *Disciplina et Institutio Puerorum* (Magdeburg, 1540), p. 209ff.

7. William L'Isle, *Virgil's Eclogues Translated into English* (London, 1628), pp. 9-11.

8. George Puttenham, *The Arte of English Poesie* (1589), ed. G. D. Willcock and A. Walker (Cambridge: Cambridge University Press, 1936), pp. 38–39.

9. But political caution was also one of Petrarch's motives for writing the *Bucolicum Carmen* as "poematis genus ambigui"; see E. Carrarra, *La poesia pastorale* (Milan: F. Vallardi, 1909), p. 88.

10. For a subtle account of the "duplicity" of Elizabethan pastoral, see Louis Montrose, "'Eliza, Queene of Shepheardes,' and the Pastoral of Power," *English Literary Renaissance* 10 (1980), 153–82.

11. See Paul E. McLane, *Spenser's Shepheardes Calender: A Study in Elizabethan Allegory* (Notre Dame, Ind.: University of Notre Dame Press, 1961).

12. E.K.'s prefatory "Epistle" to the *Calender* observes that "as touching the generall dryft and purpose of his Aeglogues, I mind not to say much, him selfe labouring to conceale it." His opening note to "January" explains that under the name of Colin Clout Spenser "secretly shadoweth himself, as sometime did Virgil under the name of Tityrus." In the "Argument" to "November" E.K. complains: "The personage is secrete, and to me altogether unknowne, albe of him selfe I often required the same." There are a dozen such warnings to the reader that the text is encoded, topical and probably dangerous.

13. *An Apology for Poetry,* ed. Geoffrey Shepherd (London: Oxford University Press, 1965), p. 116.

14. For a fuller, but still embryonic version of this argument, see my "'Under . . . Pretty Tales': Intention in Sidney's *Arcadia,*" *Studies in the Literary Imagination* 15 (1982):5–21.

15. S. K. Heninger, *Journal of the History of Ideas* 22 (1961): 254–61.

16. John Ogilby, trans., *Works of Publius Virgilius Maro* (London, 1649), p. 2.

17. David Underdown, *Royalist Conspiracy in England, 1649–1660* (New Haven: Yale University Press, 1960), pp. 30–51, 73–96.

18. Anthony à Wood, *Athenae Oxonienses,* 2 vols. (London, 1691), 2:263.

19. Underdown, *Royalist Conspiracy,* p. 87.

20. The *Guardian* was edited by Thomas Tickell; *Guardian* 31 (April 17) gave an allegorical history of pastoral that made Philips, via Spenser, the heir to Vergil and Theocritus, and excluded Pope altogether.

21. For the Hanover Club, see Robert Allan, *Clubs of Augustan London* (Hamden, Conn.: Archon Books, 1967), pp. 55–56. On the political motives of the pastoral dispute, see also W. L. Macdonald, *Pope and His Critics* (London: J. M. Dent, 1951), pp. 62, 77.

22. In a crucial eclogue in the *Arcadia* Philisides defers to his mentor "Languet, the shepherd best swift Ister knew" who had taught him "old true tales" in "oak's true shade." *The Countess of Pembroke's Arcadia,* ed. Jean Robertson (Oxford: Clarendon Press, 1973), pp. 255–56.

23. Robert J. Thornton, ed., *The Pastorals of Virgil, with a Course of English Reading, Adapted for Schools* (London: F. C. and J. Rivington, 1821), p. 13.

Thornton wrote "Mecaenas" and glossed "Addison." The poem itself gives the patron's name as Menalcas.

24. "The Second Pastoral" in *Poetical Miscellanies: The Sixth Part,* ed. Jacob Tonson (London, 1709), pp. 10–11.

25. Wordsworth, "The Excursion," 3:321–22. *The Poetical Works,* ed. E. de Selincourt and H. Darbishire, 5 vols. (Oxford: Clarendon Press, 1949), 5:84.

26. René Rapin, *Eglogue, cum dissertatione de carmine pastorali* (Paris, 1659), cited here in Thomas Creech's 1684 translation; see *The Idylliums of Theocritus, with Rapin's Discourse of Pastorals* (London, 1684), ed. J. E. Congleton (Ann Arbor: Augustan Reprints 2:3, 1947), p. 23.

27. Bernard le Bovier de Fontenelle, *Discours sur le nature de l'églogue* (1688), trans. Pierre Motteux as *Of Pastorals* (London, 1695), pp. 330–31.

28. George Crabbe assumed in *The Village* (1783), for polemical purposes, that Vergil was responsible for the "flattering dream" whose "Mechanick echoes" debase his culture, as it has degraded the rural poor. Instead of the nonexistent "happy swains" of Golden Age pastoral, he demanded that writers produce "the real picture of the poor" and of the rural labor that Fontenelle's theory excluded.

29. Thomas Rosenmeyer's *The Green Cabinet* (Berkeley and Los Angeles: University of California Press, 1969) was a late but influential summation of this view, posing Theocritus as the true father and definer of pastoral, and attempting to read Vergil as if he were Theocritus. A decade later Paul Alpers, in *The Singer of the Eclogues: A Study of Virgilian Pastoral* (Berkeley and Los Angeles: University of California Press, 1979) restored part of the Vergilian dialectic; while his new translation (facing the Latin) and his subtle synthesis of the commentary tradition from Servius onward should help to recover the text for American education.

30. Valéry, *Variations sur les Bucoliques* (Paris: Société Scripta et Picta, 1953), p. xxix. In *Dialogue de l'arbre* (1943) Valéry imagined a debate between Tityrus and Lucretius on the pastoral tree itself. The dialectic here is not idealism vs. realism or sad vs. happy, but between the two versions of meditation (simple/intuitive vs. profound/speculative) distinguished by Vergil himself in *Georgics* 2: 490–99.

The English Institute, 1982

SUPERVISING COMMITTEE

Patricia Spacks (1982), Head, Yale University
James Cox (1982), Dartmouth College
Carolyn Helibrun (1983), Columbia University
Murray Krieger (1983), University of California, Irvine and Los Angeles
Leo Braudy (1984), Johns Hopkins University
Stanley Cavell (1984), Johns Hopkins University
Frances Ferguson (1984), University of California, Berkeley
Kenneth R. Johnston, Secretary, Indiana University, Bloomington

TRUSTEES

Geoffrey Hartman, Yale University
Charles A. Owen, Jr., University of Connecticut
Helen Vendler, Boston University

ARCHIVIST

David V. Erdman, State University of New York, Stony Brook, and New York
    Public Library

The Program

Thursday, August 26 through Sunday, August 29, 1982

I. Pope and Poetic Reference
    Directed by John Sitter, Emory University
    Thurs. 1:45 P.M.   Refinement
                        Susan Staves, Brandeis University
    Fri. 9:30 A.M.   The Muse of Pain
                        David B. Morris, University of Iowa
    Fri. 11:00 A.M.   The Rape of the Sybil: Pope and Abandoned Women
                        Lawrence Lipking, Northwestern University

II. The American Renaissance Reconsidered
    Directed by Walter Benn Michaels, University of California, Berkeley
    Thurs. 3:15 P.M.   From Revolution to Renaissance
                        Eric J. Sundquist, University of California, Berkeley
    Fri. 1:45 P.M.   The Other American Renaissance
                        Jane Tompkins, Temple University
    Fri. 3:15 P.M.   Romance and Real Estate
                        Walter Benn Michaels, University of California, Berkeley

III. Rome in the English Imagination
    Directed by Annabel Patterson, University of Maryland
    Sat. 9:30 P.M.   "The Afflatus of Ruin": Meditations on Rome by
                        Du Bellay, Spenser, and Stevens
                        Margaret Ferguson, Yale University
    Sat. 11:00 A.M.   Virgil's *Eclogues:* Images of Change
                        Annabel Patterson, University of Maryland
    Sun. 9:30 A.M.   Roman Victorians, Victorian Romans, and the Vic-
                        torian Idea of Rome
                        George Landow, Brown University
    Sun. 11:00 A.M.   Romantic Rome
                        Jerome McGann, California Institute of Technology

IV. Marxism, History, Textuality
    Directed by Mary Jacobus, Cornell University

Sat. 1:45 P.M.	Marxist Theories of History
	Terry Eagleton, Wadham College, Oxford University
Sat. 3:15 P.M.	Philosophy of Modern Poetry: Poetic Technique as Social Form
	John Brenkman, University of Wisconsin, Madison
Sun. 1:45 P.M.	History and Narrative
	Pamela McCallum, University of Calgary
Sun. 3:15 P.M.	Kenneth Burke: Action, Rhetoric, History
	Frank Lentricchia, University of California, Irvine

Sponsoring Institutions

Columbia University, Princeton University, Yale University, University of Rochester, Rutgers University, Michigan State University, Northwestern University, Boston University, University of California at Berkeley, University of Connecticut, Harvard University, University of Pennsylvania, University of Virginia, Amherst College, State University of New York at Stony Brook, Brandeis University, Cornell University, Dartmouth College, New York University, Smith College, The Johns Hopkins University, Washington University, State University of New York at Albany, Temple University, University of Alabama at Birmingham, University of California at San Diego, Boston College, Brigham Young University, University of California at Los Angeles, University of California at Santa Cruz, Massachusetts Institute of Technology, Wellesley College, Stanford University, Indiana University at Bloomington, Tufts University, University of Colorado, Wesleyan University, Fordham University, University of Arizona, State University of New York at Buffalo, University of California at Irvine, University of Maryland, University of Miami, Emory University, University of Illinois at Chicago.

Registrants, 1982

Timothy J. Abraham, Board of Education, New York City; Maurianne Adams, University of Massachusetts at Amherst; Ruth M. Adams, Dartmouth College; Janet E. Aikins, University of New Hampshire; Robert Alpert, York School; Quentin Anderson, Columbia University; Jonathan Arac, University of Illinois at Chicago; Norman S. Asbridge, Central Connecticut State College; Mary Axtmann, University of Puerto Rico

J. Leeds Barroll, University of Maryland, Baltimore County; George W. Bahlke, Hamilton College; Adrianne Baytop, Rutgers University; Jerome Beaty, Emory University; Millicent Bell, Boston University; Larry D. Benson, Harvard University; J. Scott Bentley, University of Oregon; Nancy M. Bentley, La Jolla Middle School; Jerry Bernhard, Emmanuel College; Warner Berthoff, Harvard University; Walter Bezanson, Rutgers University; Morton W. Bloomfield, Harvard University;

191

Charles Blyth; Rachel Bowlby, Yale University; Frank Brady, City University of New York Graduate School; Peter Brand, Buffalo and Erie County Public Library; Leo Braudy, Johns Hopkins University; John Brenkman, University of Wisconsin, Madison; James H. Broderick, University of Massachusetts at Boston; Gillian Brown, University of California at Berkeley; Marshall Brown, University of Colorado; Betty Buchsbaum, Massachusetts State College of Art; Jane Britton Buchanan, Tufts University; Lawrence Buell, Oberlin College

Gary Carlson, Boston University; Stanley Cavell, Harvard University; Arnold H. Chadderdon, Post College; Cynthia Chase, Cornell University; Sr. Anne Gertrude Coleman, College of St. Elizabeth; Arthur N. Collins, State University of New York at Albany; Marion Connor, Tufts University; Mason Cooley, College of Staten Island; Richard Corum, Dartmouth; Rosemary Cowler, Lake Forest College; James Cox, Dartmouth; Patricia Craddock, Boston University; G. Armour Craig, Amherst College; Jonathan Culler, Cornell University

Stuart A. Davis, Lehman College; Robert Adams Day, City University of New York; Hermione de Almeida, University of Miami; Daryl De Nitto, Rutgers State University, New Jersey; Elisabeth De Nitto, City University of New York; Michael Denning, Columbia University; E. Talbot Donaldson, Indiana University; Deborah Dorfman, State University of New York at Albany

Terry Eagleton, Wadham College, Oxford, England; Delbert L. Earisman, Upsula College; Carol Ellis, University of Iowa; Martha W. England, Queens College; David V. Erdman, State University of New York at Stony Brook

N. N. Feltes, York University, Toronto; Frances Ferguson, University of California at Berkeley; Margaret W. Ferguson, Yale University; Mary Anne Ferguson, University of Massachusetts at Boston; Judith Ferster, Brandeis University; Kathe Davis Finney, Kent State University; Stanley Fish, Johns Hopkins University; Philip Fisher, Brandeis University; Jay Fliegelman, Stanford University; Marcia M. Folsom, Wheelock College; Debra Fried, Cornell University; Margaretta Fulton, Harvard University Press

Mary-Kay Gamel, University of California at Santa Cruz; Burdett Gardner, Monmouth College; Robert E. Garlitz, Plymouth State College; Byron Gassman, Brigham Young University; Blanche H. Gelfant, Dartmouth College; Carol Gesner, Berea College; Michael T. Gilmore, Brandeis University; Philip Goldstein, University of Delaware; Ellen Golub, University of Pennsylvania; James Gray, Dalhousie University; Linda Gregerson, Stanford University; Stanley T. Gutman, University of Vermont

Janice Haney-Peritz, Beaver College; Maryhelen C. Harmon, University of South Florida; Richard Harrier, New York University; Geoffrey Hartman, Yale University; Joan E. Hartman, College of Staten Island; Richard Haven, University of Massachusetts at Amherst; Carolyn Heilbrun, Columbia University; Neil Hertz, Johns Hopkins University; Margaret Higonnet, University of Connecticut; Myra Hinman, University of Kansas; John Hobbs, Oberlin College; Daniel Hoffman, University of Pennsylvania; Benjamin Hoover, Brandeis University; Chaviva Hosek, Victoria College, University of Toronto; Anne B. Howells, Occidental College; Peter Hughes, Universitat Zurich; Kathleen Noda Hulley, University of North Dakota; J. Paul Hunter, University of Rochester

Mary Jacobus, Cornell University; Abdul R. JanMohamed, Boston University; Paula Johnson, New York University; Judith L. Johnston; Kenneth Johnston, Indiana University; Sidney C. Jones, Carroll College; Bruce W. Jorgensen, Brigham Young University; Gerhard Joseph, Lehman College and Graduate Center

Marjorie Kaufman, Mount Holyoke College; James H. Kavanagh, Princeton University; Carol Kay, Amherst College; Gillian Kendall; Charles A. Knight, University of Massachusetts at Boston; Murray Krieger, University of California at Irvine.

George P. Landow, Brown University; Berel Lang, University of Colorado; David J. Langston, Trinity College; Lyman L. Leathers, Ohio Wesleyan University; Judith Lee, Brandeis University; Frank Lentricchia, University of California at Irvine; Vivien Leonard, Rensselaer Polytechnic Institute; Julie Lilienfeld; Dwight N. Lindley, Hamilton College; Joanna Lipking, Northwestern University; Lawrence Lipking, Northwestern University; J. P. Lovering, Canisius College at Buffalo

Paul Magnuson, New York University; Robert K. Martin, Concordia University; Leo Marx, Massachusetts Institute of Technology; Pamela McCallum, University of Calgary; Stuart Y. McDougal, University of Michigan; Jerome McGann, California Institute of Technology; Peter McInerney; Terence J. McKenzie, Humanities Dept., U. S. Coast Guard Academy; Cathleen T. McLoughlin, City University of New York Graduate Center; Donald C. Mell, Jr., University of Delaware; Anne K. Mellor, Stanford University; Jeffrey Meyers, University of Colorado; Ronald Meyers, East Stroudsburg State College; Walter Benn Michaels, University of California at Berkeley; W. Gordon Milne, Lake Forest College; David Minter, Emory University; Lee Mitchell, Princeton University; David B. Morris, University of Iowa; Joann Morse, Barnard College; Steven Mullaney, Massachusetts Institute of Technology; Adrienne Munich, State University of New York at Stony Brook

John Nesselhof, Wells College; Judith Newton, La Salle College; Clare Harwood Nunes, Concord Academy

James Olney, North Carolina Central University; Charles A. Owen, Jr. University of Conneticut

Stanley R. Palombo, M.D., George Washington University; Andrew Parker, Amherst College; Patricia Parker, University of Toronto; Reeve Parker, Cornell University; Annabel Patterson, University of Maryland; Vincent F. Petronella, University of Massachusetts at Boston; David Porter, University of Massachusetts at Amherst; Robert O. Preyer, Brandeis University; John W. Price, Middlesex School

Louis A. Renza, Dartmouth College; David S. Reynolds, Northwestern University; John Paul Riquelme, Southern Methodist University; Bruce Robbins, Université de Lausanne; Jeffrey C. Robinson, University of Colorado at Boulder; Ruth Rosenberg, Kingsborough; Barbara Rotundo, State University of New York at Albany, P. C. Rule, Holy Cross; John Paul Russo, University of Miami; M. PatonRyan, R.S.M., Marquette University

Elaine B. Safer, University of Delaware; Elaine Scarry, University of Pennsylvania; Daniel Schenker, Brandeis University; Eve Kosofsky Sedgwick, Boston University; Mark Seltzer, Cornell University; Sheila Shaw, Wheaton College, Mass.; Elaine Showalter, Rutgers University; Frank Shuffelton, University of Rochester; Anderson Silber, Victoria College, Toronto; John Sitter, Emory University; Carol H. Smith, Rutgers University; Sarah Smith, Boston University; George Soule, Carleton College; Patricia Meyer Spacks, Yale University; Claire Sprague, Radcliffe College; Michael Sprinker, Oregon State University; Susan Staves, Brandeis University; A. Wilber Stevens, University of Nevada at Las Vega; Holly Stevens, Peter Stine, Gordon College; Gary Stonum, Case Western Reserve; Margaret Storch, Rudolf Storch, Tufts University; Jean Sudrann, Mount Holyoke College; Sara Suleri, Williams College; Eric Sundquist, University of California at Berkeley; Tania Sundquist

Irene Tayler, Massachusetts Institue of Technology; Dennis Taylor, Boston College; J. J. M. Tobin, University of Massachusetts at Boston; Jane Tompkins, Temple Universi_y; Humphrey Tonkin, University of Pennsylvania; Lewis A. Turlish, Bates College

William Vance, Boston University; Helen Vendler, Boston/Harvard Universities; Andrew Von Hendy, Boston College; Elizabeth G. von Klemperer, Smith College

Melissa Walker, Mercer University; Donald Weber, Mount Holyoke College; Grant Webster, State University of New York at Binghamton; Sr. Mary Anthony Weinig, Rosemont College; Epi Wiese; Carolyn Williams, Boston University; Joshua Wilner, The Hebrew University; Cynthia Griffin Wolff, Massachusetts Institute of Technology

Patricia S. Yaeger, Williams College

Susan Zimmerman, University of Maryland